AFTER
THE COLD WAR

AFTER
THE COLD WAR

Questioning the Morality
of Nuclear Deterrence

edited by
CHARLES W. KEGLEY, JR., and
KENNETH L. SCHWAB
University of South Carolina

Westview Press
BOULDER • SAN FRANCISCO • OXFORD

Copyright © 1991 by Westview Press, Inc.

Published in 1991 in the United States of America by Westview Press, Inc., 5500 Central Avenue, Boulder, Colorado 80301, and in the United Kingdom by Westview Press, 36 Lonsdale Road, Summertown, Oxford OX2 7EW

Library of Congress Cataloging-in-Publication Data
After the cold war : questioning the morality of nuclear deterrence /
    edited by Charles W. Kegley, Jr., and Kenneth L. Schwab.
      p.   cm.
    ISBN 0-8133-8063-4—ISBN 0-8133-8064-2 (pbk.)
    1. Nuclear warfare—Moral and ethical aspects—Congresses.
2. Deterrence (Strategy)—Moral and ethical aspects—Congresses.
3. World politics—1985–1995—Congresses. I. Kegley, Charles W., Jr.
II. Schwab, Kenneth L.
U263.A29 1991
172′.422—dc20   90-44539
                                                                         CIP

Printed and bound in the United States of America

The paper used in this publication meets the requirements
of the American National Standard for Permanence of Paper
for Printed Library Materials Z39.48-1984.

10   9   8   7   6   5   4   3   2   1

For our children

Kempten L. Schwab
Carlton L. Schwab
Christopher L. Schwab

Suzanne Taylor Mitchell

For whom we wish to nurture
a world free of the peril
of nuclear annihilation

Contents

Preface

We know today that . . . ideas, not armaments, will shape our lasting prospects for peace; that the conduct of our foreign policy will advance no faster than the curriculum of our classrooms; that the knowledge of our citizens is one treasure which grows only when it is shared.

President Lyndon B. Johnson

The revolutionary year 1989 stands as a true historical watershed. Communism's collapse in Eastern Europe, the fragmentation of the Warsaw Pact (and, potentially, the Soviet Union itself), the progress in arms control, and the outbreak of peace generally seemed, to many, to set the stage for a new era of world politics. What began with the hope to move "beyond the Cold War" culminated in awareness that a new international system—contrary to most predictions and to the surprise of nearly all observers—had become a reality.

Change poses both promise and peril. What the emergent new global architecture will mean for world politics is highly uncertain. Particularly problematic among the many questions that the "post-postwar" era presents is the most pressing question of our time: Will the peace among the great powers that has continued without interruption since 1945 persist in the new global atmosphere created by these rapidly converging developments? It is the purpose of *After the Cold War* to address the fundamental strategic issues presented by the new global environment and to take a critical look at the morality and efficacy of that core pillar of peace—nuclear deterrence—in the new geopolitical context.

As we enter this new era, it is imperative to reconsider the superpowers' military doctrines, the moral dilemmas they pose, and how the extraordinary global changes may affect the prospects for nuclear deterrence and, ultimately, abiding peace. The questions of whether deterrence will be a cure or a curse and whether a system that requires mass annihilation for defense remains morally defensible are presently approached from widely disparate vantage points.

At the risk of oversimplification, three categories of observers may be distinguished: (1) policymakers and strategic theorists, (2) policy analysts and peace researchers, and (3) moral philosophers, religious leaders, and peace activists. Each of these groups is actively engaged in the continuing debate about nuclear weapons, and their divergent perspectives enlarge awareness of the issues to be confronted. But rarely have their views been brought together and their conclusions exposed for critical comparison. That need is more urgent than ever, because the end of the Cold War does not end the urgent need to find a basis for preventing nuclear war. The new global circumstances now require, more than ever, reexamination of conventional wisdom and established policy prescriptions.

To cover comprehensively the full range of opinion concerning these complex issues (and expose the diversity of opinion within each community of commentators) is well beyond the reach of a single volume. But a representative sample of thought on this subject by leading authorities within each school *is* possible, and perusal of their competing viewpoints can illuminate the similarities and differences within and across the three groups. It is the purpose of *After the Cold War* to present the diverse views of leading scholars, national leaders, and philosophers about the basic policy and moral questions posed by the new era, as expressed within the Atlantic community.

In order to organize inquiry, original papers by leading authorities were commissioned to explore the moral status of nuclear deterrence in the current environment. The authors of these papers were brought together at the University of South Carolina in February 1990 for a discussion taped for televised broadcast throughout the United States.

The contributors have prepared informed and informative reflections on the most important issue of our time: how peace might be preserved in a new age fraught with both great opportunity and continuing danger. They present contending ideas about how a nuclear catastrophe might best be avoided and about whether a strategy that holds innocents hostage as a means for preserving peace should be morally justified or condemned. Thus, this volume seeks to make an impact on the scholarly study of peace and on the ways policymakers think about the paths to a more orderly international system. It also seeks to make a contribution to the advancement of policy science, peace research, and moral philosophy.

The field of peace studies is changing fundamentally in response to a new global environment liberated from the threat of two superpowers pledged to destroy each other's way of life, and it is hoped that this book will respond to the instructional needs created by this change.

After the Cold War provides a set of interpretations around which discussion of the morality of alternative paths to continued international peace can, and inevitably will, focus. It is also hoped that the book's thought-provoking chapters will stimulate other people to join the contributors' search for the best means to prevent the ultimate apocalypse.

Many people made this book possible, and their contributions are gratefully acknowledged. First, Dr. James B. Holderman, president of the University of South Carolina, is to be thanked for encouraging us to conceive a theme for an international symposium and seek external support for its sponsorship. The generous support subsequently provided by the United States Institute of Peace made the project possible, and the assistance provided by South Carolina Educational Television also contributed greatly to its success. For their support we are very appreciative.

In addition, the advice and managerial support provided by Jonathan Davidson in the Washington office of the University of South Carolina and Donald Puchala, director of the Institute of International Studies at the University of South Carolina, facilitated the project's administration. The assistance provided by Steven W. Hook, Christina Payne, Chad Poteat, Susan Caldwell, and Mary George, all at the University of South Carolina, also contributed substantially to the process by which the original discussion papers were converted to manuscripts for publication. In addition, reviews of these manuscripts by anonymous referees proved supportive and constructive. Furthermore, the confidence placed in this project in response to the prospectus for this book by Jennifer Knerr of Westview Press and the professional editorial support of Megan Schoeck, Jeanne Campbell, and Steven W. Hook also facilitated the book's publication. And finally (but not exhaustively), the intellectual resources of the scholars who dedicated their energies and insights have made this volume a valuable educational resource, policy statement, and contribution to the literature. In sum, the book is a collective product made possible by the contributions of many people sharing a common commitment to the generation of knowledge and a belief in its capacity to create a more secure world. We are indebted to all of them and very appreciative of the vision, enthusiasm, and professionalism they brought to this project.

Charles W. Kegley, Jr.
Kenneth L. Schwab

1

At Issue: Deterrence in the Post–Cold War Era

Charles W. Kegley, Jr.
Kenneth L. Schwab

Since the advent of the nuclear age, to keep the peace the superpowers have depended on the doctrine of "nuclear deterrence," placing great faith in the belief that the threat of massive destruction can prevent a military attack by an adversary. Many observers have regarded reliance on the capacity to inflict widespread destruction as a necessary (if precarious and ethically questionable) strategy, which, nonetheless, appears to have prevented a recurrence of another general war of mass annihilation. Other have condemned nuclear deterrence as inherently immoral because it depends on threats that, if carried out, would be more inhumane than the evil they are designed to prevent; to them, deterrence exposes innocents, indeed, the entire human species, to extinction. Still others assume an intermediate position between these two views. They recognize that nuclear weapons have dramatically escalated the dangers posed to human survival, but they perceive the risks as being acceptable nonetheless because under conditions of mutual assured destruction (MAD—the centerpiece of nuclear deterrence), the great powers have experienced the longest period of peace since the birth of the nation-state system in 1648. This rationale was expressed by the U.S. National Conference of Catholic Bishops, which observed:

> When one looks back at the evolution of the nuclear age, it is highly unlikely that anyone would have chosen to have our present situation result. . . . Yet, any assessment of the policy of deterrence will be hard-put not to acknowledge that in a world of widespread nuclear knowledge and at least six nuclear powers, deterrence has been a significant factor in preventing the use of nuclear weapons. [National Conference of Catholic Bishops, 1989: 69]

Or has it? What have been the actual consequences of dependence on nuclear weapons, even for the avowedly defensive purpose of deterring an adversary contemplating aggression? Can deterrence be morally justified, given the risks and costs involved? Moreover, even if functional during the Cold War, is reliance on nuclear deterrence still justifiable? When the superpowers' rivalry and ideological antagonism have dissipated and the threat of war between them has vanished, are other peacekeeping strategies and even concerted great-power endeavors (as evident in their response to Iraq's aggression in 1990 in the Persian Gulf) now feasible? Is it therefore safe to turn from a preoccupation with defense and address other long-neglected problems?

The answers are not clear. If deterrence has kept the postwar great-power peace, discarding it for an alternate security system may be imprudent, which is why the United States and its allies (especially France) remain committed to retaining nuclear arsenals and relying on them for the purpose of war prevention. But retaining deterrence is also expensive, threatening, and strategically precarious. For mutual deterrence to prevent war, some ethically questionable risks must be taken: each adversary must possess the ability to inflict unacceptable damage on the opponent and be willing to expend large portions of its national treasury to preserve this capability; each must be able to withstand an enemy's initial strike and still retain the capability to retaliate with a devastating second blow; and each must threaten mass annihilation and make that threat credible by promising to carry it out. For an adversary's contemplation of a preemptive strike to be deterred, it must be assured that its aggression will result in its own destruction.

Hence, deterrence requires the preservation of mutual vulnerability. According to the theory's cardinal proposition, for each adversary to be inhibited from attacking the other, each must remain vulnerable. "What is significant about nuclear weapons," Robert Jervis notes, "is not overkill, but mutual kill. . . . Nuclear weapons have brought the superpowers both great security and enormous insecurity" (Jervis, 1986: 690). At issue, almost since the dawn of the nuclear age, therefore, has been whether there is any moral justification for a system of defense that requires, if the system is to work, leaving adversaries (and innocent noncombatants) defenseless.

This doctrine has understandably been subjected to criticism, given the dangers it created. During the 1960s and 1970s, the term "balance of terror" best described the deterrence strategy's essential property—that mutual deterrence was based on the military potential for and psychological expectation of widespread death and destruction for all contestants in the event of a nuclear exchange.

This circumstance enlarged awareness of the essential strategic dilemma created by this system of defense: the strategy's success was contingent on preservation of the high probability that if one adversary attacked the other, it would do so at the price of its own destruction. Nuclear deterrence, in the imagery of Jonathan Schell, "is like a gun with two barrels, of which one points ahead and the other points back at the gun's holder. If a burglar should enter your house, it might make sense to threaten him with his gun, but it could never make sense to fire it" (Schell, 1984: 54). This analogy punctuates the nuclear age's primary paradox, namely, in the words of former Secretary of Defense Robert S. McNamara, "to the extent that the nuclear threat has a deterrent value, it is because it in fact increases the risk of nuclear war" (McNamara, 1989: 182).

Ever since Hiroshima, states have been "conditionally viable" (Boulding, 1962) because they have been made dependent on other states for their survival. The superpowers are especially endangered as a result of the weapons and targeting doctrines they have created to protect themselves. For, as President John F. Kennedy often observed, in the event of a nuclear exchange, no matter who initiated it, the two superpowers automatically would become the primary targets. But the superpowers' territories are not the only endangered areas. Many scientists believe that an exchange of nuclear weapons would precipitate climatic changes of catastrophic proportions, producing a "nuclear winter" that conceivably could destroy the entire planet (C. Sagan, 1989; Robock, 1990). Moreover, as the Third World rushes to build weapons of mass destruction—facilitated greatly by the July 1, 1990, decision of the United States and its allies to lift export controls on the technologies and materials necessary to acquire nuclear weapons (Milhollin, 1990)—the threat of a nuclear war has become a shared threat to people throughout the world. Even as the Cold War passes from the scene, the danger of nuclear war, and the need to deter it, continue.

If nuclear deterrence leads to a *decrease* in national and global security, as some maintain, how then can states escape their hostage circumstances and free themselves from the prospect of destruction? As the preceding discussion suggests, until very recently the strategic predicament afforded little room for maneuver. There was no assurance that the "unthinkable" use of nuclear weapons would not occur, and the possibility that raging Third World conflicts could eventually set off a nuclear cataclysm made fear pervasive and seemingly permanent (Schwartz and Derber, 1990). Since the advent of the nuclear age, there has appeared no alternative to the seemingly inescapable necessity, in the phrase of the Harvard Nuclear Study Group (1983), of "living with nuclear weapons."

On the Horizon: A New Strategic Context

Despite the limitations inherent in strategies of deterrence, the great powers have steadfastly relied on the strategy of nuclear deterrence. Many people felt there was no safe alternative to that strategy—despite its dangers, questionable premises, and alleged immorality, deterrence was working, and, it was reasoned, it would be unwise to attempt to replace it. Other options did not appear available.

To be sure, a number of proposals have been advanced to free humanity from dependence on nuclear weapons for protection. Since 1945, for example, various efforts have been made to reduce or eliminate nuclear stockpiles through negotiated arms control and disarmament agreements. But these, at least until the intermediate-range nuclear force (INF) agreement, produced very marginal results (see Goldblat, 1982; Kupperman and Van Opstal, 1988) and it could be argued that these arms control agreements have *increased* rather than reduced reliance on nuclear deterrence. Moreover, arms control agreements may have rationalized continuation of the arms race under the euphemism "force modernization" (Kruzel, 1991), because defense planners have used these agreements to justify development of new military technologies (Evangelista, 1988). For example, tactical air-surface missiles (TASMs) deployed by NATO and the Soviet Union have replaced the intermediate nuclear forces that the INF agreement banned. Hence, efforts to expand military capabilities have not diminished as the Cold War has waned, and even the promise of "deep cuts" in strategic arsenals does not presage the end of deterrence (Aspen Strategy Group, 1989). As inspection of trends in the superpowers' inventories of delivery vehicles (Figure 1.1) and warheads (Figure 1.2) attests, the "age of overkill" persists. Both George Bush and Mikhail Gorbachev have remained committed to maintaining a strong, invincible force capability, and have resisted substantial transfers from the military to the domestic sectors of their economies; force modernization continues apace, as attested to by the fact that in 1990 the Soviet Union launched one new submarine every six weeks and one new missile every day (Frost, 1990).

Similarly, to escape dependence on offensive nuclear weapons for protection, some proponents foresaw the dawn of a "defense-dominant" strategy as an alternative to nuclear deterrence. President Ronald Reagan labeled reliance on offensive missiles to deter attack "morally unacceptable," and in 1983 he proposed a new antiballistic missile (ABM) defense program to make nuclear missiles "impotent and obsolete." To proponents of the Strategic Defense Initiative (or Star Wars as it became known), "defending through active defense [was] preferable to defending through terrorism—the ultimate mechanism by which deterrence through

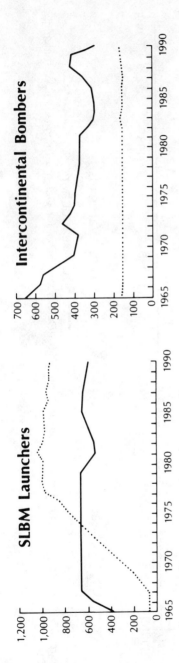

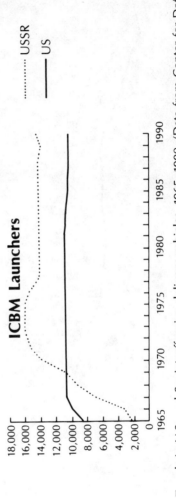

Figure 1.1 Trends in U.S. and Soviet offensive delivery vehicles, 1965–1990. (Data from Center for Defense Information, Washington, D.C.)

6

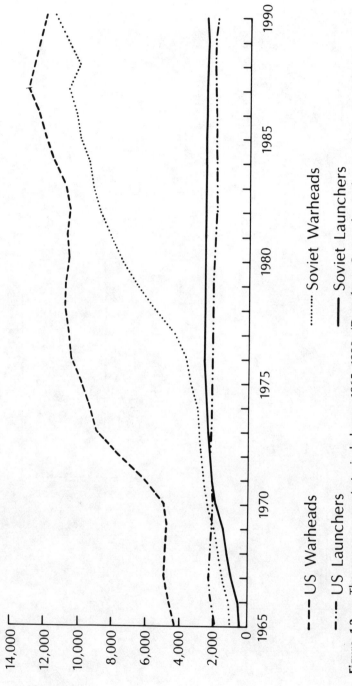

Figure 1.2 The superpower strategic balance, 1965–1990. (Data from Center for Defense Information, Washington, D.C.)

--- US Warheads
...... Soviet Warheads
-·-· US Launchers
—— Soviet Launchers

threat of retaliation operates" (U.S. Office of Technology Assessment, 1989: 111). But faith in the feasibility of a defense-dominant strategy has steadily eroded since its proclamation, and the heralded transition in a postnuclear system from offense to defense (Goldberg, 1989) has halted. "No one now proclaims," McGeorge Bundy reports "that there can be a leakproof shield, and those who proclaim the value of enormously expensive partial protection are each year less persuasive in Washington" (Bundy, 1990: 208). Hence, the elusive quest for "absolute security" (Chace and Carr, 1988) has lost its momentum as "most experts agree that no system will be available for the foreseeable future that would support a strategy based on a defensive shield against nuclear attack. . . . The United States will contiue to rely on deterrence provided by offensive nuclear weapons well into the next century" (Doty and Chayes, 1989: 1). Nuclear deterrence thus remains the accepted method by which the United States and the other nuclear powers seek to avoid destruction, even though the search for an antiballistic defense system continues and President George Bush has remained a fervent supporter of the Strategic Defense Initiative (Seib, 1990).

Until now, the basic parameters of debate about the morality of the deterrence strategy remained confined within a fairly stable range of discourse. Given the pervasive superpower tensions throughout the Cold War, the nuclear *problématique* was thus framed within largely invariant intellectual boundaries. People disagreed about what to do with and about nuclear weapons—and about their purposes, utility, and morality— but agreed on the basic questions about their existence.

But in 1989 and 1990, dramatic changes swept world affairs, preceded by President Mikhail Gorbachev's pursuit of a more open society (glasnost) and a fundamental economic and political restructuring (perestroika) in the Soviet Union and, later, the Warsaw Pact countries. Gorbachev's subsequent "peace offensive" set in motion revolutionary and far-reaching developments that arguably were not altogether part of his original intent. The forces his reforms unleashed led not only to eased superpower relations and progress in arms control but also to the dismantling of the Berlin Wall, the crumbling of the Warsaw Pact, the "spinning-off" of the Soviet Union's Eastern European satellites, the unification of the two Germanys, a push for independence and democratic governance by republics of the USSR, a rejection of communist principles, and an endorsement of reforms to permit market economies to take root. Gorbachev set the stage for the end of the Cold War—a victory for all humanity for which Gorbachev deserves primary credit (Bundy, 1990: 208).

The changes prompted President Bush to respond, however hesitantly and cautiously (see Kegley, 1989; Kegley and Wittkopf, 1991). "Now

[that] danger from Moscow [was] no longer the driving force of debate, [the United States had] to decide what role it [wished] to play in the world when there is no overwhelming danger to national security and no clearly identifiable enemy" (Hyland, 1990: 2). The stage was set to proclaim that the time had come for U.S. policy to move "beyond the Cold War" and beyond the containment of communism, which had formed the cornerstone of the U.S. approach to the Soviet Union for four decades. Instead of a continued arms race, President Bush signaled receptivity to new priorities within a postcontainment policy. He proposed in April 1990, for example, the abolition of land-based missiles with more than one nuclear warhead and pledged at the NATO summit in July 1990 to terminate the Cold War by treating the Soviet Union as a partner in security instead of as a competitive adversary. As other initiatives in arms control and tension reduction followed, peace broke out, and Secretary of State James A. Baker began to speak optimistically about the advent of what he termed an emergent "post-postwar era."

At first glance, these promising developments might seem to resolve the moral and policy issues surrounding the nuclear dilemma, which have preoccupied national leaders and scholars since the Manhattan Project first conceived of a superweapon and forced onto the global agenda the questions about how they could be used. Under conditions of peace, when the prospect of a full-scale nuclear exchange had disappeared, it appeared possible for the first time to ask if nuclear weapons were needed and to question what those weapons were designed to deter. But on closer inspection, peace in the 1990s has not answered the fundamental questions about strategic requirements. Rather, in the post–Cold War era, the traditional issues are that much *more* salient. And the propitious prospects for peace have made the question of *Why Peace Breaks Out* (Rock, 1989) more rather than less puzzling.

The era "beyond the Cold War" does not entail the necessary abandonment or reformulation of the doctrine of nuclear deterrence. Mutual assured destruction remains the foundation of the superpowers' defense strategies, and the realpolitik priority of operating from a position of military strength remains a pillar of strategic thinking in the West.

The West explicitly reaffirmed this reliance in the communiqué of the Economic Summit in July 1989. That commitment was reinforced in Secretary of Defense Dick Cheney's *Annual Report to the President and the Congress,* which proclaimed that "deterrence of nuclear attack remains the cornerstone of U.S. national security. Regardless of improved U.S.-Soviet relations and potential arms control agreements, the Soviet ability to initiate strategic warfare against the United States will persist" (D. Cheney, 1990: iv). This adherence was confirmed further by the Bush administration's strategic initiatives at the July 1990 NATO summit, which, "By shifting to a pledge to use nuclear weapons only as a 'last resort,' [sought] to keep the nuclear option but show an awareness that the likelihood of a Soviet ground attack [had] virtually disappeared" (Hoagland, 1990: 8). Hence, for its part, the United States has reaffirmed its faith in nuclear deterrence and quietly revived it as the foundation of its grand strategy (Hoagland, 1989). Revealingly, the United States, on October 1, 1989, put into place a new Single Integrated Operational Plan (SIOP) to govern the targeting policy for U.S. nuclear forces. These revised nuclear employment policies placed *greater* emphasis on targeting the Soviet leadership and relocatable assets at the very time when the threat from the Soviet Union had dissipated. Because these developments in U.S. strategic targeting "threaten to take U.S. war-fighting doctrines to dangerous extremes," they reveal that the moral problems underlying nuclear weapons have not vanished as the Cold War has thawed—"U.S. strategic war planning has involved a continuing effort to make nuclear weapons 'usable' " (Ball and Toth, 1990: 66). Consequently, the ethical issues associated with U.S. nuclear deterrence doctrines have taken on a new coloration as the Cold War rivalry has subsided, but the changed climate has not resolved the issues; it has, in fact, increased the need to assess the moral implications in light of the new changes in global circumstances and in U.S. policy.

In addition, there is little to suggest that the Soviet Union, for its part, has jettisoned its dependence on nuclear deterrence either. Indeed, with the fragmentation of the bipolar bloc structure and potential end of the postwar alliance systems (see Kegley and Raymond, 1990b), the Soviet Union's dependence on nuclear deterrence for defense has increased rather than diminished, even as Soviet military doctrine has recently undergone revolutionary changes (see Garthoff, 1990).

Moreover, the relaxation of superpower tensions, accompanied by vigorous Soviet wooing of Western European opinion, has reopened many old internal rifts in the Atlantic alliance. Controversy about basing the defense of Western Europe on nuclear weapons, to be used first by the NATO alliance if invaded from the east—a "first use" policy long the subject of intense moral and political debate—has intensified, and a new and seriously divisive issue surfaced early in 1989 within NATO over the modernization of short-range nuclear weapons based in West Germany. These issues became instantly more complex and divisive as German unification proceeded and negotiations about how a united Germany would align itself in restructured alliance structures rose in importance on the global agenda (see Kegley and Raymond, 1990a). The need for a new architecture for European peace became, in addition, more complicated when U.S. military planners (in response to the Soviet Union's dismantling of its conventional forces in Europe and in the face of the fact that now "no Soviet general can plan for an invasion when the supply lines run through a thousand miles of openly hostile territory" [Barnet, 1990: 49]) acknowledged "for the first time in the postwar era that the Western alliance could now defeat any conventional Soviet military invasion of Europe without resorting to nuclear weapons" (Moore, 1990: A12). (This acknowledgment prepared the way for President Bush's May 1990 decision to abandon plans to modernize short-range nuclear weapons in Germany while pledging to keep U.S. nuclear weapons in Europe, despite pressure to reduce superpower arsenals there.)

Hence, the issues on the horizon—given the uncertainties posed by rapidly changing conditions and superpower ambitions and policies— are as complex and problematic as ever. The end of the Cold War has not ended reliance on deterrence, but it has altered the classic strategic equation and the calculations on which strategic doctrines have heretofore been based. The answers about the most moral and prudent path to continued peace in this new epoch are therefore as uncertain and hypothetical as ever.

John F. Kennedy once stated that the splitting of the atom changed all the questions and all the answers. That adage is applicable in today's world, as the rush to terminate the Cold War and drastically reduce strategic arsenals (alongside the stubborn fact that those weapons continue to exist) likewise changes the questions and challenges the validity of conventional wisdom. A new age raises new ethical and policy issues, even while old ones persist.

Given the entrenched reality of nuclear arsenals, how might the great powers best frame deterrence and other strategic doctrines in order to avoid the outbreak of war? *After the Cold War* seeks to address that question and the basic policy and moral issues surrounding it. Relevant to any analysis of the moral evaluation of deterrence in the era *After the Cold War* is a review of several empirical and epistemological questions:

- Has deterrence been responsible for the great-power peace? Or has it perpetuated the Cold War, the arms race, and international tension?
- Why has deterrence worked until now?
- Can deterrence keep the peace in today's changing circumstances?
- How do we evaluate the consequences of technological innovations in weapons systems?
- If nuclear deterrence remains official doctrine now, has it become a truly *permanent* fixture of modern superpower relations?
- What processes of disarmament and/or arms control are most stabilizing?

In addition, persistent ethical questions call out for attention.

- Can deterrence be reconciled with the principles of proportionality and discrimination?
- Is a consequentialist rationale for deterrence—that an immoral means is justifiable if it obtains a moral end—acceptable?
- Is nuclear deterrence, morally dubious at a time of global tension, even more "immoral" when relations are calm?
- What are the realistic alternatives to nuclear deterrence? Do strengthened conventional forces qualify as a "moral" alternative?

Such questions must be addressed with awareness that judgments about nuclear weapons cannot be divorced from the broader political context in which deterrence policies are framed and that any proposed alternative to deterrence has inherent moral costs.

The debatable virtues and vices of deterrence strategies which in order to prevent warfare, threaten the use of weapons that would exterminate not only the attacker and the attacked but also neutrals and noncombatants are certain to remain on the global agenda even at a time when the prospects for great-power peace are highly auspicious. Consensus is unlikely to emerge on the moral status of nuclear deterrence even given the rapidly changing, propitious conditions, in part because no school of thought appears able to formulate a position capable of cogently addressing all the dilemmas posed until agreement is reached about the nature of the post-postwar world before us.

It is not reasonable to expect experts to concur about the nature of the new strategic environment or to agree about the most moral and effective means to prevent nuclear war. Consensus is unlikely because the emergent circumstances are more complex and changing than were the relatively simple and stable bipolar Cold War conditions "and there has not been enough time to work out a new strategy that supports post–Cold War foreign policy goals and priorities" (Hyland, 1990: 8).

Readers will discover in the following chapters a range of new questions and new perspectives that are worthy of contemplation. The authors advance rival interpretations of the nature of military strategy in the post–Cold War era whose validity must be weighed, for collectively they represent positions that define the agenda for future debate. To introduce the contents, we will put this book's chapters into context and outline their purpose and relationship to one another. For that purpose, we shall first describe more fully the concept of deterrence that must now be reevaluated.

Responding to the
New Security Environment

On the surface, the concept of nuclear deterrence is disarmingly simple. Yet, by the 1980s, theories of deterrence had splintered into "a state of confusion amounting almost to disintegration" (Schell, 1984: 48), and the war-fighting aspects of nuclear weapons and their deterrent value were preceived by some people as being "bankrupt" (Summers, 1989).

The fragmentation of deterrence theory has accelerated even further since the Cold War has terminated. The Cold War has added a cohesive force to the debate about nuclear strategies by making geostrategic calculations of military preparedness a noncontroversial preoccupation. But with the conclusion of the Cold War struggle, that coherence has been lost and even the primacy of national security policy is being questioned. Now the United States and its allies "will be required to conduct a 'normal' foreign policy for which there is almost no precedent, with limited resources in an increasingly competitive world in which the threat that held together the various anticommunist alliances will have vanished" (Hyland, 1990: 3). Hence, today "no conception of nuclear strategy enjoys consensual support. As a result, debate concerning strategic issues defies easy characterization, and comparison of viewpoints is difficult" (Kegley and Wittkopf, eds., 1989: 10).

At its core, "deterrence in a more or less pure form consists of the following threat: 'Do not attack me because if you do, something unacceptably horrible will happen to you' " (Rothschild, 1983: 40). Beyond this underlying meaning, deterrence refers to a number of discrete phenomena. It is, alternatively, a condition, a strategy, a doctrine, a goal, or a "policy involving... weapons systems, force posture, declaratory policy, targeting doctrine, and the relationship of these to the objectives of security policy and . . . arms control" (National Conference of Catholic Bishops, 1989: 69). As President Reagan's Commission of Integrated Long-Term Strategy added: "Deterrence is not an abstract notion amenable to simple quantification. . . . Deterrence is a set of beliefs in the minds of . . . leaders, given their own values and attitudes, about capabilities and will" (1988: i).

Deterrence After the Cold War:
The Contributors' Perspectives

Deterrence is a multidimensional political-military-psychological construct. To appreciate the differing perspectives taken on its different facets as the Cold War passes from the scene, let us consider, in turn, the views represented by three groups of participants and observers in the new dialogue—policymakers and strategic theorists, policy analysts and peace researchers, and moral philosophers and religious leaders.

Policymakers and Strategic Theorists

To a remarkable extent, since the beginning of the nuclear age policymakers and strategists have interpreted the problems and paradoxes of nuclear weapons through the lens of realpolitik. To political realists, the dictum "if you want peace prepare for war" is axiomatic. Although they disagree on the balance of strategic forces required for deterrence to succeed, realists agree that the acquisition of military might is critical to national security. "The basic philosophy of [U.S.] deterrence policy is that in no way can or should [the United States] trust [its] adversary. Contrary to most other forms of human intercourse, behavior [in the realm of national security] cannot be governed by moral means. Distrust is the basis of this philosophy, and trust is considered irrational" and faith in weapons imperative (Gralnick, 1988: 176).

Realists, in other words, expect the worst in international affairs and counsel that it is prudent to prepare for amoral international conduct by others. Their Hobbesian vision springs from the convictions that conflict is a natural state of affairs, that relative military capabilities (force ratios) are decisive variables, and that states pursue power and national interests through "rational" ends-means calculations (see Holsti, 1989). Modern realist and neorealist thinking has guided the superpowers' embrace of nuclear deterrence as a path to security, even if, as some allege, "nuclear strategizing" emanates from "a misconceived rationality" (Cimbala, 1988; see also Jervis, 1984).

To many policymakers, adherence to realist principles allowed containment and deterrence to succeed—producing the longest period of great-power peace in modern history (see the analyses in Kegley, ed., 1991) and the West's "victory" in the Cold War (see Kegley, 1991). To others (e.g., Vasquez, 1991), of course, containment was unnecessary and deterrence irrelevant to postwar peace: "Things would have turned out much the same had nuclear weapons never been invented" (Mueller, 1991). According to these skeptics, the realpolitik formula produced and perpetuated the Soviet-U.S. rivalry, the Cold War conflict, and the arms race; moreover, these observers aver, preparations for war *decreased* international security (Johansen, 1989 and 1991).

Given this difference of opinion, it is not surprising that policymakers have taken diametrically opposed positions on the axioms they believe ought to guide deterrence doctrine in a post–Cold War world. In "Military Power and the Passing Cold War" (Chapter 2), Richard Perle advances realpolitik recommendations that reaffirm the need for military preparedness and continued reliance on nuclear arsenals to keep the peace. To him, the new climate does not resolve *The Nuclear Dilemma in American Strategic Thought* (Osgood, 1988) nor does it diminish the need to preserve a position of relative strength. Nuclear deterrence through military capabilities is still required, as is continued vigilance, Perle argues, because "it would be premature to conclude that Soviet military preparations have fundamentally changed" (McGeehan, 1990: 11). "Extreme proposals . . . that would disarm the West after the Cold War," continues Perle, would "run the risk that [the West] might yet again make Europe safe for the exertion of Soviet military power."

In principle, Perle would agree with the view that any assessment of the effects of cuts on the strategic balance "depends on how deep the proposed cuts are and how they relate to one's definition of deterrence" (Nye, 1989a: 196), but he would disagree with the corollary that effective counterforce targeting would permit substantial reductions in strategic forces. "We would be wise," Perle advises, "to wait a little longer before confidently predicting that we can afford to be weak in the face of uncertainty." Perle, who was often seen as the catalyst behind the Reagan administration's ability to double U.S. defense spending and its flirtation with a "prevailing" strategy for waging a nuclear war, aligns himself with others (e.g., C. Gray and Payne, 1980; C. Gray, 1984) who believe that to deter nuclear war, the United States must be prepared to wage it. Acknowledging that the threat of a massive Soviet invasion "of NATO territory is no longer plausible," Perle pleads that we "remember that Soviet military power remains formidable and growing even as the Warsaw Pact disintegrates." Hence, Perle concludes that "a dismantling of Western defenses in ways that would make them difficult or impossible to reconstruct should the need arise" is the new threat that has come "to replace those to which we had become accustomed." Advising "moralists . . . to steer clear of issues that [are] not essentially moral ones," Perle urges that we not "succumb to the siren call of the unilateralists and pacifists whose policies, had we followed them previously, would surely have kept the Cold War going or even allowed the Soviet bloc to win it."

Of course, reasonable people may disagree about what is reasonable and about "What Should We Do in the World?" (Hoffmann, 1989b). In contrast to Perle, for example, Sir Hugh Beach, who served as director of the Council for Arms Control in the United Kingdom, approaches the options and risks that present themselves *After the Cold War* and arrives at a different set of conclusions. In "What Stakes Would Justify the Use of Weapons of Mass Destruction?" (Chapter 3), Beach concludes that relaxed superpower tensions warrant reduced reliance on nuclear weaponry and on the threat to carry out a nuclear attack.

This conclusion derives from Beach's reading of historical lessons about the sources and scenarios from which past wars have sprung and from his evaluation of the moral arguments that have been developed about whether it could ever be ethically justifiable to fight a nuclear war. Similar to Perle, Beach perceives continuing peace to be contingent, to some degree, on the retention of nuclear capabilities. He ascribes to the view that

> as areas of agreement in Soviet-American relations have expanded, the occasions on which either side has felt the need to deter the other have become rare, and that trend has in turn raised the possibility of getting by with far fewer nuclear weapons and delivery systems than each side has now. . . . [Americans] and the Russians would do well, though, to resist the temptation to abolish nuclear weapons altogether, or even to reduce our stockpiles to a level approximating that of the next largest nuclear power. The reason for this is simple: nuclear weapons have played a major role in bringing about the evolution from Cold War to long peace. They have . . . induced caution. [Gaddis, 1990: 51, 54]

Noting, and dismissing, four popular rationals for the initiation of a nuclear war, Beach therefore suggests that there exists a variety of circumstances in which the use of nuclear weapons "could be both reasonable, in the sense of producing the effect intended, and proportionate, in the sense that the evil prevented by stopping the war [would] probably [be] far greater than the damage inflicted, horrifying though that [would be]." There are principles worth dying for, he contends, and people should remain willing to make great sacrifices on behalf of them. Hence, some stakes could warrant the use of nuclear weapons.

But those stakes have lessened, Beach continues, given President Gorbachev's "determination to move away from the world of closed societies." In such a world, he concludes in a statement that differs from the position of Richard Perle, "the use or threat of force would no longer be a valid instrument of foreign policy." For Beach, even though the Soviet Union is perceived as still being dangerous (especially if it collapses or returns to authoritarian rule), the important new reality from which strategic doctrines must proceed is that "even if the most dismal scenario is accepted, it is hard to see a major military threat confronting the West." The encouraging facts "that both the Soviet Union and the United States are engaged in strenuous nuclear arms reduction exercises and that doctrines of minimal deterrence are being increasingly discussed," create hope. Although nuclear weapons will be with us for decades yet, possibly forever, Beach would advise, as an interim ethic, that it is difficult to improve upon the position that a nuclear war not only cannot be won but must not be fought.

This latter view steadily gained adherents as the Cold War thawed. The shift was signaled in 1984 by Ronald Reagan himself, when he challenged the tenet about the "winnability" of a nuclear war with the phrase, endorsed at the same time by his newfound friend, Mikhail Gorbachev, "A nuclear war cannot be won and must never be fought" (Reagan, 1984).

Still, old thinking colors much of the thinking about the new post–Cold War strategic environment. As McGeorge Bundy observes:

> Yet not even a president with a gift for phrase-making and an earned immunity to criticism from conservatives can undo a whole strategic mindset by a single sentence. There is much serious work to be done in thinking through what it means, in terms of strategic doctrine, planning and procurement, to start from the proposition that a nuclear war cannot be won. The central tradition of military thought in both countries is that what you must do in war is win. In the particular version adopted as a formal service credo by the U.S. Air Force, you must win by the resolute and decisive application of strategic air power—nuclear since 1945 and including submarine-launched missiles since 1960. Unless Reagan and Gorbachev are all wrong about nuclear war, such pursuit of victory is quite literally nonsensical. You cannot win, and if you try to, you will only commit national suicide.
>
> Senior military men are obviously not blind to that reality. In practical terms what they expect from strategic strength is deterrence, not victory. Nonetheless they have been slow to address the habits of mind that lead planners and service leaders to seek ways and means of attack that might in some numerical sense "win." [Bundy, 1990: 209]

Indeed, habitual mindsets and conventional wisdom govern thinking, both in the United States and, to an unknown extent, in the Soviet Union, about the goals that nuclear weapons shall serve, even as conditions are transformed and purposes that once seemed reasonable may no longer be warranted. For example, "Washington's national security establishment," warns Fred Charles Iklé, who served as undersecretary of defense for policy in the Reagan administration, "continues to see the world in terms of the 1947 mindset. . . . Our nuclear strategy is still under the curse of Joseph Stalin. Few realize the extent to which the design and purpose of our nuclear armaments, doctrine and war plans date from the same old mindset that since 1947 shaped and governed the bulk of our conventional forces. . . . The obsolete dogma that our nuclear retaliation must be prompt is responsible for the Pentagon's insistence that we must maintain a large force of land-based missiles" (Iklé, 1990: 14, 19, 20). New strategies, these observers argue, are required, strategies that respond to the questions, after the Cold War ends, "What, now, are the threats against which the Pentagon should prepare?" and "How should America's strategy and military forces . . . be changed to take account of the transformed environment?" (Iklé, 1990: 13).

Of particular importance is redefinition of the nature of the threat that strategic forces are designed to deter. To many, if there are no threatening rivals, strategy should logically shift from the goal of "winning" or "prevailing" to the exclusive goal of defending or deterring. This change, in turn, requires rejection of a nuclear war-fighting strategy and acceptance of only a retaliatory use of nuclear arsenals.

In the spring of 1982, four eminent, former high officials of the U.S. government—McGeorge Bundy, George F. Kennan, Robert S. McNamara, and Gerald Smith (1982)—advocated an explicit shift to only that purpose when they called for a declaratory policy of "no first use" of nuclear weapons, thus challenging the long-standing doctrine of the United States and its NATO allies. This doctrine is based on the premise that the collective defense of the West depends on the strategy of initiating the use of nuclear weapons should the West's conventional, or nonnuclear, forces be threatened with defeat in Europe or elsewhere. These leaders instead urged that a no-first-use policy be adopted in Europe, which would also have required that NATO's conventional forces be increased to balance and repel the Warsaw Pact's forces.

This proposal to prohibit the initial use of nuclear weapons, even in retaliation, was criticized by others in policymaking circles because, in part,

> conventional defeat is the Achilles' heel of no first use. A policy of no first use thus can never really live up to its name. There is always an invisible asterisk attached, referring us to a footnote that reads, "Unless we start to lose." Without this qualification, a policy of no first use would really be a form of unilateral nuclear disarmament by verbal means, in which the foe was invited to take what he could, provided only that he did it with conventional forces. [Schell, 1984: 53–54]

But this perceived liability may have lost its relevance in the wake of the Cold War. With the threat of a Soviet surprise attack on Western Europe or the United States now virtually inconceivable, and with the elimination of short-range nuclear missiles in Europe as a result of the INF Treaty and the disintegration of the Warsaw Pact, the situation has been drastically altered. If a conventional attack from the east is no longer a realistic scenario, then "no first use" may now be an idea whose time truly has come.

In "Now More Than Ever: No First Use" (Chapter 4), Paul Warnke, who headed the negotiations during the Strategic Arms Limitations Talks (SALT), explains why the principle of first use—the doctrine that would authorize a preemptive or retaliatory nuclear strike—must be permanently rejected. To rely on the pledge to escalate a conventional war across the nuclear threshold (official NATO doctrine) is dangerous and unnecessary, Warnke argues. If ever that threat made sense, it has now become, with the end of the Cold War, invalid. However, "the regrettable, and unacceptable, fact," Warnke reminds us, "is that we have never made up our minds about the purpose of nuclear weapons. While pursuing arms control, we continue to cling to the illusion that nuclear weapons can be used to fight and win a war. [U.S.] weapons decisions have been and are still based on this fallacy."

At the July 1990 NATO summit, President Bush came closer to a "no first use" position when he proposed reversing three decades of defense doctrine by classifying nuclear arms as "weapons of last resort." "By moving to a strategy in which the alliance would wait to use tactical nuclear weapons only as a last resort, NATO would in effect commit itself to no *early* first use of nuclear weapons, without formally renouncing the right to strike first. [Hence] the Bush administration . . . again emphasized that it [would] not agree to a declaration that would formally rule out first use" (Hoagland, 1990: 1, 8). As Warnke observes, the doctrine of nuclear first use, "though badly wounded, still lives."

Like the doctrine of massive retaliation, Warnke believes, first use has also become obsolete. A nuclear war-fighting strategy is "both farce and folly" because, Warnke argues, the Soviet Union could absorb a first strike and retaliate with devastating force. Moreover, the threat of first use is not needed to preserve the peace; in fact, it increases the risk of nuclear war. And war among major powers is no longer a realistic means of resolving differences or achieving national objectives. The likelihood of escalation makes first use of tactical battlefield weapons or contemplation of limited strategic strikes an incalculable danger to human existence. Particularly in view of accommodation and even collaboration between the former Cold War enemies, the first-use doctrine, Warnke concludes, has become "an embarrassing anomaly."

To be sure, this principle is only one among many keys to deterrence and peace after the Cold War. It illustrates, and is linked to, many other difficult choices confronting policymakers in the new era. To broaden the picture, let us explore the observations and recommendations put forth by academic experts on the subject.

Policy Analysts and Peace Researchers

Removed from the inner corridors of power, academics who specialize in the scholarly analysis of peace, and who advise governments, also diverge on how national strategies can be adapted to fit the new post–Cold War circumstances. In the past, their analyses have contributed to the development of nuclear doctrines and force levels, and today, as before, their expertise remains at the cutting edge of inquiry and guides policymakers.

To understand what is new and different about deterrence in the post–Cold War period, it is useful to first look backward and extract lessons and theories applicable to the emergent new global context. That is the purpose of John Mueller's rich contribution, "Deterrence, Nuclear Weapons, Morality, and War" (Chapter 5).

To Mueller, conceptual misunderstanding of the Cold War and the role assigned to nuclear weapons poses a real danger to the prospects for peace in the 1990s and beyond, for, he demonstrates, great faith has accumulated in the untested proposition that nuclear weapons and targeting doctrines have prevented great-power war. The more powerful causal force inhibiting great-power war, Mueller cogently argues, has been the great powers' lack of appetite for waging one, and their aversion has eliminated any temptation they might otherwise have harbored to expand their territories by force. "Where people once saw great glory and honor in war—particularly in victory—they are now more inclined to see degradation in it instead." As a consequence, nuclear weapons and nuclear deterrence have lost their appeal and value, and war has been largely rendered "obsolescent" (see also Mueller, 1991).

To organize analysis and refocus theorizing, Mueller critiques the ambiguous concept of deterrence (Morgan, 1983) and broadens it to include nonmilitary considerations. Demonstrating that the vast majority of wars that never happen are deterred by factors which have little or nothing to do with military considerations, he focuses on nuclear deterrence by distinguishing "crisis stability" (see Hermann, 1988) and "general stability" and concludes that nuclear weapons have been essentially irrelevant to the remarkably long peace that has existed in the developed world since 1945: "even without nuclear weapons, the United States and the USSR would have been deterred from a war with each other."

From this revisionist perspective, Mueller derives insightful hypotheses about the future of deterrence in the post–Cold War period. Iconoclastic in temper, he illuminates the deficiencies in conventional realpolitik analysis while at the same time echoing the realist assumption that state behavior is not a fit subject for moral judgment. Mueller maintains that moral argumentation is better left out of the dialogue so that a relatively detached examination of nuclear strategies can be conducted and "the unintended—even perverse—results" of moralistic reasoning can be avoided. To Mueller, "wars would be less frequent and less murderous if moral and religious precepts had never been applied to them" because "a belief in the existence of a guiding and an instrumental God has helped to facilitate the sacrificial, uncertain, masochistic, improbable, and fundamentally absurd activity known as warfare." Seven arguments are developed to support the conclusion that war will be less frequent and destructive if theologically inspired analysis of the morality of deterrence is avoided. Ironically, this nihilist posture leads to conclusions that are largely compatible with those derived from normative inquiry and moral justifications (especially those guided by a consequentialist ethic, such as the moral pacifism that Richard Perle berates).

Other dimensions of the ethical and policy predicament presented by the post–Cold War era are equally basic: under conditions of *Stable Peace* (Boulding, 1978), it must be asked, What legitimacy can be claimed for the possession of nuclear weapons? How can nuclear arsenals be justified, if the threat of attack truly disappears in a post–Cold War system?

In "What Power Do Nuclear Weapons Give Their Possessors? The Basic Instability of Deterrence" (Chapter 6), Kenneth E. Boulding maintains that the instruments of nuclear destruction are dysfunctional. Rather than conferring security, they increase their possessors' vulnerability and breed instability. Boulding's critique of deterrence points to the problem that

> deterrence rests on a perilous paradox. What is perceived as an impossible war has to be perceived as possible if it is to be impossible. On the one hand, a nuclear war entails an unacceptable holocaust for all parties. It is assumed to act as a deterrent from aggression and to render impossible any and every military use of nuclear weapons. On the other hand, deterrence is not credible if these weapons cannot be used. [Tunander, 1989: 354]

To escape the dangers of this paradox, Boulding recommends that it be recognized that an entrenched "deterrence myth" (Vasquez, 1991) has dominated thinking—blind faith in the plausible, simple, and therefore appealing conviction that nuclear weapons have kept the peace. A counterargument is that nuclear weapons have not deterred war (largely because no superpower has desired since 1945 to wage a major war) and that they have bred instability instead; it is possible to have global security without nuclear deterrence (Johansen, 1989). The new post–

Cold War age therefore necessitates global learning and the discarding of cherished myths about the usefulness of weapons of mass destruction.

Nonetheless, faith in the logic of deterrence through threat clearly remains entrenched (as Chapter 2 illustrates). That belief persists for a variety of cultural, institutional, and conceptual reasons, including especially, Boulding argues, some common fallacies about the nature of power and misunderstandings about the sources from which it truly derives. Power is often equated with military capability, Boulding submits, when in fact that simple equation is inappropriate.

Power, he explains, is a complex phenomenon and must be looked at as a total system involving three elements: threat power, economic power, and integrative power. The distribution of power does not depend on the decisions of a single actor but on the interactions of the individual units composing the whole system. This distribution is related to the technology of destructive power (Pilat and White, 1990), which also has a profound effect on political institutions and, ultimately, the ability of nations to avoid *The War Trap* (Bueno de Mesquita, 1981). The development of the effective cannon destroyed the feudal system, and, Boulding contends, the development of aerial warfare and nuclear weapons have made national defense obsolete. National military organizations are now justified mainly on the grounds of deterrence. But, he shows, a system of deterrence cannot be stable in the long run, only the short run. "Now that communism has collapsed, the next candidate for the loss of legitimacy is the military," Boulding concludes: after the Cold War, the threat system of nuclear deterrence and the principles on which it rests must be jettisoned.

In "MAD (Minimum Assured Deterrence) Is *Still* the Moral Position" (Chapter 7), Paul M. Kattenburg argues against these conclusions and maintains that whereas the world is on the threshold of real change, the threat of nuclear weapons and need for deterrence will continue. Like Mueller, Kattenburg contends that whereas "MAD or the conditions of MAD themselves [did not cause] superpower peace in the years since World War II," nonetheless mutual assured destruction "can be viewed as a condition empirically producing a moral or an ethical outcome, regardless of its abhorrent logic": "the morality of the ends justifies the apparent immorality of the means." "Would a world in which both superpowers were nonnuclear," Kattenburg asks, "be not only more peaceful but also a better, more just world?" In his view, "there is very little to support that thesis." "There is therefore nothing unethical or immoral," Kattenburg concludes, "about a continued—though minimized—balance of terror among the superpowers" because "such a balance [can] be viewed as the most moral means of enhancing humanity's self-preservation."

Profoundly pessimistic (given the opportunity to err and the probability that a tactical nuclear war "would almost certainly escalate to wholly unacceptable levels of destructiveness"), Kattenburg calls for "a super-power entente" to create and lead a rudimentary world government empowered to deter conflicts elsewhere through its "continued possession of only minimal nuclear forces." The need for such a "security regime" (Jervis, 1982) is especially acute, Kattenburg warns, because "worldwide proliferation of nuclear technology and materials in recent decades has made it possible to envision the threat or even the actual use of nuclear as well as chemical weapons" by some desperate party—a condition that makes the practice of nuclear terrorism more probable (Beres, 1990). This prescription for a supranational organization led by the two super-powers is not, Kattenburg argues, "too visionary." (Perhaps the U.N. Security Council's imposition of a military and trade embargo on Iraq following that country's invasion of Kuwait in the summer of 1990 provides an example of the kind of transnational collaboration for the maintenance of international security that Kattenburg envisions.) His proposal for international peacekeeping by supranational entities, more-over, is not unprecedented, in that it follows the advice Albert Einstein voiced in 1946 when he recommended that "Everything that is done in international affairs must be done from the viewpoint of whether it will advance or hinder the establishment of world government" (cited in Nathan and Norden, 1960: 117).

In one sense, therefore, Kattenburg advocates the necessity of adhering to nuclear deterrence even while he also recognizes the need to move beyond it and pare back nuclear forces "to a minimum deterrent" (Maynes, 1990: 12; see also A. Bailey, 1989). The primary dangers stem from the risks of accident and miscalculation; the longer a threat lasts, the greater the probability that such an event will occur—with the likelihood of an eventual nuclear war a statistical certainty given the absence of nuclear disarmament and the passage of sufficient time (Avenhaus et al., 1989). The risks inherent in the preservation of nuclear weapons to which Kattenburg refers are suggested by Carl Sagan's imagery:

Imagine a room awash in gasoline, and there are two implacable enemies in that room. One of them has 9,000 matches; the other has 7,000 matches. Each of them is concerned who's ahead, who's stronger. Well, that's the kind of situation we are actually in. The amount of weapons that are available to the United States and the Soviet Union are so bloated, so grossly in excess of what's needed to dissuade the other, that if it weren't so tragic, it would be laughable. What is necessary is to reduce the matches and to clean up the gasoline. [Cited in Kegley and Wittkopf, eds., 1989: 4]

To reduce the risk, Kattenburg perceives the need to reduce force levels to a minimum deterrent and to forge a new supranational authority led by the superpowers. Because crisis management is not always possible and a dangerous illusion (LeBow, 1987a and 1987b), Kattenburg concurs with the Soviet view that stability requires finding "some agreed definition of what constitutes minimal deterrence in various strategic circumstances through expert discussions among representatives of nuclear powers and from countries that have such weapons deployed on their territory" (Trofimenko, 1990: 32). To secure minimum deterrence after the Cold War, "the size of the U.S. deterrent and the vigor of weapons research would depend upon cooperative measures Americans and Soviets could devise to reassure each side that the other was not cheating or on the verge of a breakout" (Maynes, 1990: 12).

This line of reasoning is extended and broadened in Bruce Martin Russett's wide-ranging contribution, "An Acceptable Role for Nuclear Weapons?" (Chapter 8). Russett, a political scientist who helped write the Catholic bishops' much-discussed 1983 pastoral letter on nuclear war, maintains that its "analysis should be adapted to current conditions" and suggests that "recent events call the acceptability of even [the bishops'] limited role [for nuclear weapons] into question."

Russett argues that most normative and policy problems with nuclear weapons arise from extended deterrence, that is, deterrence of attacks on friends or allies of a nuclear power. He traces the historical evolution of and contradictions in the West's extended deterrence strategy, which in the post–Cold War period has come under increased challenge as many Cold War alliances have ceased to function for the original purposes for which they were built. In addition, Russett outlines the sources of differences and similarities in the perspectives on the issues of nuclear weapons of U.S. and West German bishops. He presents a logical schema of types of deterrent situations and, after drawing some lessons from history about deterring conventional attack, evaluates some historical evidence which indicates that the utility of nuclear weapons for many of these situations is often exaggerated. After assessing alternative strategies, Russett suggests a role for a very restricted "countercombatant" deterrence in the post–Cold War era. Acknowledging that "such a countercombatant deterrent is [not] at the moment politically feasible, given the present levels and types of nuclear weapons," it "could become feasible sometime in the future, given the will of governing authorities to make it so." Such a deterrent may be possible because "the threat of a deliberate Soviet attack on Western Europe has dropped to the vanishing point for the foreseeable future." As a consequence, "it is hard now to imagine what it is that nuclear weapons must deter." The Soviet threat has receded, which provides "room for substantial progress."

"Under these new circumstances," he concludes, "very substantial reductions in the Soviet and U.S. nuclear armories appear both needed and likely."

Russett closes his timely chapter by noting that it is now time for the Catholic bishops (and other observers) to face the issues created by these hopeful developments, and he notes that "Cardinal Bernardin forcefully argues for greater vision on this and other dimensions of a new world order." Let us now consider the vision that Cardinal Bernardin and other moral philosophers and religious leaders propose.

Moral Philosophers and Religious Leaders

The study of nuclear deterrence has been monopolized by strategic theorists and policy analysts, even though it inescapably entails profoundly moral issues. "Behind all the issues of security we find questions about values" (Higgins, 1990: 205). For both strategists and moral philosophers, deterrence lies at the center of concern about the means to a preferred end, human survival: "Many analyses of the morality of nuclear deterrence—both defenses and condemnations—try to use a consequentialist method of moral argument. They assume that a correct moral judgment prescribes the choice of that option likely to lead to an overall preferable state of affairs—one in which benefits are maximized and harms minimized" (Finnis, Boyle, and Grisez, 1988: v).

The nuclear age and the Cold War placed consequentialist ethical accounts center stage. During the early 1980s, when superpower relations reached their most frigid state, how to avoid the most dreaded consequence of the nuclear age assumed special salience, and the escalating strategic arms race provoked widespread commentary from moral philosophers and religious groups.

The most ambitious probe of the moral problems of nuclear strategy at that time was the celebrated pastoral letter published in 1983 by the National Conference of Catholic Bishops, drafted under the leadership of Joseph Cardinal Bernardin. It compared the superpowers' strategic doctrines with the principles of Christian doctrine and found the former largely unacceptable. The plans then officially endorsed were perceived to violate a number of principles central to the "just-war" tradition in Christian theology, especially the stipulations that resort to violence be (1) *discriminate*, by giving noncombatants immunity; (2) *proportionate*, by limiting any collateral harm caused by war to a level commensurate with the good intended or the evil to be avoided; and (3) *reasonable* in its probability of success. As the pastoral letter then made clear, these norms prohibited acceptance of many of the strategic plans then in place or under consideration, and they challenged such prominent features of the U.S. strategic doctrine as counterpopulation (countervalue) warfare and unrestricted counterforce warfare.

When released in 1983, the moral position adopted in the pastoral letter provoked great controversy. By recommending a strategy for peace that severely limited the use of nuclear weapons (never!), by restricting how the threat of their use could be expressed (only to deter an attack), but by allowing nuclear weapons to be possessed nonetheless, the bishops arrived at a "strictly conditioned" acceptance of nuclear weapons, one that came close to a "you can have them but you can't use them" position (Russett, 1984). This statement generated both favorable and critical commentary (see the literature review in Chapter 12 of this book).

To keep abreast of changes, the bishops prepared a revised statement in 1988 entitled *Building Peace*. This comprehensive assessment alluded to the possibility that a new, more peaceful era could materialize at some point in time, which might provide a climate for many of the problems of nuclear deterrence to be meaningfully confronted. But that 1988 prediction addressed global conditions as they then existed. The new report once again repeated the "absolute categorical" prohibition against the deliberate targeting of civilians and reaffirmed the strong disapproval of the first use of nuclear weapons, while arguing that the threat of nuclear weapons for retaliation under certain "strict conditions" was acceptable to deter war. The new report sought "to build a barrier against nuclear use" by challenging those who ascribed to the view that nuclear weapons are "normal" or "controllable" instruments of military policy.

The hopeful new conditions that this revised statement envisioned as a future possibility became a sudden reality in 1989, and the momentous changes that swept the globe caught the bishops and nearly everyone else by surprise. As the superpowers lowered their fists, clasped hands, and talked seriously about beating their swords into plowshares, what had very recently been only a far-fetched dream had become a reality.

In "Ordering Our Destiny: Politics, Strategy, and Ethics" (Chapter 9), Joseph Cardinal Bernardin examines the Catholic interpretation of the nuclear dilemma in light of these changes. Maintaining that "the next decade of analysis and action will clearly not be a continuation of the nuclear debate of the last four decades" because "the historical fault line marked by 1989 is real," Cardinal Bernardin addresses the intellectual and political changes that must be made "to adapt nuclear policy in the post–Cold War world." As he sees it, to "construct an order that works, but one that works justly and can be maintained peacefully," an "ethic of control" is needed, which "requires cooperation, and cooperation, in turn, must be built on a common conception of a shared destiny." This, it is argued, necessitates recasting the issues, which "does not mean moving away from the ethics of deterrence but addressing it in a different context."

Although clearly the most visible religious interpretation of the morality of nuclear deterrence, the Catholic bishops' statement does not stand alone. Indeed, most of the world's major religious groups have put forward position-statements on the morality of nuclear weapons and nuclear deterrence, interpretations of these capabilities and doctrines in accordance with their individual theological traditions. In "From Pacifism to Apocalyptic Visions: Religious Perspectives on Nuclear Deterrence" (Chapter 10), Janice Love, who serves on the Board of Directors of the World Council of Churches, provides the most comprehensive comparative survey of those groups' attitudes ever undertaken. Her examination of the official positions taken by forty-seven Christian and Jewish governing bodies reveals the cleavages and areas of consensus among their perspectives. From the evidence, categories of moral positions are delineated, and the ideas associated with "pacifism," "nuclear pacifism," "interim deterrence," "minimum deterrence," "just nuclear war," and "apocalyptic militarism" are described. In addition, the organizations' proposals for peacemaking programs are compared.

Love's empirical research is enlightening. Instead of finding, as she initially expected, religious organizations in the United States to be far to the left on issues, in fact most groups were not. Although many of the groups reproach states' almost-worshipful attitude toward nuclear weapons (see Chernus, 1987), the evidence indicates that most religious organizations also believe the world is passing, and should pass, through "a period of transitional deterrence." In the short term, these religious bodies accept the need for nuclear weapons in order to maintain political equilibrium, but they urge the need for disarmament in the long term. In addition, these groups share a deep concern—verging on outrage—about the social, economic, and ecological costs of nuclear weapons, which have left many human needs unmet and possible remedies underfunded. They also recognize and berate the psychological costs as well, for it is costly for people to live with the knowledge that they have the capacity to end life as they know it on earth and possibly in the cosmos. Love concludes that if tensions between East and West continue to diminish in the 1990s, the groups that make a moral presumption against war are likely "to press further for nuclear restraint and disarmament, [and] should the superpowers and other states possessing nuclear weapons succeed in moving toward substantial or complete reductions in their nuclear arsenals, those who make a moral presumption in favor of war will need to find new justifications for that stand." "With a lessening of East-West tensions," Love believes that "the future would also seem to point to increasing adherence to moral positions that advocate a holistic accounting of the impact of nuclear war preparedness rather than those that focus more narrowly on the ethics of how and when to use various forms of these weapons."

Love's moral evaluation speaks to the fundamental ethical issue of nuclear weapons in our time, namely, whether such strategies can be justified. In "Can Contemporary War Be Just? Elements in the Moral Debate" (Chapter 11), James Turner Johnson reviews the applicability of traditional moral precepts regarding the just-war doctrine to the present post–Cold War era. His ethical assessment demonstrates the continuing relevance of that doctrine as interpreted by both Catholic and Protestant religious bodies in light of today's circumstances— circumstances that make the classical distinctions between the just and the unjust uses of force as pertinent as ever. Noting that "each argument reflects the political and technological conditions of the historical period in which it was prepared as well as the shape of the moral debate in each of those periods," Johnson identifies "at least five types of armed conflicts" that need to be included in the post–Cold War analysis of war and shows how changed conditions have modified the cogency of the arguments made on their behalf during the Cold War period. "The question," he concludes, "is whether this same level of deterrence preparedness can be justified today, in the light of altered East-West relationships, changed patterns of Soviet behavior, and modified perceptions of Soviet intentions and capabilities. I think not," he asserts, and accordingly, "one of the priorities in the moral debate . . . is to consider how mutually the two superpowers might reduce their deterrent forces and scale back their readiness for strategic retaliation."

That, indeed, is now *the* most prominent moral issue. The nature and role of deterrence must be rethought, Johnson convincingly argues, and "one of the ironies about strategic nuclear deterrence" must be confronted, namely, "that it attempts to protect values while at the same time it sharply contradicts other values, notably, the value of not putting innocent life at risk. A moral defense policy should seek the end to that irony."

Johnson's sobering analysis suggests the contribution timeless moral principles can make to the preservation of peace in the 1990s, while reminding us of the fact that such precepts cannot make a contribution unless policymakers take cognizance of them and voluntarily comply with their strictures. In the last analysis, then, peace *After the Cold War* will depend on the perceptions and values leaders embrace as they attempt to fashion strategies for deterring nuclear war.

New Thinking and Old Questions

In 1789, the framers of the Constitution of the United States proclaimed the advent of a *novus ordo seclorum*. Two hundred years later, in 1989, it became fashionable again to envision the advent of still another new world order. The founding fathers of the new democracy sought to wrestle with the new order that they had inherited by turning to the ideas and ideals that had inspired it during the Enlightenment. Similarly, today's policymakers are destined, to some extent, to be influenced by the experiences and dominant ideas of the first fifty years of *Danger and Survival* (Bundy, 1988), during which time they have lived in the shadow of nuclear-tipped missiles. The post–Cold War period is new, but how it is viewed will be profoundly shaped by how nuclear deterrence was evaluated during the protracted Cold War. The world faces a new world order, perhaps demanding a new architecture and new grand strategies, but the old questions and issues survive and will exert an impact on how the new realities and options are viewed.

To gain insight into the evolutionary course of strategic thinking since the beginning of the nuclear age, Steven W. Hook and William A. Clark examine the literature on the morality of deterrence. Their systematic survey, "On the Scholarly Study of Nuclear Deterrence: Historical Roots of the New Discourse" (Chapter 12), provides a backdrop against which the basic strategic and ethical questions are likely to be approached in the 1990s. Tracing the evolution of the literature as it has unfolded in discourse among U.S. strategic theorists, just-war students of international morality, and U.S. policymakers, Hook and Clark identify the intellectual antecedents to today's new dialogue. In the process, they provide not only a summary of the literature that informs contemporary discourse but also a review of concepts and a typology for classifying schools of thought so that today's dialogue can be better understood. As their review of the strategic dialogue demonstrates, the spectrum of issues being debated widened as the Cold War neared conclusion, and "nuclear moralism" has undergone a resurgence after a prolonged period in which "explicitly moral aspects of the nuclear debate [were] held in abeyance." "In an odd twist of Herman Kahn's (1966) admonition that Americans should 'think about the unthinkable,' " Hook and Clark explain why "the new challenge . . . may be to consider the *peaceful* possibilities that only yesterday were scarcely imaginable."

This survey of the existing literature provides a useful introduction to Jonathan Davidson's postscript to *After the Cold War*, "The Post–Cold

War Context: The Contributors' Dialogue in Perspective" (Chapter 13). Davidson broadens the printed material presented in the other contributors' chapters by summarizing the ideas they exchanged when they convened on February 8–9, 1990, at the University of South Carolina to discuss and critique the first drafts of their chapters. Davidson's overview of this dialogue provides supplementary statements that further explain the contributors' positions and permit the areas of their agreement and disagreement to be better understood. Furthermore, this postscript to *After the Cold War* records opinions about nuclear deterrence not available elsewhere. The overview will enable readers to better understand the contributors' positions, and it gives background information from which subsequent scrutiny of the morality of deterrence in the post–Cold War era can proceed.

The readers of this book are asked to assess the many contending ideas put forth in order to discern for themselves whether nuclear deterrence can be morally justified as the Cold War ends. In the final analysis, the answers are likely to remain ambiguous. But the promise of a new era makes it imperative to resolve the issue of whether, as the Palme Commission on Disarmament and Security Issues (1989) argued, "war is losing its meaning as an instrument of national policy, becoming instead an engine of senseless destruction that leaves the root causes of conflict unresolved" (cited in Zuckerman, 1989: 26). As the commission (1989) also admonished, "A doctrine of common security must replace the present expedient of deterrence through armaments. . . . International security must rest on a commitment to joint survival rather than on a threat of mutual destruction." The world must now judge the wisdom or folly, and morality or immorality, of that prescription. If *After the Cold War* provokes serious consideration of this proposition, it will have succeeded in its basic purpose.

Part I

The Views of Policymakers and Strategic Theorists

The passing of the postwar era [as well as the] new world which we are approaching present us with a new mix of challenges and concerns. As we celebrate the revolution of 1989 and the triumph of our policy of containment, we cannot afford to postpone the development of a new set of policies. [To] address this new world we must take advantage of the myriad opportunities that present themselves and deal with the new problems that are arising and the dangers that remain.

With creativity tempered by prudence, we can help in the creation of a safer, more peaceful, and more rewarding world.

Paul H. Nitze
Special Adviser to the President

2

Military Power and the Passing Cold War

Richard Perle

As we ponder the need for military power in the aftermath of the Cold War, remember this: the collapse of the Soviet empire in Eastern Europe is in large measure a result of the postwar strength and determination of the alliance of Western democracies. Those who argued for nuclear deterrence and serious conventional military capabilities contributed mightily to the position of strength that eventually led the Soviet leadership to choose a less bellicose, less menacing approach to international politics.

Now that we see the military power of the Warsaw Pact ebbing with the receding tide of communist rule and Soviet domination, there will be those who argue that the Soviet empire never amounted to much, that Western estimates of the strength of the Warsaw Pact were exaggerated, and that we can now go shopping for new programs with the savings the demise of the Soviet threat will allow us to achieve.

This argument is of more than passing, historical interest. For it will be necessary for some time to come to gauge correctly the threat still posed by Soviet military power in judging how to protect the security of the United States and how to shape the military budget. So before running to the bank with the elusive "peace dividend," it would be wise to remember that Soviet military power remains formidable and growing even as the Warsaw Pact disintegrates.

Soviet Military Threat

Even as the influence of the Soviet Union declines, the Soviets continue to spend massively on military power. While the United States invests about 6 percent of GNP in defense and our allies something like 3 percent, the Soviets, in my judgment, are spending 25 percent or more.

This debilitating Soviet investment in defense, which has proceeded apace despite the absence of any plausible threat, has produced, and continues to produce, a formidable array of military systems of all sorts, including an aggressive program of nuclear force modernization. General James Galvin put it well when he observed that

> every month the Soviets still produce enough tanks to outfit an entire division and enough artillery to equip four artillery regiments. Since Gorbachev assumed power in March, 1985, the Soviets have fielded more tanks and artillery pieces than currently exist in the combined armies of Britain, France and West Germany. [Galvin, 1989: 85–86]

The slight slowing observed recently seems to reflect Soviet anticipation of a strategic arms reduction treaty. Even so, it is a slowing that comprehends significant further investment within the levels contemplated by a treaty—if not beyond.

I do not mean to imply that nothing has changed. The transformation of Poland and Hungary, Czechoslovakia and East Germany, Rumania and Bulgaria; the tearing down of the Berlin Wall; the rising demand in Eastern Europe for a withdrawal of the Soviet troops that kept corrupt and stagnating communist regimes in power against the will of their own citizens, all these changes have profound implications, mostly beneficial, for Western security. The threat of a cohesive Warsaw Pact, led by Soviet troops, forcing its way through the center of Europe in a massive invasion of NATO territory is no longer plausible. As we consider how to respond, we must take care not to revive that threat by so depleting Western defenses that the advantage once enjoyed by the Warsaw Pact will now belong to the Soviet Union alone.

Extreme proposals, immune to the lessons of history, that would disarm the West after the Cold War as it was disarmed after World Wars I and II would run the risk that we might yet again make Europe safe for the exertion of Soviet military power. A careless rush to disarm in which we throw caution to the winds of change, shipping technology and capital to Moscow even as that country reels under the weight of a massive military budget; a disregard for the importance of verification of international agreements; a dismantling of Western defenses in ways that would make them difficult or impossible to reconstruct should the need arise—these are the new threats that have come to replace those to which we had become accustomed.

But the situation has vastly improved. It should prove far easier to fight an improvident, dangerous euphoria than the Warsaw Pact divisions whose eastward movement we now anticipate celebrating—not so much, by the way, because we've sent an army of diplomats to Vienna, but because the emerging independent nations of Eastern Europe are quite determined to throw them out.

There is a second threat that also seems to me much diminished. That is the threat of a massive Soviet nuclear strike, out of the blue, against the strategic retaliatory forces of the United States, a strike that would entail thousands of nuclear weapons exploding on American territory. I believe that Soviet attitudes toward nuclear weapons have been evolving, by and large, away from the contemplation of a massive, disarming strike mounted in peacetime and prepared in secrecy. The days when Soviet doctrine considered that nuclear weapons differed little except in explosive power from conventional ones are past.

For the foreseeable future I believe the United States can reduce the amount it invests to provide a high degree of protection against a massive surprise Soviet nuclear attack. But that can only be done safely if sensible principles are adopted to guide the shaping of a diminished defense budget. And it cannot be done at all, of course, if we now succumb to the siren call of the unilateralists and pacifists whose policies, had we followed them previously, would surely have kept the Cold War going or even allowed the Soviet bloc to win it.

U.S. Response to Changes

The rapidity of recent changes should humble us as we make sweeping predictions, although, if experience is any guide, it will spur more people to rashness than it will temper with caution. My vote is for caution as we greet the millennium and divvy up the "peace dividend." That caution has to do with the instability that has resulted from Moscow's loosening grip—not only in Eastern Europe but in the Soviet Union itself—and the uncertainty about the future of Soviet leadership.

President Gorbachev has set in motion centrifugal forces that have reawakened old ethnic and national allegiances. In Lithuania, Latvia, Estonia, Georgia, Azerbaijan, Moldavia, and elsewhere, there are hapless, restive people who have suffered under Soviet imperial domination. They see what is going on in Eastern Europe. They have seen the hammer and sickle torn from national flags; they have seen statutes and regimes toppled, tyrants shot or imprisoned. In a world of instant communications the revolution in Eastern Europe is on display in the most distant corners of the Russian empire.

No one can say where these forces will lead, but an unstable Soviet empire could be a dangerous place. We've waited a long time for an opportunity to throw off the burden of providing security for ourselves and our allies; we would be wise to wait a little longer before confidently predicting that we can afford to be weak in the face of uncertainty.

So how, then, should we shape the defense budget to take full and creative account of the political changes in Eastern Europe and the beginning of a change in attitude—not yet matched by a change in investment—in the Soviet Union? How can we manage the cuts in defense spending that everyone knows are coming in a way that protects our security and encourages further change in the Soviet Union?

Two principles should guide the shaping of a national strategy and the defense budget that goes along with it. First, we should reduce force structure to reflect the lessened Warsaw Pact threat while maintaining the quality of the smaller residual force, especially as regards the cadre necessary to reestablish larger forces should that become necessary. Second, we should protect research and development and the defense industrial base so we can reconstitute advanced military capabilities should the need arise. The application of these two principles would mean a cut in overall military forces, especially ground forces, in order to assure that a smaller armed force will be adequately equipped and trained and poised for rapid growth if our hopes for a less menacing Soviet Union should be disappointed.

Such a response may mean forgoing some planned weapons systems now on the grounds that the increased risk in the near term of "making do" with the current generation of equipment is manageable while the future is murky. It is this murkiness and the dismal record of clairvoyance in these matters that so clearly counsels caution.

Some of the new weapons should be continued. The B-2 aircraft is one. So is the Trident II. I would not proceed with either the Midgetman or the rail-mobile MX: the current generation of intercontinental ballistic missiles (ICBMs) should prove adequate, and the next generation—for we will need a strategic deterrent as far as the mind can see—will benefit from further research and development if it is delayed for a few years.

The same should hold true for some conventional weapons systems: making do with the current generation should not entail an intolerable risk while we press ahead with research and development and gain a better sense of how the world is evolving. I doubt that a new tactical fighter is worth the cost at this moment, given a shrinking budget. We should be able to keep the current planes flying, but I think it wise to develop a new fighter later.

There is one program in which the United States should be investing more rather than less: the Strategic Defense Initiative (SDI). As the prospect of nuclear proliferation draws closer, we should be reminded that the threat is neither exclusively Soviet nor, for that matter, exclusively deliberate. There are other countries and there are accidents; these two reasons alone would justify a vigorous research and development program to push back even further the frontiers that have recently been yielding to impressive research results.

It is, I believe, unprecedented in human history for a nation with the technical and financial resources to protect against a known mortal danger to decide as a matter of national policy to do nothing. A serious program of research and development reoriented toward limited, partial defenses can and should go forward even in the face of a shrinking defense budget.

Moral Arguments in Perspective

The period of the Cold War was marked by a most extraordinary inversion of moral argument applied to complex questions of military strategy. We had the bizarre spectacle of clergy marching against ballistic missile defenses in the late 1960s and early 1970s as the nation debated whether to proceed with the Safeguard antiballistic-missile defense system—a system that would have protected our retaliatory forces by shooting down missiles aimed at destroying them. This "moral" opposition to ballistic-missile defense, which resurfaced in the 1980s after the SDI was proposed, would have had the effect of leaving the United States with only offensive weapons with which to deter attack. It was never clear by what moral principle offensive weapons were to be preferred to defensive ones; one's intuition would seem to lead in precisely the opposite direction.

The most likely explanation is that the judgment of the moralists was, not a moral, but a strategic one, one that followed from the belief that the deployment of strategic defenses by the United States would lead the Soviet Union to deploy additional offensive weapons with which to attack the U.S. deterrent. This was a doubtful conclusion, and in any case, even after a treaty was concluded in 1972 that all but banned strategic defenses, the Soviet Union went right on building more offensive forces anyway. The lesson for the moralists should have been to steer clear of issues that were not essentially moral ones.

But it is a lesson that went unheeded as the moralists soon lined up again to oppose the "neutron bomb" in the mid-1970s. This time, the moral authorities who took to the streets to protest were demanding that the United States not replace its tactical nuclear weapons with weapons whose effects would be confined to the battlefield—or at least to an area substantially smaller than the weapons they would have replaced. Thus, the moral position seemed to be on the side of a greater radius of destruction.

Another example of misapplied moralism is provided by the objections moralists voiced concerning the 1981 Israeli destruction of Iraq's nearly completed atomic reactor. I find this reaction among the moralists even more bizarre than their reaction to strategic defenses or the neutron weapon. Israel did all countries a favor when it bombed an Iraqi nuclear installation in order to forestall the Iraqi program to develop a nuclear weapon.

If ever there was a simple moral tale it is to be found in the Israeli attack. There appeared to be no other way to deflect Saddam Hussein from his reckless course, and moral suasion on the part of the people who voiced indignation at the Israeli action would have been about as useful as a candle in a hurricane. The United Nations was not about to take action, and the International Atomic Energy Authority is wholly ineffective in dealing with aggressive countries bent on acquiring nuclear weapons, such as Iraq.

In retrospect, it is clear that had Israel not acted to destroy the Iraqi reactor—and had Iraq obtained a nuclear weapon—it would almost certainly have been used during Iraq's war with Iran. When one compares the admittedly aggressive act of dropping bombs on a site in Baghdad with the use of a nuclear weapon, how can one argue about the essential moral correctness of the Israeli action?

The dilemmas posed by the role of power in an amoral world will continue to animate moralists even as the Cold War winds down. One hopes that these moralists will become more subtle as the issues with which they have to contend are scrutinized more closely. Maybe a calmness will now descend where urgency and anxiety once plagued careful judgments about morality and power.

3

What Stakes Would Justify the Use of Weapons of Mass Destruction?

Sir Hugh Beach

The Artful Dodgers

The most perplexing issue in the debate over the acceptability of nuclear deterrence is whether it is or could ever be morally permissible to fight a nuclear war if deterrence should fail. There are four ways at least of dodging this issue, and since all of them find favor, in one form or another, it is worth disposing of them.

The first dodge is to sweep the problem under the carpet with the reflection that deterrence, provided that it is "robust" enough, will always in fact work. In other words, provided that NATO, for example, keeps its nerve and its guard up, no question of fighting a nuclear war need ever arise. A weaker form of this argument, but a more insidious one, is to aver that the whole object of possessing a deterrent is to ensure that it shall never be used. A French view might be that since deterrence is a logically consistent doctrine, it cannot fail; since the aim is dissuasion, no question of immorality exists. But the argument founders on the rock of uncertainty—*how* can one be so sure? As is well known, this argument, if one is to take it seriously, has to assume that the actors in the drama are rational, that there is no question of miscalculation or overreaching, and that the technical mastery of warheads, missiles, and so forth is such that the chance of an accident leading to inadvertent use is negligible.

If anyone were disposed to take that position, two recent misadventures should be enough to put them off. The Chernobyl reactor disaster and the Challenger debacle stand as suggestive surrogates for a nuclear warhead and its delivery means. At Chernobyl, it seems that, for no good reason, technicians embarked upon an unauthorized and unnecessary experiment, with insufficient knowledge, and when things went wrong utterly bungled the recovery procedures. In the case of Challenger, it appears that a known point of technical difficulty (the O-ring joints in the booster casing) was never sufficiently acknowledged in the risk assessments at high level, and in the particular conditions of the final launch the judgments of those who did know were overridden for reasons of managerial expediency.

In both of those cases, the stakes were high and known to be so; the best qualified people in the Soviet Union and the United States were involved; and the type of accident that occurred had shortly beforehand been publicly and explicitly proclaimed to be impossible. The conclusion is self-evident: so long as nuclear weapons exist, there must also exist the risk that, for whatever reason, one will be deployed. Such an event need not, of course, lead to a nuclear war, but it would be rash to say that it could never do so. It simply cannot be true that deterrence, so long as it is in place, is certain to work.

The second approach is to rely on bluff, and this dodge is surprisingly popular. It takes the form of saying, in effect, that it is perfectly acceptable to possess nuclear weapons, and thus to derive the benefits of deterrence, provided that it is recognized that in the event, they would be unusable. A more dignified description of this doctrine is "existential deterrence"—which presumably means that so long as these things exist, no question need ever arise of being prepared to use them, because the opposition could never be *sure* that one would not and that fact alone would be sufficient to deter.

But that type of reasoning overlooks two crucial difficulties. The first is that these things are weapons, and it is as weapons that they exercise their deterrent effect—not simply as a reassuring context (like an impassable range of mountains) within which the normal traffic of diplomacy can be conducted in perfect safety. Since they are weapons, there has to be a policy for their use, and in the case of nuclear weapons, the policy is a highly complex, extensive, and sophisticated one. It embraces the technical experts who design, test, manufacture, store, service, and repair the warheads and their delivery means. It involves a huge apparatus of geodetic and terrain survey, intelligence gathering, surveillance, command and control communications, and the means for governmental decision making whether to fire or to forbear. It involves the service and civilian crews who operate all these facilities: their selection, training, management, and motivation. It involves the development of doctrine, plans, policy, and exercises covering every aspect of the weapons' possible deployment and use. If the weapons are never, in fact, to be used, how is that fact to be handled? Who is in on the secret? Who is supposed to be fooling whom? And so far as the West is concerned, with its quasi-open society that appears to be highly susceptible to espionage, is it not probable that the real, but presumably secret, policy of non-use will be as well known to any potential enemy as it is to those in command on our side? One can not run an enterprise of this magnitude as a gigantic spoof.

The second crucial difficulty is even more compelling. Bluff is appropriate enough in a poker game where the stakes are affordable; it is totally inappropriate when the survival of peoples and civilizations is involved, since a bluff may always be called.

The third way out is to accept that the possession of, and conditional intention to use, nuclear weapons on the part of the West are justified (and indeed necessary) as such weapons provide much the best guarantee of not being involved in a war—and above all a nuclear war—with the Soviet Union *but* that no morally acceptable use can be realistically envisaged. Indeed, it is precisely the threat of escalation to morally impermissible levels that constitutes the sure element in deterrence. This argument is the more compelling to the extent that "escalation" is taken seriously: once place one's foot on the lowest step of the moving staircase, and there can be no turning back, no emergency stop button; one will be carried willy nilly to the top.

But there is a logical nonsense in that argument. How can it, at one and the same time, be right and necessary to form a conditional intention which, if it came to carry it out, is impermissible? This way of thinking has been characterized, understandably, as incoherent. Another way of describing it is as an inescapable paradox. But sane people could hardly accept that reasoning as the basis for a Christian survival policy unless they could be assured that it is indeed inescapable. All the more reason, therefore, to attempt to think through the possibilities for morally permissible use—even if they are all ultimately discarded.

The fourth way of dodging the issue, and arguably the only logical consequence of accepting that no morally acceptable use of nuclear weapons can be found, is to follow the path of despair. If we believe that the existence of nuclear weapons is bound to lead one day to their use, that bluff is not a viable option, and that their use could never be morally justified, then the natural conclusion is that we in the West should give them up and submit to what might follow. This is an unwelcome conclusion.

First, save in the unlikely event that all other countries possessing nuclear weapons (notably Russia and China) were shamed into following suit, this course of action would put a monopoly of nuclear military power into hands arguably less scrupulous than ours. Second, it would lay us open to nuclear blackmail in ways that are impossible to foresee in detail but which could prove disastrous in practice. Third, it is far from self-evident that the existence of a nuclear monopoly is the best guarantee against eventual use, as historically, it was only during the existence of a monopoly (by the United States) that the actual use of nuclear weapons occurred. So this conclusion is a counsel of despair indeed, a renunciation that might render more likely the very contingency that it is designed to obviate. Thus, the presumption is very strong that we should seek some concept for the use of nuclear weapons in war that is consonant with the precepts of a "just war."

Just-War Doctrine in the Atomic Age

The criteria of *jus ad bellum* (just resort to war) imply both a just cause and a reasonable prospect of success, and they should, in theory, be comparatively simple to fulfill. The requirement of a just cause implies, first, that the war should be one of self-defense, and it is difficult to suppose that NATO would undertake any other type of war. It is a truism that the correlation of conventional forces on the central front is such as to rule out absolutely any aggression by the West, whatever the provocation. No plans, policies, training, or logistical preparations could possibly support such an act. Soviet commentators have made much of the U.S. plan called Dropshot, current in the early 1950s, whereby the strategic bombing of Russia with atomic weapons would have been followed up with a conventional invasion. This plan has absolutely no credibility today, if indeed it ever did. One need not believe, for its own sake, the declaration by leaders of the NATO governments that "none of our weapons will ever be used save in self-defense." The transparent fact is that political support in the West simply does not exist for any attempt to roll back the frontiers of the Soviet empire by force of arms.

It follows that the purposes for which the military establishments of NATO have been maintained are indisputably just. They have existed to prevent either the physical destruction of one or more of the countries of the West (say, West Germany), their military occupation and the imposition of regimes totally alien to their preferred systems, or their coercion or blackmail whereby the fundamental freedoms and values that constitute their concept of nationhood would be lost. The question of *how bad* the alien regimes imposed in the event of defeat or appeasement might have been is another matter.

The other criterion of a just cause ought also to be attainable, at least in theory: there should be a reasonable prospect of a successful outcome. It is fashionable, and certainly true, to say that in an all-out nuclear war between the superpowers there could be no "winners." It is true because the term "all-out," as things stand at present, must imply the use of a substantial proportion, if not the greater part, of the strategic nuclear arsenals of both sides. Each possesses tens of thousands of such warheads, and it is not necessary to invoke the hypothesis of nuclear winter to demonstrate that the use of nuclear warheads on anything approaching that scale could never be considered a part of any definition of success. Nor is such an outcome one that either of the protagonists could rationally desire.

The aim of the Soviet Union in going to war with the West could only be to bring about surrender—either to remove a threat judged to be intolerable or, more improbably, to subjugate, if it were foreseen that no substantial defense would be offered. On the other side, the aims of the West could only be to compel the aggressor to cease and desist. The West might hope to enforce a return to prewar boundaries and a promise of future good conduct, but such outcomes would not be essential. It would be a sufficient concept of success to have brought the war to an end as quickly and as economically as possible. It is by no means obvious a priori that a readiness to use, or indeed an actual use of, nuclear weapons by the West could not have these effects. In fact, it has been persuasively argued, not least by Leonard Cheshire (1985), that the use of nuclear weapons by the Americans against the Japanese in 1945 did precisely that.

We move on then to the criteria of *jus in bello* (just use of force), that any use of nuclear weapons should be both discriminate and proportional. The principle of discrimination rules out any direct intentional attack on noncombatants or nonmilitary targets. The principle of proportionality requires both that the damage resulting from any operation must be proportional to the military ends sought and, more demandingly, that the overall costs of the war be proportionate to the good accomplished by conducting it—that is to say, by resisting rather than appeasing, surrendering, accepting defeat, or suing for peace. These criteria are closely interrelated. The principle of discrimination forbids any attack upon noncombatants or nonmilitary targets *as such* and would thus rule out the type of attack variously described as "countervalue," or "counter city," and prohibit any such attack undertaken to comply with the doctrines of "mutual assured destruction" or "minimal deterrence."

The British government, in justifying the possession of an independent strategic nuclear force capable of striking the USSR, has explained that its concept of deterrence aims at threatening "key aspects of Soviet state power." The U.S. government has spelled out its potential targets as being the military forces of the aggressor, that opponents' war-supporting industrial and economic base, and the political entities whereby control by the Communist party is maintained. These two concepts seem to mean much the same thing and do not necessarily amount to a strategy of striking indiscriminately.

The difficulty is that such targets, while unquestionably military and combatant in themselves, are collocated with centers of population so that any attack upon the targets would result in extensive civilian casualties. It is not much help to say that such casualties are unintended if they are in fact certain. It is, of course, useful to develop weapons that, by virtue of their accuracy and comparative freedom from radioactive fallout, can reduce unintended casualties to a minimum, and such development has been precisely the trend in warhead, missile, and aircraft design for the past several decades. Perhaps the point has now been reached at which it is permissible to merge this principle with that of proportion and to say that just-war doctrine would allow the use of nuclear weapons against military targets provided unintended damage to nonmilitary people and things was held down to a proportional level.

On that basis, it can be argued that sufficient legitimate targets could be found, in Russia and the Eastern bloc, whose destruction would do damage to the Soviet system out of all proportion to any benefit those countries could anticipate by going to war and would thus constitute a legitimate strategy of deterrence (Fisher, 1985: 178). Although that argument may be true, it gets us only part of the way. To be legitimate, a strategy must not only threaten the aggressor with an unacceptable amount of damage but also satisfy the further condition that the total damage suffered—by the belligerents, by the neutrals, and by the world at large—must be proportional to the good that is achieved.

Thus, the whole trend of the argument to this point requires that we focus on the issue of proportion. "The *calculus of proportion* between the values of the polities to be defended and their just causes and the costs of such just defense, in the light of the probability of success, is the central moral exercise in just war analysis" (O'Brien and Langan, 1986: 165). Yet such an analysis seems seldom to be attempted. If it is, it tends to be in some such simplistic terms as "you cannot put a price on a principle" or "better to be red than dead," which is conspicuously unhelpful. Yet the reason for shying away from this type of analysis is also clear enough. Who indeed is qualified to evaluate the goodness of the values to be defended, the badness of the regimes that would supervene if those values were not defended, and the damage to be anticipated in the act of defending them—let alone to strike a balance between these essentially incommensurate entities? But if such an evaluation is not carried out, then the whole analysis fails.

Another awkward feature of this argument must be acknowledged before the central issue is confronted directly. If defense of one's nation could not, so far as anyone can judge, be conducted within the limits of justice—that is, if the costs of defending were held to exceed the damages that would be suffered by conceding—then to appease, surrender, or sue for peace would become not simply a despairing gesture but a moral duty. Herbert Butterfield catches the essence of the problem precisely. In speaking of the eighteenth-century theorists, he says:

> They rejected the fanaticism which felt that God and all His angels would be thwarted if you failed to defeat the enemy; and they argued that it was better to say clearly that you were fighting for a province, fighting for Alsace for example, and then when you were tired of fighting you could divide the territory or arrange a system of compensation while in a "war for righteousness" you could never compromise. Don't awaken the moral indignation of the masses, they said, because you may want to withdraw from the war and public opinion will be at fever heat and will not allow it. They even said that you must keep the moral element out of war since, like religion, it only multiplied the number of the atrocities. [Butterfield, 1949: 179]

It follows that if, at the moment of transition to war, the prospective costs outweigh the expected benefits, it is morally imperative to turn back. If during the conduct of war the same condition applies, it is morally necessary, and generally far more difficult, to cease and desist and to pay the price. And so far as deterrence is concerned, it is not sufficient to assert that *some* morally acceptable uses of nuclear weapons can be envisaged (as plainly they can) and that this fact in itself suffices to justify their possession. The condition to be satisfied is a far stiffer one: the possessor nations must be able to conceive of a war policy, involving the use of these weapons, that in its totality can satisfy the tenets of both discrimination and proportion—and one that, within these limits, is sufficient to deter. It is not of the essence that such a policy be published, least of all to potential opponents, but one clearly must exist. And in devising such a policy, there can be no justification for assuming an optimum outcome for any move that might be made, rather the reverse.

So, to restate the question, How much death and destruction is it morally licit to threaten to inflict and to sustain as the price of preventing one's country from falling under the sway of another? This question is quite different from that implied by the calculations of strategic analysis that the destruction of, say, 30 percent of an adversary's population and 70 percent of the industrial capacity would constitute unacceptable damage. The question posed here is quite different because there is now the possibility of suffering and inflicting almost literally infinite punishment. In past wars, exhaustion or the overrunning of one side by the other has generally brought an end to the war well before total destruction occurred. So, while just-war criteria might well have dictated an earlier accommodation, at least the ultimate damage was confined.

Such an outcome might be no longer possible. The limits of acceptable damage that it makes sense to contemplate need now to be brought out into the open and compared with the benefits of resisting. It is not a question of how much is it worth in blood and treasure to win. It is more a question of how much resistance is worth. If a nation goes to war, it should be because the alternative is worse. In present circumstances, what *could* be worse than a war?

"Total" War and History

In getting at an answer to that question, it may be helpful to examine the very few historical instances when something approaching the scale of devastation that might be suffered in a nuclear war has been experienced. Four examples come to mind. The first episode occurred at the Jewish fortress at Masada in the year A.D. 73. It seems that the whole garrison, under siege, preferred to commit suicide rather than surrender to the Romans. Was this a preference for death rather than dishonor or simply a preference for death at one's own hand rather than life imprisonment or death by torture? It is difficult to judge, the more so because the miseries of the Jewish nation seemed so largely of the Jews own making. Was the mass suicide a principled gesture in the face of intolerable oppression or a collective act of paranoia more akin to the episode at Jonesville?

The second instance is the Thirty Years War, fought mainly in Germany between 1618 and 1648. This war had its origins in religious disputes— between the Catholic and Protestant branches of the western Christian church—but developed into a struggle for power between the Holy Roman Emperor, supported by Bavaria and Spain, and France, which was supported by various Protestant states as well as by the pope. When the war ended, France had gained most; Sweden and Brandenburg emerged as major powers; and the Holy Roman Emperor became little more than the ruler of Austria. The price paid by the people of Germany was fearful. Because the armies involved were larger than their own administrative capacities could cope with, devastation was for thirty years a logistical necessity. Religious passion was not necessarily a civilizing influence, and no moral sanctions appeared to prevail. At the sack of Magdeburg, 30,000 people were burned to death. In Germany as a whole, 8 million people perished. In Bohemia, only 6,000 out of 35,000 villages survived. In all of Germany, the richest areas suffered most. Protestantism was preserved, but in most other respects German civilization suffered deeply, perhaps ruinously, and the effects were felt for at least a hundred years.

The political issues involved, including control of the Rhineland and the organization of Germany as a unitary state, continue to bedevil Europe to this day. Most historians would no doubt judge that the Thirty Years War went over the top—the damage suffered by Germany was out of all proportion to any benefit gained—and, indeed, the eighteenth-century views applauded by Butterfield were a reaction to the excesses of that war. The issues involved—as between Catholic and Protestant, between Hapsburg and Bourbon—though we can view them with dispassion, were as compelling to contemporaries as are the issues between East and West today, and for much the same reasons. They were issues of faith, style, and nationality. Can the history of that war then afford some clue to our question? Even in disputes of this kind, maybe the sacrifice of five places of civilization in every six is just too much.

The third episode worth citing is that of Paraguay, though the parallels here are less close. In 1865, the then-president, Francisco Solano López, by ill-judged declarations of war, succeeded in combining against his country the triple coalition of Argentina, Uruguay, and Brazil. The war went on for five years, only to end with the death of López in an obscure skirmish and the virtual destruction of his country. The economy was in ruins, the population had been halved, and nine out of every ten adult males had been killed. Women, in despair, were reduced to mating casually with any available sailor at the riverfront. Militarist groups fought each other for power; presidents were compelled to resign or were deposed or assassinated. The Bill of Rights, drawn up in reaction to dictatorship, remained a dead letter for forty years. The country is still poor and underpopulated, and it only recently escaped from yet another authoritarian military regime. Obviously the War of the Triple Alliance was unjust by any canon, whether of cause or conduct, but it teaches one sad and salutary lesson: President Francisco Solano López, megalomaniac, is revered as a national hero to this day, so, in assessing the limits of justifiable sacrifice in war, it may not be much help to trust the people.

The last instance is that of World War II, fought to destroy the rule of Adolf Hitler over one of the most civilized countries on earth. This regime obliterated people systematically on racist grounds alone—because they were Jews—and it believed in locking away people of whom it disapproved in concentration camps. It was determined, as gradually became apparent, on extending its country's borders (whether by conquest or intimidation) without limit. For too long the French and the British, with the World War I battles of the Somme and Passchendael in mind, failed to define even to themselves where to draw the line. In the end, when there was plainly no other way of stopping Hitler, they went to war to do so. The price is said to have been 50 million dead (50 megadeaths in the jargon), of whom 20 million were Russian. If it had been known at the outset that this would be the price, would the combatants have been prepared to pay it? And would it have been right to do so? One cannot interrogate the dead, but among the living, even among Germans and certainly among Russians, the general opinion seems to be that it was. With hindsight, it would have been even more right if they had made their determination clear, and acted upon it, five years earlier.

The last example presents the case for deterrence. But what does it say about the just war and the fair price? To answer, one need not defend all that was done on the Allied side; indeed, it is important that one should not. But on the central issue, it seems to say that tens of megadeaths need not be a disproportionate price to pay, if that is the only way of stopping in its tracks a regime as evil, arrogant, and aggressive as that which staged the Holocaust.

To carry the argument forward, let us now consider two hypothetical instances taken from the mythology of the 1970s and 1980s. The first is that devised by General Sir John Hackett (1978). In this tale the Soviets having attempted to overrun Western Europe with conventional forces and run out of steam, stage a single attack utilizing an SS-17 missile airburst over Birmingham, England. The immediate casualties are 300,000 killed, 250,000 with blast or burn injuries of a very serious nature, and another 500,000 with lighter injuries requiring no more than first aid. The radiological aftereffects are small. In retaliation, the British and U.S. governments, with the concurrence of the French, launch two missiles each from submarines to explode in an airburst over Minsk. The damage is as for Birmingham only many times worse. The result is the dissolution of the Soviet Union and the end of the European war.

Of course, this story was written to point up certain morals—among them, no doubt, the ethical justification of the British and U.S. submarine-based nuclear deterrents—and one should not make too much of this aspect. But if the tale has any plausibility, it may perhaps be taken as an instance when use of nuclear weapons, at least in theory, could be both reasonable, in the sense of producing the effect intended, and proportionate, in the sense that the evil prevented by stopping the war was probably far greater than the damage inflicted, horrifying though that was. There was, moreover, a sort of rough justice involved. The Soviets both started the war and were the first to use nuclear weapons, and when they did so, they struck indiscriminately. They must have foreseen at least the possibility of retaliation, yet they chose to go ahead. What they got they asked for, on the basis of tit for tat. But is the application of rough justice good enough? The Allied attack upon Minsk was clearly indiscriminate, and thus flatly in breach of one crucial principle of *jus in bello*: it could never be justified in the strict sense. The intentional destruction of innocents by the hundred thousand must always, in itself, be evil. The question is whether such damage can be redeemed by proportionality if it succeeds. Or did the Allies have a duty to surrender?

The second hypothetical instance is even more difficult, however, in that it involves NATO governments' opting for a first use of nuclear weapons in response to a conventional assault they have otherwise failed to stop. This scenario lies at the heart of the NATO strategy of flexible response, the official doctrine for over twenty years. In defending this doctrine, it has been usual to propose that at a point before the Allied defense breaks up and becomes incoherent, NATO commanders would apply for and NATO governments would collectively accede to what is ghoulishly known as nuclear "release." What might follow is the detonation of a small number (say six or twelve) airburst weapons of low yield, designed to destroy military targets (airfields, bridges, tank concentrations, missile launchers, radars, or headquarters) in Eastern Europe, with minimal collateral damage. The aim would be, by shock/horror effect, to stop the Warsaw Pact in its tracks and compel it to sue for peace.

If the strategy worked, of course, it could be justified as both rational and moral. But in this case we are not writing the plot. If we were, we could not overlook some of the obvious implausibilities in the story: the improbability, for instance, of getting agreement on the part of NATO governments at large for such an undertaking or the objection that in the highly foreseeable event of Warsaw Pact retaliation, the West would have obtained no military advantage, rather the reverse. Setting these difficulties to one side, we must confront the moral issue. Bearing in mind the range of probable responses to first use by the West, and their consequences, what would be the likelihood of good being done in proportion to the wrong inflicted? Here everything turns on the issue of escalation.

In military circles, the likelihood has been rated very high that the Soviet Union would retaliate on at least the same scale as NATO's attack. But perhaps everyone has been brainwashed by the automaticity implied by the very term "escalation." Delving more deeply, it is contended on the one hand that to pay the West back, at least like with like, is the declared doctrine of the Soviet forces, set out in training manuals and practiced during innumerable exercises. On the other hand, others say it could not possibly be in the Soviet interest to raise the ante since their only motive for invasion would be to annex one or more of the NATO nations as a going concern, not as a wasteland. But this argument is demonstrably false. Annexation was always a most improbable motive for Soviet military adventurism, so long as NATO kept its nerve and kept up its guard. Almost the only plausible circumstance for a Soviet incursion would have been under grave duress, when they had grounds for apprehending something far worse, such as the imminence of a nuclear attack upon their country. A more worrying thought, perhaps, is the possibility of escalation by inadvertence, through panic or plain loss of control.

The truth is both simple and unwelcome. Given the first use, by NATO, of nuclear weapons in the circumstances postulated by the strategy, no one could possibly know, or even hazard a plausible guess, as to what the consequences might be. That they would be fraught with danger is self-evident. Could such an action ever be deemed proportionate—short of the most culpable wishful thinking? It is interesting that William O'Brien, at the end of a long and rather hawkish defense of nuclear war-fighting under just-war credentials, nevertheless concluded that nuclear weapons must be reserved exclusively for countering threats and attacks with nuclear weapons and opted categorically for an operational policy of no first use. "Given the risks of nuclear war it is long overdue to sacrifice the 'creative ambiguity' of a mixed nuclear/conventional deterrence posture in NATO" (O'Brien and Langan, 1986: 182). O'Brien's opinion is not definitive—no one's is—but the thought of Germany, East and West, reduced through escalation to the condition of Bavaria in 1648, or Paraguay in 1870 (not to mention Masada), is to go so far beyond any conception of "preserving Western values" or "defending democracy" as to make mockery of just-war criteria. Does this consideration not deserve the benefit of the doubt?

Contemporary Prospects

I turn now to the application of the previous ideas to the central confrontation of the 1990s between East and West. How good are the values to be defended? It is obviously unhelpful to contrast a "Christian" West with an "atheistic" East, at a time when church life at some points in the Soviet bloc is thriving and when Britain, for example, is arguably one of the most highly secularized societies on earth. And if recourse is had to democratic values, it is worth recalling that not all NATO governments have at all times been democratic. In defining what it is the West seeks to defend, the simplest and most truthful thing to say is that it wants to defend its countries from being overrun by foreigners. No one should underrate this goal as a matter of practical politics.

From the earliest recorded wars in history to the successful ejection of the Argentinians from the Falkland Islands, that motive has had the utmost potency. Men and women die willingly for their country and their flag, and it is the essential founding principle of NATO that an attack upon any member state, no matter by whom, will be treated as an attack upon all. That principle simply extends the concept of territorial integrity to embrace the alliance as a whole, but more is at stake here than simply land and nation. Again and again, in the literature and even more certainly in popular perception, the issue of values is seen as central. On the one hand, there are those who have professed to regard the Soviet Union and the United States as "morally equivalent," and on that ground they have decried the efforts of the Western nations to defend their own system. On the other hand, there is the view of the USSR as an "evil empire" whose encroachments it is morally imperative for all free peoples to resist. Both of these views have been discredited, and something more perceptive must be attempted.

The societies of the West are capitalist and pluralist; they produce prosperity and individual liberty to a quite unprecedented degree. The martial virtues are generally discounted, because believing in ideals that are peaceful, law-abiding, commercial, and libertarian, we tend to play down the heroic. The spirit is one of small gains and losses, prudence and mutual regard, practical accomplishment and compromise. Self-government is cherished and imperialism despised. With every one of these terms the Soviet system has seemed to be at variance. Its spirit is collectivist; life, liberty, and the rule of law appear to be subordinate to state and party. The USSR has been considered a mysterious country, alien, inhospitable, inaccessible, self-contained, and dangerous.

President Gorbachev has made plain his determination to move away from the world of closed societies in search of a new world order based on consensus, in which the use or threat of force would no longer be a valid instrument of foreign policy. The Political Consultative Committee of the Warsaw Treaty Organization renounced interference with the internal affairs of its member states at its meeting in Bucharest in the summer of 1989 (see Almquist, 1990), and it stood by that undertaking, cost what it might, throughout the turbulent episodes of the succeeding months. Its stated aim is now to move, in cooperation with the West, toward a military posture of reasonable defensive sufficiency backed by minimal nuclear deterrence. A beneficial spiral could then be set in motion whereby negotiated arms reductions and the relaxation of tensions mutually reinforce each other. NATO and the Warsaw Pact could increasingly become instruments for the political management of a newly emerging European order, and the West must do all that it possibly can to encourage this process.

But there are other more somber possible outcomes (J. Gray, 1989, 10). For the Soviet Union there is the prospect of chaos on the Yugoslavian model: economic collapse compounded by nationalist and ethnic conflict. There is then the possibility of mutation to an authoritarian regime, shorn of ideology and relying alternately upon such repression as the KGB (the State Security Committee) can still afford and tactical concessions. Eastern Europe may fall victim to rampant nationalism of the Peronist type: weak populist governments, with wages indexed and prices still controlled, succumbing to syndicalism and hyperinflation. Both types of regime, having squandered whatever Western aid is offered, might then be tempted to shore up their crumbling legitimacy by means of military adventures.

What forms these might take is much harder to foresee. NATO for the past forty years has taken as its canonical threat a rolling advance of Warsaw Pact forces, on the blitzkrieg model (Stoll, 1990), with or without prior reinforcement. Improbable as this possibility may have seemed in recent years, it now passes all belief. The reductions in the Soviet armed forces announced by President Gorbachev in December 1988 were driven by the imperative need to save money and are most unlikely to be reversed by any future Politburo, however dominated it may be by military-industrial interests. Although the Soviet armed forces may emerge more efficient, they will certainly be smaller and more defensively oriented. The Warsaw Pact countries appear for the moment to be literally incapable of mounting coordinated operations. It is therefore generally agreed that the threat of short-notice attack upon the West has vanished. Assuming the successful conclusion of present negotiations on conventional forces in Europe (CFE), it is unlikely that the risk of any large-scale offensive action will remain.

Even if the most dismal scenario is accepted, it is hard to see a major military threat confronting the West. There is the possibility of fighting, perhaps on a substantial scale, within and between countries of Eastern Europe, and there is a need for sufficient conventional forces to contain any risk of spillover of that fighting. A unified Germany, whether neutral and disarmed or within NATO, should pose no dangers to the West, provided it is not allowed to become (what the great majority of Germans in any case do not want) an independent nuclear-weapon state. The Soviet Union has already been dragged, contrary to its own expressed intentions, into military involvement with the Muslim south. The lessons of Afghanistan, Azerbaijan, and Tadzhikistan have not been happy ones, but the need for further such involvement may increase in coming years. Even so, it is difficult to see how any of these types of problems could throw up the possibility of nuclear action by the Soviet Union, still less by the West.

It is certainly possible that at some future date, for some reasons presently impossible to foresee, Russia—perhaps shorn of even its closest subordinate republics (Byelorussia, Ukraine) but still a military super-power with a vast nuclear arsenal—might again turn wholeheartedly hostile to the West. If there should be no other way of stopping aggression then, what would be a proportionate price for the world to pay, and who is to decide?

And so we return to the central moral exercise—the *calculus of proportion* between the value of the polities defended and the costs of just defense. If it is true that World War II was a just war on the Allied side but that the Thirty Years War was unjust, where can one draw the line? Specifically, how much death and destruction is it morally licit to inflict and to sustain as the price of preventing one's country from falling under alien sway or, more problematically still, to prevent a global tyranny? To essay a specific answer (say twenty or fifty megadeaths) is simply to expose the near impossibility of attempting to measure the incommensurable.

There may be some comfort in the facts that both the Soviet Union and the United States are engaged in strenuous nuclear arms reduction exercises and that doctrines of minimal deterrence are being increasingly discussed. Perhaps there is no escaping from the paradox that, ad interim, the "city-busting policy" that underlies a minimal deterrent posture, while the most unacceptable in terms of just-war theory, is nevertheless the only practicable route to a regime in which actual use of nuclear weapons is utterly discounted. They would then be, in actuality or in potential, no more than an ultimate lethal sanction and would make any recourse to war between possessors (those who have weapons or could quickly and easily acquire them) as unthinkable as a nuclear war has already become in practice. The answer could then confidently be given to our question about what stakes would justify the use of weapons of mass annihilation—none.

Notes

This chapter is a revision of a chapter entitled "What If Deterrence Fails?" in Richard J. Bauckham and R. John Elford (eds.), *The Nuclear Weapons Debate: Theological and Ethical Issues;* London: SCM Press, 1989. Published here by permission of SCM Press.

4

Now More Than Ever:
No First Use

Paul C. Warnke

A strategy based on starting a nuclear war never made much sense. Today it makes none. The doctrine of "first use" should join that of "massive retaliation" as a historical oddity.

Early in the administration of President Dwight Eisenhower, Secretary of State John Foster Dulles announced that communist aggression against the United States or its allies could result in massive retaliation against the Soviet Union (Arms Control Association, 1989: 21). At the time, of course, the United States had great and meaningful nuclear superiority. By the late 1960s, however, the Soviet Union was acquiring a credible ability to launch a retaliatory strike of its own in the event of nuclear attack. Accordingly, the NATO defense ministers working in the Nuclear Planning Group recognized that the threat of an all-out nuclear attack in response to Soviet conventional military action was no longer credible. The deterrent strategy was therefore changed to one of "flexible response" involving "a range of appropriate responses, conventional and nuclear, to all levels of aggression or threats of aggression" (Arms Control Association, 1989: 24).

In a volume based on six years of meetings between U.S. and Soviet international security experts, Henry Trofimenko, of the Soviet Institute for the Study of the U.S.A. and Canada, notes: "When the Soviet Union achieved real parity in second-strike capability . . . the United States came to understand a new common interest in mutual security and thus to change the rules of the game" (Trofimenko, 1989). Despite this inescapable realization, however, first use of nuclear weapons remains the declaratory policy of the United States and its allies in the North Atlantic alliance. The NATO summit in June 1990 resulted in a rhetorical refinement whereby nuclear weapons are described as "weapons of last resort," but the alliance refused to abandon the threat of first use.

Nuclear Weapons as Peacekeepers:
A Persistent Myth

Some seasoned strategic analysts continue to contend that nuclear weapons, and the threat of their first use, are what has maintained peace among the major powers for more than forty years. I would suggest that many more persuasive reasons exist, among them the changed role of Germany with the integration of the Federal Republic into the North Atlantic alliance along with the continued significant U.S. military presence on the continent of Europe. More important, however, is the recognition by the great military powers that a world war, even in the unlikely event that it could be kept to the use of conventional military weapons, would devastate all of Europe and leave the putative victor with no spoils. War, like empire, is no longer worth what it costs.

Unquestionably, the very existence of nuclear weapons provides a kind of "existential deterrence," since any nation contemplating the initiation of hostilities would have to take into account the chance of escalation. This deterrent factor, however, requires no policy of deliberate first use. Indeed, the existence of such a policy in fact lessens the deterrent efficacy.

To elaborate on this point, consider a situation in which each of the possible antagonists has an enunciated doctrine of willingness to resort first to nuclear use and suppose that each believes that the other means it. At a time of high crisis, both sides would have a powerful incentive to strike first in the hope that doing so might reduce the damage that would be caused by a retaliatory strike and in the expectation, at least, that this damage would be less than that caused if the other side launched a first strike.

The regrettable, and unacceptable, fact is that we have never made up our minds about the purpose of nuclear weapons. While pursuing arms control, we continue to cling to the illusion that nuclear weapons can be used to fight and win a war. Our weapons decisions have been and are still based on this fallacy.

The Continuing Belief in War-Fighting
with Nuclear Weapons

Early in the Reagan administration, the then-secretary of defense, Caspar Weinberger, said in the *Annual Report of the Secretary of Defense to the Congress, Fiscal Year 1983* that among the minimum purposes our nuclear forces had to serve were "to help deter major conventional attack against U.S. forces and our allies, especially in NATO" and "to impose termination of a major war—on terms favorable to the United States and our allies—

even if nuclear weapons have been used" (Weinberger, 1982: I-18). An earlier secretary of defense, James Schlesinger, had announced in 1974 a new strategic doctrine involving the creation of nuclear strike options to provide a strategic "flexible response." He argued that the ability to conduct counterforce strikes against Soviet military targets was needed to maintain the credibility of the U.S. threat to use nuclear weapons (Arms Control Association, 1989: 30).

The persistence of this notion of the practical military utility of strategic weapons was shown in the issuance of Presidential Directive 59 in the last year of the presidency of Jimmy Carter. PD 59 contemplated the maintenance of nuclear forces capable of conducting a "limited and protracted" nuclear war. In seeking to rationalize this oxymoronic concept, Carter administration officials asserted that although they recognized that a nuclear war could be neither limited nor protracted, the Soviet leadership exhibited no comparable recognition and therefore deterrence required that we maintain a war-fighting strategy.

The dichotomy between reasoned analysis and established strategic doctrine continued throughout the Reagan administration. Although President Reagan became a convert to the cause of arms control and, like most converts, a devout practitioner, his administration continued to espouse the first use credo. In 1988, a Pentagon blue-ribbon commission recommended the development of "small, highly accurate nuclear weapons" that would be "politically usable, and could be paired with the Strategic Defense Initiative" (Commission on Integrated Long-Term Strategy, 1988). The commission appears to have disregarded the problem of using small, highly accurate nuclear weapons if the other side has nothing to respond with except big, ugly ones.

Moreover, the commission's proposed pairing of new nuclear missiles and SDI can only by interpreted as a contradiction of President Reagan's insistence that Star Wars was intended solely for defense and not to make a preemptive strike more plausible. It should also be noted that President Reagan proposed to share SDI technology with the Soviet Union so that they, too, would have what he envisioned as an impenetrable shield that would render nuclear missiles "impotent and obsolete"—and thus do the same for the threat of their first use (Reagan, 1983: 74).

The schizoid nature of U.S. strategic thinking is illustrated most dramatically by the history of intermediate-range nuclear forces and the development and implementation of the INF Treaty that banned them. In the late 1970s, the Soviet Union embarked on an ambitious buildup of nuclear missiles that had less than a strategic range. The triple-warhead Soviet SS-20 could not strike North American targets, but it could devastate all of Europe and most of Asia. The purported reason for deployment of the new missile was that existing Soviet SS-4s and

SS-5s were obsolete, liquid-fueled, and dangerous to maintain. The SS-20 deployment, however, rapidly exceeded the mere replacement of the warheads on the older missiles. This deployment was consistent with a nuclear war-fighting strategy on the part of the Soviet Union, and it threatened to become a divisive factor within the NATO alliance.

In 1977, the then-chancellor of West Germany, Helmut Schmidt, made a speech under the auspices of the International Institute for Strategic Studies in London. He explained his concern that while the United States and the Soviet Union were negotiating reductions and limits in the nuclear missiles that could strike each other's territory, the Soviet Union was increasing the separate nuclear threat to the European members of NATO. He saw this combination of action as a "decoupling" of the security of the West Europeans from that of the North Americans.

In late 1979, the NATO defense ministers, meeting as the Nuclear Planning Group, announced what became known as the "two-track decision." An effort would be made to achieve strict limitations on Soviet SS-20s, and failing that, NATO would deploy its own force of U.S. intermediate-range missiles, consisting of 464 ground-launched cruise missiles and 108 Pershing II ballistic missiles.

Alarmed by the early reluctance of the Reagan administration to resume arms control negotiations, the European allies urged that the two-track decision be carried out and that the United States seek to negotiate strict limits on intermediate-range missiles in Europe. When the INF talks resumed late in 1981, the United States proposed the worldwide elimination of all intermediate-range nuclear weapons—defined as those with ranges between 1,000 and 5,000 kilometers. This proposal became known as the "zero-option."

The NATO decision to deploy intermediate-range nuclear forces was thus undertaken as a specific response to a specific and ominous action by the Soviet Union. For many years, the West had seen no need to base nuclear missiles in Europe. They could strike no targets that were not already redundantly covered by strategic-range forces, including submarine-launched ballistic missiles dedicated to NATO defense. In the face of heavy-handed efforts by the Soviet Union to frighten the governments of West Germany, the Netherlands, Belgium, Italy, and the United Kingdom out of accepting deployment of the new missiles, NATO had no choice but to persevere. Soviet pressure could not be allowed to nullify NATO military decisions taken in response to provocative Soviet deployments.

But, as part of the campaign to ensure acceptance of these deployments, other arguments were advanced to try to persuade the proposed host countries of their essentiality to European security. Some administration spokesmen stressed that the cruise missiles and Pershings would improve deterrence by more securely coupling European defense to the U.S. strategic arsenal. U.S. allies were told that the Soviets would regard first use of such missiles as a more plausible threat than that presented by weapons based in the great plains of the United States or in international waters. The incompatibility of this reasoning with the zero-option, which the United States had tabled in the Geneva talks, was simply ignored.

This remarkable ability to entertain at one and the same time two completely inconsistent ideas was rudely challenged when, after the entry on the scene of Mikhail Gorbachev, the Soviets not only accepted the zero-option but included all missiles with ranges as low as 500 kilometers. For a time, there appeared to be some possibility that the United States would not take yes for an answer. Some security savants, including former President Richard Nixon and former Secretary of State Henry Kissinger, maintained the first use faith and argued for reduction rather than elimination of intermediate-range missiles.

But the prospect of the elimination of an entire class of nuclear weapons, and the late-blooming enthusiasm of Ronald Reagan for an arms control accomplishment, carried the day. The United States abandoned the argument that its INF weapons were needed for improved deterrence because they made first use more plausible. The acceptability of the INF Treaty to our friends in Europe is perhaps best explained by their recognition that the first use option is not reserved to the West's side. If, indeed, Soviet leaders accepted the argument that preemptive strikes from European-based nuclear missiles are more likely than a strategic launch from U.S. territory, then cruise missile and Pershing launchers, particularly those based in West Germany, would become highly attractive targets. A Pershing warhead launched from Germany and striking Soviet territory would almost inevitably produce a retaliatory nuclear strike against the missile bases in the Federal Republic. The Soviet leaders might well conclude that such retaliation would not automatically lead to a strategic response from the United States. The INF Treaty thus ended a discrete and serious threat to the European members of NATO.

Arms Control and First Use

But the first use doctrine, though badly wounded, still lives. Its durability could be seen in the debate in 1989 about the modernization of NATO's nuclear weapons. The INF Treaty does not affect some 4,000 U.S. nuclear warheads based in Europe, including about 80 Lance missiles with a range of less than 150 kilometers. The "beanbag" phenomenon of arms control—when you push one weapon down another pops up—showed up again in the proposal that a "follow-on-to-Lance" be deployed. This entirely new weapon system would have involved about 995 launchers of missiles, some 700 of which would carry nuclear warheads and have a range just under the floor of the INF Treaty. In addition, there have been calls for heavy deployment of sea-launched cruise missiles.

As late as spring 1989, the modernization issue seemed destined to cause a wrenching debate within NATO. Some U.S. officials and the Thatcher government in the United Kingdom were pressing hard for an early decision on deployment of the Lance follow-on, and West Germans of all political stripes were resisting. In a sound move at the May summit that year, President Bush and his advisers managed to defer the issue pending progress in the talks on conventional forces in Europe (CFE). Modernization of theater nuclear forces, particularly the follow-on-to-Lance, has since been overtaken by the rapidly developing events in Eastern Europe. West German Foreign Minister Hans-Dietrich Genscher asked whether the new missile would be aimed at Lech Walesa. And, indeed, its targets would be mainly in Czechoslovakia, Poland, Hungary, and East Germany. Bonn's earlier alarm about providing a base for such weapons had rightfully turned to ridicule of the idea. On "Meet the Press" on Sunday, December 3, 1989, Senator Sam Nunn, chairman of the Senate Armed Services Committee, pronounced that the Lance replacement program was dead. The Bush administration thereafter dropped it. There may be some mourners in the United Kingdom and a few in the United States, but they would be hard to find in Central Europe.

In his arms control odyssey from 1981 to 1989, President Ronald Reagan started off "from Missouri." As he went on to Geneva, Reykjavik, Washington, and Moscow, he clearly enjoyed the trip, but for advocates of a nuclear war-fighting capability, he enjoyed it all too well. Even before his first summit meeting with Gorbachev, in Geneva in November of 1985, Reagan was giving clear signs of rejecting any strategy of extended deterrence based on first use of nuclear weapons. On January 25, 1984, in his State of the Union address, he directed the following comments to the people of the Soviet Union: "A nuclear war cannot be won and must never be fought. The only value in our two nations possessing nuclear weapons is to make sure that they will never be used. But then would it not be better to do away with them entirely?" (Reagan, 1984). This statement presaged his willingness at the second Reagan-Gorbachev summit in Reykjavik to discuss not only deep cuts in the strategic arsenals but the elimination of all nuclear ballistic missiles and even of all nuclear weapons.

The Reykjavik summit in October 1986 came to an impasse over the issue of Reagan's Strategic Defense Initiative, to the undisguised relief of the nuclear aficionados. But the dramatic impact of the revelation that such an idea was even discussed by the president is still deeply felt. Former President Richard Nixon, in an article in *Foreign Affairs* in early 1989, complained:

> At the Reykjavik summit, the Reagan administration undermined public support for nuclear deterrence by advocating the idea of eliminating all nuclear weapons. We must renounce the Reykjavik rhetoric in unequivocal terms and explain to Western publics the realities of the nuclear age. We should pursue the so-called competitive strategies on the conventional level to undercut the significance of Soviet quantitative superiority and thereby raise the nuclear threshold. But nuclear deterrence, both strategic and tactical, remains imperative. [Nixon, 1989: 208–209]

It may indeed be unrealistic to talk about the total elimination of nuclear weapons at a time when the world order and international institutions are inadequate to police a global ban. Not even the names and numbers of the nations that now have such weapons is known. Neither the Soviet Union nor the United States could take the chance that their mutual nuclear disarmament would leave some erratic or beleaguered leader as king of the nuclear hill. But common sense compels the conclusion that the search for "discriminate nuclear war-fighting capability" be ended. Indeed, if nuclear weapons are in fact intended and needed to deter conventional hostilities, if we must have the ability to conduct a "limited and protracted" nuclear war, then pursuit of nuclear arms control measures is either farce or folly.

There are, however, thoughtful experts in the field of international security who have come to the conclusion that it is a nuclear war-fighting strategy that is both farce and folly. Buttressing Reagan's instinctive rejection of the notion of resort to nuclear war for military advantage are the reasoned comments of former West German Chancellor Helmut Schmidt, also a former defense minister, and the late Andrei Sakharov, both a renowned nuclear physicist and a gallant defender of human rights.

In an article (*New York Times*, April 8, 1987), Chancellor Schmidt observed that the armed forces of the Federal Republic of Germany could be counted on to fight valiantly in a conventional war but that their efforts would end if nuclear warheads began exploding in their homeland. He asked why the Germans should be expected to be more fanatic than the Japanese after Hiroshima and Nagasaki. In a subsequent speech (*International Herald Tribune*, December 17–18, 1988), he said, "I deeply believe that nuclear weapons in our hands—the West's hands—have one purpose only; to put the onus of nuclear first use on the opposite side of the Iron Curtain."

Andrei Sakharov, in an open letter published in *Foreign Affairs* in 1983, made his position unequivocally clear: *"Nuclear weapons only make sense as a means of deterring nuclear agression by a potential enemy, i.e., a nuclear war cannot be planned with the aim of winning it.* Nuclear weapons cannot be viewed as a means of restraining aggression carried out by means of conventional weapons" (Sakharov, 1983: 1006; emphasis in original). He ended his open letter as follows: "In conclusion I again stress how important it is that the world realize the absolute inadmissibility of nuclear war, the collective suicide of mankind" (Sakharov, 1983: 1016). Sakharov elaborated on this theme in accepting the Albert Einstein Peace Price in Washington on November 15, 1988, when he called on the NATO nations to abandon the policy of first use of nuclear weapons, calling it an "incalculable risk for mankind" and emphasizing the infeasibility of preventing escalation from tactical use to an all-out strategic exchange.

On the assumption that the escalatory potential could be controlled, it is possible to make a case for first use of tactical battlefield nuclear weapons, such as the 4,000 that remain in NATO Europe. They present no threat to the homeland of other nations. They could be used only against an invading army, and the damage would be confined to the aggressor's forces and to the host nation. In discussions of the Nuclear Planning Group in the late 1960s, tactical nuclear weapons were described as those that would blow up in friendly territory. Representatives of the Federal Republic of Germany found this definition less than amusing, and this sensitivity was aroused anew in the debate about inclusion of short-range nuclear weapons in East-West arms control talks. There was strong support in West Germany for a third zero, which would end what is described as the singularization of Germany as a theater for nuclear war, even before unification appeared inevitable. It now also seems inevitable that a united Germany will find no room for either Soviet or U.S. nuclear weaponry.

In theory, an invading aggressor might not respond in kind to the use of tactical nuclear weapons. The invader's homeland would remain unscathed, and it would have the option of calling off the war and bringing its forces back there. But the circumstances that led the aggressor to undertake so risky an action would have to be so powerful that the option of using its own battlefield nuclear weapons would inevitably be considered. The distinction between tactical and strategic use would be difficult to discern if enemy warheads were going off in NATO territory. The destruction of a German city by battlefield nuclear weapons or by strategic missiles would merit the same strategic nuclear response. Chancellor Schmidt's cautionary comments should not be ignored, nor should Sakharov's prediction that "if the 'nuclear threshold' is crossed, i.e., if any country uses a nuclear weapon even on a limited scale, the further course of events would be difficult to control and the most probable result would be swift escalation leading from a nuclear war initially limited in scale or by region to all-out nuclear war, i.e., to general suicide" (Sakharov, 1983: 1006).

Yet, it is still possible for an experienced defense analyst, Earl C. Ravenal, to describe the North Atlantic alliance in the following terms: "The essence of NATO is the American nuclear commitment, that is, the coupling of America's strategic nuclear retaliatory force ultimately to the outbreak of a conflict in Europe" (Ravenal, 1989: 220). Ravenal states further, "A consistent policy of no first use implies the dissolution of the American defense commitment to NATO" (Ravenal, 1989: 231).

First Use: An Embarrassing Anomaly

As previously indicated, I do not believe that the defense of Europe or the U.S. commitment to that defense rests on first use of nuclear weapons. But this remains NATO's declaratory policy, and it is a policy devoid of thought content. As pointed out by the same defense analyst, "A design for stability must include an unconditional doctrine of no first use of nuclear weapons" (Ravenal, 1989: 231).

Whatever colorable rationale can be asserted for first use of tactical battlefield nuclear weapons, I find none possible for the deliberate initiation of a strategic nuclear exchange. In his book *Thinking Tuna Fish, Talking Death* (1988), Robert Scheer vividly describes an arms control conference held at the Lawrence Livermore National Laboratory in the fall of 1981. A luncheon discussion led by Herman Kahn of the Hudson Institute speculated about the likely response to the nuclear destruction of New York City by a five-megaton Soviet weapon. Kahn suggested that the war would cease after Leningrad had been eradicated in retaliation but that the Soviet leadership would consider a strike on Moscow as a disproportionate response and, in that event, would proceed to take out Philadelphia. Other participants suggested a less apocalyptic scenario in which each side would target five minor cities in the other country. But another participant counseled Scheer not to get "sucked into this megatonnage and throw-weight business or you'll be lost and will never be able to get back to what is important—which is that life as we know it could easily be destroyed over stupidities" (Scheer, 1988: 314).

The fact is that no one can know what either Moscow or Washington would do if its territory came under strategic attack of any scale. Rather than selecting from a smorgasbord of cities, the nuclear victim might conclude that its best hope was an all-out attack designed to destroy as much as possible of the aggressor's missile fields, military infrastructure, and command and control. Moreover, it strains credulity to suppose that a preemptive strategic strike would be limited in nature and would leave the other side's nuclear arsenal intact rather than being a massive attack in an attempt to lessen the magnitude of the retaliatory strike. I am sorry that Andrei Sakharov and Herman Kahn are not around to debate the issue of limited nuclear war, but I have no doubt who would be the winner.

It is long since time that we terminated our love affair with the bomb. The encouraging developments in international relations and the easing of tensions between the nuclear superpowers may make increasingly irrelevant the debate about the military utility of nuclear arsenals and what number and types of weapons they should include. Perhaps the most important result of the arms control negotiations that have now been going on for over twenty years is the education that has been provided to both sides. The abandonment of the Brezhnev doctrine and its replacement by what the Soviet Foreign Ministry spokesman, Gennadi Gerasimov, has dubbed the "Sinatra doctrine" (according to which any Eastern European country can sing "I did it my way") would not have been possible at a time when the Soviet Union feared that the elimination of its buffer zone of satellite states would be taken advantage of by the West and thus present a serious threat to Soviet security.

World leaders must now recognize that mutual security is the only security that can exist in an age of modern weaponry. This mutual security can be best obtained by a military standdown in Europe and by strict controls on and dramatic reductions in nuclear weapons. Further tinkering with nuclear weaponry and threats of their first use are not needed to keep the peace. They can only increase the risk of nuclear war. Shortly after his retirement as chairman of the Joint Chiefs of Staff, Admiral William Crowe said in early 1990, "I do not believe the theory that [a strategic arms accord] is just going to make it safe for conventional war—that theory has now become hollow" (Crowe, 1990).

The threat of first use has been thoroughly exposed as a hollow one. The United States resorted to first use once, to end a war that had ravaged two continents and at a time when it had a nuclear monopoly. It did not use nuclear weapons in Korea, even after Chinese intervention when U.S. nuclear dominance remained unchallenged, and their use in Vietnam was never seriously considered. They have no utility in low-level conflict. Nuclear weapons could have disposed of General Noriega, but Panama and the Canal might have gone along with him.

The threat of first use has thus been directed exclusively at the Soviet Union. At a time when Gorbachev and his colleagues are moving toward elimination of the offensive attack capability of the Warsaw Pact forces, and when the Warsaw Treaty Organization itself can no longer be regarded as a cohesive military alliance, the NATO first use doctrine is an embarrassing anomaly. Its repudiation would do no damage to our security or that of our allies; it would only improve our world image as both a great power and a responsible one.

Part II

The Views of Policy Analysts and Peace Researchers

From time immemorial through the Nazi holocaust to a by-no-means-improbable World War III, human organizations have shown a propensity for inflicting the most unbelievable destruction on one another. That the latter has not yet occurred is no ground for either self-congratulations or optimism, and despite recent developments in the East-West relationship, everything is in place for the ultimate crime against humanity. It will require an impressive amount of intellectual and moral autonomy if the doomsday machine is to be dismantled in time.

J. David Singer

5

Deterrence, Nuclear Weapons, Morality, and War

John Mueller

Deterrence is almost always looked at strictly as a military issue; a typical definition characterizes it as "the threat to use force in response as a way of preventing the first use of force by someone else."[1] Starting with a definition like that, most discussions of deterrence quickly get bound up with analyses of various military force levels and postures that make war more or less likely to be successful or profitable. Ideally, a common argument runs, each side should have a secure second-strike capability: it should be able to absorb a surprise attack fully confident that it will be able to respond with an effective counterattack. Thus each side, rationally fearing costly and punishing retaliatory consequences, can be expected to refrain from initiating war.

This chapter seeks to broaden the concept of deterrence to include nonmilitary considerations. In the first section, deterrence is recast in an effort to demonstrate that the vast majority of wars that never happen are deterred by factors that have little or nothing to do with military considerations. The second section focuses on nuclear deterrence and concludes that a major war has been highly unlikely in the postwar world and that nuclear weapons have been essentially irrelevant to the remarkably long peace that has enveloped the developed world since 1945. The third, and final, section develops a set of exploratory propositions about war, morality, and religion, some of which reflect the broadened concept of deterrence.

Deterrence and Stability

The notion of deterrence has inspired two kinds of criticism. Some people find it immoral and/or absurd to seek to prevent a destructive war by threatening to launch destruction that could be even greater than the war itself. Other critics argue that the idea of deterrence is inadequate because it simply doesn't explain very well how states actually behave. Sometimes countries start wars even when they have little reason to believe they will be victorious; at other times they remain supremely cautious, refraining from war even though they feel threatened and even though they enjoy a substantial military advantage (Jervis, 1985: 6, and Lebow, 1985: 204; see also Rosecrance, 1975: 33–35). But instead of abandoning the notion of deterrence because of these important criticisms, it can easily be developed to deal with, or perhaps obviate, them. A broader and more fully pertinent concept would vigorously incorporate nonmilitary considerations as well as military ones, making direct and central application of the obvious fact that states do not approach the world solely in military terms.

Specifically, deterrence can be defined as a state of being—the absence of war between two countries or alliances.[2] If they are not at war, then it is reasonable to conclude that each is currently being deterred from attacking the other. We observe, for example, that the United States and the Soviet Union are not currently at war with each other, and we conclude that the United States is being deterred (by something or other) from attacking the Soviet Union while the Soviet Union is similarly being deterred from attacking the United States. Then, by the same reasoning we can also say that the United States is currently being deterred from attacking Canada, and that Canada is currently being deterred from attacking the United States. We can also observe that Pakistan is currently being deterred from attacking Bolivia even while Bolivia is similarly being deterred from attacking Pakistan.

This unconventional way of looking at deterrence substantially recasts the moral issue. Deterrence becomes simply a description of a situation— neither moral nor immoral. One may want to debate the wisdom, efficacy, or morality of certain *kinds* of deterrence, but deterrence itself is not the issue. More important, this concept tends to draw one's attention to nonmilitary forms of deterrence, and it immediately highlights an important central consideration, one that has attracted remarkably little attention. If countries are principally deterred by military considerations from attacking one another in our chaotic state of international "anarchy," as so many people have suggested ("if you desire peace, prepare for war"), why is it that there are so many cases in which a militarily superior country lives contentedly alongside a militarily inferior one?[3]

The United States obviously enjoys a massive military advantage over its northern neighbor and could attack with little concern about punishing military retaliation or about the possibility of losing the war. Clearly, something is deterring the United States from attacking Canada (a country, it might be noted, with which the United States has been at war in the past and where, not too long ago, many war-eager Americans south of the common border felt their "manifest destiny" lay), but obviously this spectacularly successful deterrent has little to do with the Canadians' military might. Similar cases can be found in the Soviet sphere. Despite an overwhelming military superiority, the USSR has never been anxious to attack such troublesome neighbors as Poland and Rumania. To be complete, a concept of deterrence ought to be able to explain common instances like these, as well as those in which military elements are presumably dominant—such as the considerations that deter Syria from attacking Israel (see also Rosecrance, 1975: 35).

Components of the Deterrence Calculation

In contemplating an attack, it can be said, a would-be aggressor considers two central conditions and compares them: what its world is likely to be like if it goes to war, and what that world is likely to be like if it remains at peace. If, after making this assessment, the aggressor decides the war condition is preferable to the status quo—that is, if it feels it can profit from war—it will go to war. If it finds the status quo preferable to war, it will remain at peace—that is, it will be deterred from starting a war.[4]

The would-be aggressor's calculations about the war half of its considerations can be broken down into three considerations. One is the net value it would achieve by winning the war: the benefits gained from victory minus the costs entailed in achieving it. Another is its net value should it lose the war: the benefits gained in losing (sometimes there are benefits) minus the costs (usually considerable and unpleasant) entailed in losing. Finally, it must make some effort to calculate its chances of winning. These three considerations are blended together, and the result is a general conclusion about what war would probably bring.

There is likely to be a great deal of guesswork in these calculations, but something like them will normally be made. In general, a would-be aggressor is likely to be deterred when it finds (1) the status quo to be pleasant, (2) the net value of winning a war to be rather low, (3) the net value of losing to be very low—penalizing, in fact—and (4) the probability of winning to be low.

Each of these four components can vary over time, and each can be manipulated by other countries. A policy of deterrence involves a conscious effort by one country to manipulate another country's incentives to go to war so that the potential aggressor, in thinking things over, finds the virtues of peace to be, on balance, substantially greater than those of starting a war. But, of course, two countries may very well be deterred from attacking each other even if neither has anything like a policy of deterrence toward the other: Bolivia and Pakistan enjoy a firm deterrence relationship though neither, it seems reasonable to presume, gives much thought to the issue one way or the other.

And, more important for present considerations, the absence of war—successful deterrence—does not necessarily prove that a *policy* of deterrence has been successful. The United States has a clear and costly policy in which it tries to deter the Soviet Union by threatening nuclear punishment for any major Soviet aggression. But the fact that the Soviet Union has not started a major war cannot necessarily be credited to the U.S. policy; indeed, as will be argued later, the USSR has had little interest in getting into any sort of major war, no matter how the United States chooses to array its nuclear arsenal.

The net value of the status quo. To consider now the four components of a would-be aggressor's calculations, it is useful, if unconventional, to begin with the value it places on the status quo, on not going to war. Peace is most secure when a potential aggressor finds the status quo to be substantially preferable to the value it places on victory. In other words, if the blessings of peace seem to be even greater than those of going to war and winning (much less losing), the potential aggressor will surely be deterred even if it has a high probability of winning. The persistent U.S. unwillingness to attack Canada is surely principally explained by such reasoning. The United States finds the independent existence of its huge northern neighbor to be highly congenial. Although there may be disagreement on various issues from time to time, on the whole Canada contributes very significantly to the U.S. sense of economic, political, and military well-being, and since there is little hankering in the United States for a fifty-first state anyway, cheer, contentment, and peace prevail between these militarily unequal countries. To get invaded, Canada would probably have to do something to dramatically lower its neighbor's pleasure with the status quo. Agreeing to become an outpost for Soviet missiles—as Cuba did in the early 1960s—might do the trick.

A would-be aggressor's sense of the value of the status quo includes estimations of the future—a country may be basically content at present, but fearing a future attack by its opponents, it may be led to preempt while in a position of comparative strength. The perceived value of the status quo also varies over time, and it is a quality that can be manipulated by a country trying to deter war. Canada, of course, does plenty of things that encourage the United States to prefer the status quo over aggression—for example, establishing a beneficial trading relationship that war would painfully disrupt. Although Canada's actions are probably not conscious enough to be considered a policy of deterrence, they do have the effect of lowering the U.S. incentive to invade by raising its value of the status quo—that is, they help to deter war.

There was a conscious effort to deter by manipulating a would-be aggressor's estimate of the value of the status quo during the Cuban missile crisis. The United States loudly let it be known that its satisfaction with the status quo had just fallen precipitously: it had a severe grievance—the pending implantation of offensive nuclear arms by the Soviet Union in Cuba—and it was apparently prepared to go to war to rectify this grievance. It was deterred from carrying out its threat when the USSR agreed to improve the United States' evaluation of the status quo by removing the offending arms. Similarly, the United States has sought to deter Egypt from attacking Israel by raising Egypt's evaluation of the status quo through extensive aid, which war would terminate.

Except when a country goes to war for the sheer fun of it, *all* wars can be prevented by raising the potential aggressor's estimation of the status quo. Pearl Harbor could have been prevented by letting the Japanese have Asia, Hitler's aggression might have been deterred simply by giving him the territory he wanted, and Israel could make Syria peacefully contented at almost any time by ceasing to exist. As these examples suggest, a policy of deterring war by raising a would-be aggressor's estimate of the status quo closely resembles what is commonly known as "appeasement," a word that has picked up extremely negative connotations. More neutrally, it can also be called "deterrence by reward" or "positive deterrence" (Milburn, 1959; see also Baldwin, 1971; Jervis, 1979: 294–296, 304–305).

But however labeled, such a policy contains both dangers and appeals. Clearly, if the aggressor's price is higher than the deterrer is willing to pay, appeasement is simply not feasible. Furthermore, to apply the central lesson usually drawn from the Munich crisis of 1938, even if the price is bearable, serving the demands of an aggressor may be unwise and ultimately counterproductive, because the aggressor's appetite may grow with the feeding and thus it may be enticed to escalate its demands the next time around, ultimately demanding a price too high to pay. However, the discredit heaped upon appeasement as a result of its apparent misapplication in the 1930s doesn't mean that the policy is always invalid. The policy obviously worked in 1962: the Soviet withdrawal of offensive forces in Cuba satiated the U.S. appetite for concession, it did not whet it.

The net value of victory. Against estimates of the value of the status quo—the value to be found in remaining at peace—the potential aggressor balances its estimates of what war would most probably bring. For present purposes, its thinking about war is broken down into the three estimates of the net value of victory, of the net value of defeat, and of the probability of winning. All three of these qualities can change with time, and all are potentially manipulable by a country that is pursuing a policy of deterrence.

The first of these, the net value of victory, is rarely discussed, yet it is probably the most important of the three and a close examination of it in juxtaposition to the value of the status quo helps to explain why there is so much peace in so much of the world. For, simply put, many countries much of the time prefer the status quo to fighting a war and *winning*, and thus they are comfortably deterred no matter how big their military advantage. Spectacular cases in point, again, are the noninvasions by the United States of Canada and by the USSR of Rumania or Poland: the big countries believe, probably quite accurately, that they would be *worse* off after the war even if (as seems highly likely) they were to win handily.

There are quite a few policies a country can adopt to deflate a would-be aggressor's anticipated value of victory. It can make threats that either reduce the benefits the aggressor would gain upon victory or increase its costs for achieving victory.

Presumably, an aggressor will see some sort of gains—territorial, economic, or whatever—in a victory. The deterrer could announce a scorched-earth policy, in which it pledges to burn everything as it retreats, and thus significantly lower the potential aggressor's anticipated gains. The Dutch have threatened from time to time to greet invasion by destroying their dikes, thus inundating the victor's newly acquired territory. Fearing encroachment by the United States during the petroleum crisis of the 1970s, some poorly armed Arab states pledged to blow up their oil wells if invaded (see Rosecrance, 1986: 11). Another device, promoted by pacifists, is to be able credibly to threaten passive, nonviolent resistance after losing the war. If an invader is interested in taking over a country because it seeks the productive capacity of the people of that country, it will be deterred if it believes its invasion would cause the country to become unproductive (Holmes, 1989; Brown, 1987: 127–131; Sharp, 1973; Johnson, 1987: 248–253). Like all deterrent threats, policies of scorched earth, economic destruction, passive resistance, and so forth will be effective only if they are believed by the would-be aggressor. Since these threats involve a certain amount of self-destruction by the deterring country, there is an inherent problem with credibility. The Dutch never did blow up their dikes in World War II, and aggressors who are sufficiently bloody-minded may feel confident they can break down passive resisters.

A country can also seek to increase a victor's costs. As war becomes more destructive in general, the pain suffered even by the victor increases.

If the war is sufficiently terrible, victory can quickly become Pyrrhic, with the costs outweighing the gains. In the age of long-range bombing, a losing country can often embellish the usual costs of war by threatening to visit destruction upon a victor's cities far behind the lines of battle. If the bombers carry nuclear weapons, this threat becomes highly dramatic indeed. This approach—often called deterrence by punishment—was more difficult to carry out before the advent of airpower, though punitive raids could be conducted (Schelling, 1966: 178–180). One analogous earlier procedure was for kings who were potential combatants to have their heirs brought up at each other's court, i.e., making them hostages against an outbreak of hostilities.

There are policies even small countries can adopt to increase a victor's costs considerably and thus to enhance deterrence. Switzerland is surrounded by countries that have at various times been militarily strong and aggressively inclined, yet its last battle was fought in 1798. In considerable part, this situation is owing to the fact that the Swiss have a large, dedicated, well-trained civilian army: "Switzerland does not have an army," Metternich is reported to have said in the nineteenth century, "It *is* an army" (Perry, 1986). The country does not threaten so much to defeat an invader as to make the costs of invasion, even a successful invasion, very high—and this threat has apparently been effective against even such devoted aggressors as Adolf Hitler. If defeated in initial battles, the Swiss army has been trained to fall back into a network of secluded bases and installations in the Alps; from this bastion, it would foray out to harass and obstruct the occupiers (Quester, 1977: 174; Perry, 1986). Moreover, were the Swiss to fight as tenaciously as they threaten, an invader could conquer the country only by destroying it as a productive society, thus lowering the gains of victory (unless, of course, the aggressor wanted to control the country solely for its scenery and/or its strategic location).

Other small countries have used similar threats in an attempt to deter. At various points in its postwar history, Yugoslavia has had reason to fear a Soviet invasion. At those times, Yugoslavian officials have been quick to let the potential invader know that, if attacked, they will revert to the kind of guerrilla warfare they used so effectively against the German invaders during World War II (Quester, 1977: 174–175). Fearing an attack by the United States, the Sandinistas in Nicaragua made similar threats, as has Castro in Cuba.

A victor's costs may be substantially and importantly raised by factors other than those developed by the invaded country. The Soviet Union has doubtless noticed that its surrogate invasion of South Korea in 1950 caused great alarm in the West and set in motion a substantial anti-Soviet military buildup worldwide; it surely could anticipate similar undesirable, costly developments were it to seek to conquer Yugoslavia or Switzerland or Iran. The Soviet invasion of Afghanistan in 1979 was met not only with an enervating guerrilla campaign in the country itself but also with trade boycotts, and the USSR suffered costly reductions in credibility, trust, and prestige in important Muslim areas. A winner could also become so weakened by victory that it might become tempting prey to other states.

Furthermore, a victor has to live with itself after success has been achieved. If its victory is treated by its own population as a productive achievement, a thing of glory, a symbol of virility, an economic or a political gain, then the victory will presumably end up on the plus side of the ledger for the leaders. But if the victory were to engender a domestic political upheaval—of the sort, for example, that the British suffered after their brief, successful war against Egypt in 1956—it could come at considerable cost. An adventurous U.S. victory over Canada would likely cause just such a domestic crisis because it would be seen as an outrage by those people in the United States who would hold such an intervention to be unjust and unwise.

In fact, as Michael Doyle (1983, 1986), Bruce Russett (1990b), and others (Streit, 1939; Russett and Starr, 1981: 439–441; Quester, 1982: 253–254; Rummel, 1983; Weede, 1984) have argued, Immanuel Kant's assertion in *Perpetual Peace* (1795) that liberal regimes are disinclined to go to war has held up—at least insofar as war among liberal countries is concerned. For the 200 years during which there have been liberal countries, no constitutionally secure liberal states have ever gone to war with each other. Liberal states tend to regard each other as legitimate and unthreatening (the British, after all, could destroy U.S. cities with nuclear weapons almost as readily as the Soviet Union could, yet the United States does not seem to worry much about that prospect). And since the population of a liberal state can directly affect the government, an invasion of one liberal state by another will be effectively protested by many of the people in the victorious country, thus raising—perhaps devastatingly—the costs of victory. For this subset of countries, one that has increased markedly in number over the last two centuries, deterrence has held firm. And it is extremely unlikely that military factors have had much to do with the separate, perpetual peace that these liberal countries so far have worked out among themselves.

It also appears that the psychic costs of war have increased dramatically over the last 200 years or so, at least in the developed world. Where people once saw great glory and honor in war—particularly in victory— they are now more inclined to see degradation in it instead as war has increasingly come to be regarded as an enterprise that is immoral, repulsive, and uncivilized (Mueller, 1989). In deterrence terms, this change means the value of victory has been sharply reduced.

The net value of defeat. A would-be aggressor will also be deterred if in its estimation the net value of defeat is sufficiently low—very negative, one might say. Sometimes an aggressor might envision gains in defeat: a well-fought, but unsuccessful, war might recoup lost prestige or self-respect for a country, or the test of war might have beneficial domestic consequences. German General Friedrich von Bernhardi argued before World War I that "even defeat may bear a rich harvest" because often "it leads to healthy revival, and lays the foundation of a new and vigorous constitution."[5] Or perhaps the loser can anticipate a generous postwar aid program from the victor: There are Japanese who argue that losing World War II was the best thing that ever happened to their country. Perceived gains like these will be reduced and war deterred if the would-be aggressor can be credibly assured these benefits will not accompany its defeat.

The main method for reducing the net value of defeat is to raise the costs of defeat, that is, to make war as painful as possible. A would-be aggressor is less likely to be deterred if it concludes that the costs of defeat will be unpleasant but bearable—the loss of a bit of unimportant land, perhaps, or the payment of some not-terribly-expensive reparations—than if it anticipates the kind of total loss legendarily suffered by ancient Carthage at the hands of the Romans.

War is more likely to be deterred if prohibitively high costs are the likely consequence of war itself rather than simply something tacked on at the end, as at Carthage, which suffered the total destruction of the state, the execution of the men, the sale of women and children into slavery, and the salting of the earth so that nothing would grow there again. Although it might make sense from a deterrence standpoint to lower a would-be aggressor's value of defeat by threatening it before the war with a Carthaginian "peace" should it be defeated, the threat will be successful only if the potential aggressor believes the deterring country will actually carry out its threat. However, an army that anticipates extermination after defeat has every incentive to fight to the last, thereby raising the costs to the victor and giving the winning country a strong incentive to cut a deal before the war is over. If the aggressor understands this possibility before the war, a Carthaginian threat will not be credible. This dilemma reaches its ultimate in the age of the "doomsday machine"— the threat to blow up the entire world should the aggressor start a war. Even if the technology exists, the aggressor may well refuse to believe the deterring power will ever carry out such a self-destructive policy. Similar credibility problems arise with lesser nuclear retaliatory threats. In general, threats that require massive costs to be borne by the threatener—whether trade boycotts or suicidal destruction—are not likely to be very believable, and if they are not believable they may not be effective.

If, however, tremendous costs are a necessary consequence of any war—if extremely destructive warfare is the only kind likely to develop no matter what policy either side adopts—then the would-be aggressor can anticipate with some certainty that its costs will be very high, and it is therefore more likely to be deterred. Furthermore, while Carthaginian costs are paid only by the loser of the war, costs that arise out of warfare itself accrue to both loser and winner; that is, *both* the aggressor's cost of winning and its cost of losing are raised.[6]

It is important to note that this factor is more a matter of escalation than of technology. Countries armed with nuclear weapons could still fight inexpensive wars with each other—thermonuclear weapons are destructive only if they actually go off. However, if a would-be aggressor anticipates that a war is likely to escalate until it becomes intolerably costly (in all, or virtually all, cases well below the nuclear level), it will be deterred. As is discussed in the next section, insofar as World War III has been prevented by military considerations, it is this fear that conflict will escalate that has been crucial.

Raised psychic costs lower the value of defeat as well as the value of victory, and unlike the physical costs, they suffer no problem of credibility. If war is no longer held to be an honorable and invigorating test of bravery and strength of character but is considered instead to be repulsive and uncivilized, one can only engage in it—win or lose— with a distinctly unpleasant sense of repugnance, and therefore at high cost.

The possibility of winning. Finally, the would-be aggressor must reflect upon its chances of winning the war. Normally, it will be more likely to be deterred if its chances of winning seem low.[7] By increasing its armed strength, a country with a policy of deterrence can seek to manipulate the calculations of a would-be aggressor in a favorable direction since better arms will lower the aggressor's probability of victory (while perhaps also raising its anticipated costs of war).

As with appeasement, this policy could be counterproductive. If the country one is trying to deter misreads the signal and sees the arms buildup, not as deterrence, but as preparation for an armed attack, then it might actually be tempted to launch an attack before its opponent can do so—the nightmare of arms races and arms buildup that rightfully haunt so many discussions of military matters, particularly since the advent of nuclear weapons.

Deterrence as Expected Utility

The four deterrence variables discussed—the net values of the status quo, of victory, and of defeat and the probability of victory—can be neatly and simply interrelated by means of an expected-utility formulation. The exercise leads to some nonobvious conclusions—for example, that countries with little chance of winning might still want to go to war.

Football. Expected utility can productively be illustrated with an example from football. After scoring a touchdown in the college version of the sport, a team is given another down, and it can attempt one of two things: to placekick the ball through the goalposts, garnering one point if successful, or to move the ball past the goal line by passing it or running with it, in which case two points will be awarded. Now, a football team wants to get more points than the other team, and since two is greater than one, one might suppose that teams would invariably go for the two-point play. But in fact they don't: they almost always kick.

The reason is that the desirability of an option is not determined only by its value but also by the probability one will be successful in obtaining it. Kicking is far more likely to be successful than running or passing, and thus, all things considered, kicking is a more certain choice. What the team is trying to maximize is, not points, but expected utility. If one assumes that the kick has a probability of 0.9 of being successful, the expected utility for the kick option is calculated as follows: the value of success (1 point) is multiplied by its probability (0.9), and to this quantity is added the value of failure (0 points) multiplied by its probability (0.1). Thus, the expected utility for a kick is $1 \times 0.9 + 0 \times 0.1 = 0.9$. If a running or passing play has a 0.4 probability of success, its expected utility is the value of success (2 points) multiplied by its probability (0.4), to which is added the value of failure (0 points) multiplied by its probability (0.6). Thus, the expected utility for running or passing comes out to be $2 \times 0.4 + 0 \times 0.6 = 0.8$. If those probabilities are reasonable real-life estimates, it is wise to kick, and football coaches are doing the sensible thing when they pursue the less valuable but more probable option. They may not use the term, but they are seeking to maximize expected utility.

War. It is true that war is not the same as a football game, but the same logic can be used to sort through the decision-making process. Using the deterrence variables already discussed, a would-be aggressor's expected utility for war is the value it places on victory multiplied by its estimate of the probability of winning, to which is added its value of defeat multiplied by its estimated probability of losing (the last is calculated by subtracting its probability of winning from 1). This expected utility for war is then compared to the expected utility for nonwar, or the status quo, which is the value the would-be aggressor places on the status quo (multiplied by its probability, which is 1). If the aggressor finds the expected utility of war to be higher than that of the status quo, it will go to war, and vice versa.

The usefulness of this approach is that it is comprehensive. It makes room for all the considerations discussed earlier—cost and benefit; reward and punishment; concerns about warfare, morality, trade boycotts, domestic political turmoil—and then interrelates them. It also allows one to sort through some of the puzzles deterrence critics have brought up.

For example, some analysts have suggested that the decision of the Egyptians to go to war against Israel in 1973 made no sense from a deterrence standpoint because the Egyptians knew they were likely to lose (for a discussion, see Stein, 1985). But a country goes to war, not because it feels it can *win*, but because it feels it can *profit*—that is, emerge better off. This consideration can work either way. On the one hand, the United States refrains from attacking Canada because the former could not profit from the encounter even though it could surely win militarily. On the other hand, the Egyptians may have felt, on balance, that they could profit from a war against Israel in 1973 even if they stood little chance of winning it, for it seems clear the Egyptians had come to feel that the status quo after their defeat by the Israelis in 1967 was intolerably humiliating. They saw some benefits in defeat, because if they fought well, their self-esteem and prestige would at least be raised. It's possible, in fact, that they even preferred defeat to the unsatisfactory status quo, in which case war would have been entirely sensible from their perspective and could not have been deterred no matter how low their chances of winning.[8] Or even if they preferred the status quo to defeat—but not by much—they might well have chosen war even if they stood only a small chance of winning it. Suppose, to put things in numerical form, the Egyptians could be said to have placed a value of 50 on the expected utility of the status quo, 500 on the value of victory, and -10 on the value of defeat. In that case, they would have gone to war even if they believed they stood only a 0.2 chance of victory. In their estimation, the expected utility of the status quo (50) would have been far less than the expected utility of war: $500 \times 0.2 + (-10) \times 0.8 = 100 - 8 = 92$. The same sort of logic could be used with the Japanese decision to attack Pearl Harbor (see Mueller, 1968).

Deterrence apparently failed in 1973, not because the Israelis were unable to convince the Egyptians that Egypt would probably lose a war between the two countries, but because the Egyptians' value of defeat was insufficiently unpleasant in comparison to their rather low expected utility for the status quo while their visions of the value of a victory over Israel were extremely high. To deter, the Israelis' best hope was probably to make the Egyptians' value of defeat far more penalizing, perhaps by promising devastating destruction of Egyptian values or society. But the Israelis were unable to do so credibly because of their own obvious preference for quick, decisive, and inexpensive wars. For the Arabs, even defeat was not all that bad given their apparent misery with the status quo.

Crisis Stability and General Stability

The above approach can be used to distinguish between two kinds of stability: crisis stability and general stability. Discussions of deterrence and of defense policy in general have been preoccupied with crisis stability, the notion that it is desirable for disputing countries to be so militarily secure that they can adequately deal with a surprise attack: even if successfully surprised, they can absorb the attack and rebound from it with an effective counteroffensive. If each side is militarily confident in this way, then neither side would see much advantage in launching a surprise attack, and thus neither side would be tempted to start a war because of the fear that the other might do so first. Crises, therefore, would be "stable"—both sides would be able to assess events in a luxuriously slow manner and not feel compelled to act hastily and with incomplete information. In expected-utility terms, crisis stability means that a country's expected utility for a war it starts is not much different from the utility it expects from a war the other side starts: there is, then, no great advantage in going first.

In the nuclear period, discussions of crisis stability have centered around the technological and organizational problems of maintaining a secure second-strike capability—that is, developing a retaliatory force so well-entrenched that a country can afford to wait out a surprise attack fully confident it will be able to respond with a devastating counterattack. Many have argued that crisis stability is "delicate," easily upset by technological or economic shifts (Wohlstetter, 1959; see also Snyder, 1961: 97–109), and a great deal of thought has gone into assessing whether a given weapons system or military strategy is "stabilizing" or "destabilizing."

General stability is concerned with broader needs, desires, and concerns and is essentially what Kenneth Boulding (1978) calls Stable Peace. It prevails when two countries, taking all the various costs, benefits, and risks into account, vastly prefer peace to war: their expected utility for peace, for the status quo, is much higher than their expected utility for war. This is the type of stability that prevails between the United States and Canada (see also Boulding, 1978: 44–45).

For peace, one would ideally like both crisis stability and general stability to prevail in a relationship between two countries. But efforts to improve one form of stability may weaken the other. For example, in an effort to enhance crisis stability, a country may try to improve its second-strike capability by building up its military forces; an opponent may find this buildup provocative and conclude that it is actually a prelude to an attack. On the other hand, generous appeasement concessions, designed to raise a potential aggressor's satisfaction with the status quo by reducing provocation and thus enhancing general stability, may tempt that aggressor to attack by giving it reason to believe it could win cheaply in a quick strike: in a spectacularly futile effort to placate the Germans in the 1930s, Holland decided to remain quiet and neutral while, to decrease "provocation" to Hitler, Belgium broke off its alliance with France and Denmark disarmed.

However, when general stability is high, crisis instability is of little immediate concern. Thus, many concerns about changes in the arms balance, while valid in their own terms, miss the broader issue. An antimissile defense may increase or decrease crisis stability but may not alter the broader picture significantly. Consider the case of a millionaire who loses or gains $1,000; he is now poorer or richer than before, but his overall status has not changed very much. When general stability is high, the question of who could fight the most ingenious and effective war becomes irrelevant. Deterrence, and therefore peace, prevails.

Deterrence, Nuclear Weapons, and the Long Peace

The application of an expected-utility approach helps to bring deterrence considerations into closer conformity with the realities of decision making in war initiation (or avoidance), and it comfortably builds into the discussion not only military aspects but also such important nonmilitary considerations as economics, morality, goodwill, prestige, inertia, international opinion, and national pride and self-image. These considerations can be used as background in looking at the long peace that has prevailed between the Soviet Union and the United States since World War II. Because both of these countries have huge nuclear arsenals and because the proclaimed purpose of these arsenals has been to deter an attack by the other side, it is natural to conclude that the weapons have produced the peace. Indeed, the prospectus for the February 1990 conference at the University of South Carolina began with these words: "Since the advent of the nuclear age, world order and peace have rested on the foundation of 'nuclear deterrence.' " It seems likely that peace has enjoyed firmer foundations and that the deterrence calculation has been affected by many other elements. Stability—general stability—has been very firm: even without nuclear weapons, the United States and the USSR would have been deterred from a war with each other.[9]

To begin with, each has had a high estimation of the value of the status quo. The United States and the Soviet Union emerged from World War II as the big winners and had much to be content about: the United States was by far the richest country in the world, and the Soviet Union controlled a vast new empire. Each had a lot to lose in any new war.

Next, while there are important, even visceral, differences between the two countries, direct war has never made much sense as a method for resolving those differences. During the Cold War the Soviets were devoted to the notion that international capitalism, or imperialism, is a profoundly evil system which must—and will—eventually be eradicated from the face of the globe. Although the Soviet leaders were fully committed to aiding in that "struggle" (which they thought would often be violent), they never visualized a major war—that is, a direct war against the advanced capitalist states—as a remotely sensible method for carrying it out.[10]

Finally, if nuclear weapons hadn't been invented, the worst conflict either side could threaten to inflict would be one of the size and scope of World War II. Since the United States and the Soviet Union went into that war only when it became a grim necessity, to expect them willingly to embrace a repetition of its massive destruction seems absurd: the costs of that war, even to the victors, were clearly prohibitive. Both sides have been fully aware that any severe conflict between them could easily escalate to an all-out fight, and each has adopted deterrence policies designed to make that threat credible to the other. Insofar as military considerations are relevant, then, the key issue is escalation— the conviction on both sides that a war between them would become massively costly—not the precise qualities of the horrors that wait at the end of the escalatory ladder. As long as the two sides anticipate that they would be worse off with war than with the rather pleasant status quo, deterrence has held. Nuclear weapons have not been required to bring these two cautious contestants to this elemental conclusion.

None of this discussion is meant to deny that the sheer horror of nuclear war is impressive or compelling, particularly the speed with which it could bring about massive destruction. Nor is it meant to deny that decision makers, both in times of crisis and otherwise, are fully conscious of how horribly destructive a nuclear war could be. I simply want to stress that the horror of repeating World War II is not all that much *less* impressive or dramatic and that countries that are essentially satisfied with the status quo will strive to avoid war if they feel it could escalate to *either* calamity. It is probably quite a bit more terrifying to think about a jump from the fiftieth floor than about one from the fifth floor, but anyone who finds life even minimally satisfying is extremely unlikely to do either.

War, Morality, Justice, Religion, and Deterrence

In various ways, the following discussion applies notions from deterrence theory to considerations about the interrelationships among religion, morality, and war.

1. *Any development that appears to make war more humane increases its likelihood.* Deterrence theory suggests that, all other things being equal, any measures designed to make war more civilized or humane will also make it more likely to occur. By lowering potential war costs, such measures raise the value of defeat as well as the value of victory, and thus they tempt the aggressive. Too often the quest for the "just war" has led instead to what might be called the "nice" war—wars in which the only people who die are young men in uniform—and the threat to do minimal, proportionate damage may not be enough to deter war.

It should not be forgotten that war has often been taken to have many positive and beneficial qualities (see Mueller, 1989: chap. 2), and some useful testimony on this point comes from the nineteenth century. In his famous 1910 essay, "The Moral Equivalent of War," the pacifist William James called war "supremely thrilling excitement" and "the supreme theater of human strenuousness," observing that "so far," war had "been the only force that can discipline a whole community" (James, 1911: 282, 288). Even the most zealous of war enthusiasts, however, have been willing to acknowledge that war does have its downside as well—the extensive destruction and bloodshed.[11] Consequently, small and decisive wars have often been taken to be ideal—supreme theater at low cost.

A hundred years ago in Europe, in the wake of various efforts to make war more civilized and humane and after a century in which wars there had been limited and manageable, many of the people who reveled in war had convinced themselves that what they took to be civilization had advanced to just such a blissful condition. For example, the quintessential war glorifier, Heinrich von Treitschke, idealized war in considerable part because he believed "wars will become rarer and shorter, but at the same time far more sanguinary" (Treitschke, 1916: 2:443). He found it inevitable that "the God above us will see to it that war shall return again, a terrible medicine for mankind diseased." He observed, however, that war "strike[s] us as appalling, because it involves a complete break with our accustomed conditions. The highly cultured man realizes indeed that he must slay the antagonists whose bravery he honors, and he feels that the majesty of war lies in the absence of passion from the slaughter, therefore it is a far greater effort to him than to the savage to enter upon such a conflict." Fortunately, he concluded, wars would become "both shorter and rarer" because of the "progress of culture," which "renders men's lives ever more harmonious," and because of the burgeoning, interdependent economic system. "Therefore," he concluded, "wars must become rarer and shorter, owing to man's natural horror of bloodshed as well as to the size and quality of modern armies, for it is impossible to see how the burdens of a great war could long be borne under the present conditions. But it would be false to conclude that wars can ever cease. They neither can nor should, so long as the State is sovereign and stands among its peers" (Treitschke, 1916: 1:69–70).

In England, the Reverend Father H.I.D. Ryder pointed out that war "is calculated to evoke some of the best qualities of human nature, giving the spirit a predominance over the flesh," and he observed cheerfully that "under the touch of civilisation war has lost some of its most offensive features." In particular, he felt, noncombatants could now be regarded "as henceforth excluded from the casualties of civilised warfare" (Ryder, 1899: 726–727). It was the terrific horrors of World War I, not dedicated moralizing about the institution of war, that severely undercut the force of those arguments (see Mueller, 1991).

To a considerable degree, the moralists of war and the deterrers of war are talking past each other, perhaps in part because of the different historical eras in which the two ideas grew up. The idea of making war bearable is an old one, as is the idea that one should wage only good wars. But the idea of preventing them entirely by threatening massively punishing retaliation is probably rather new. As noted earlier, it seems to have taken the technique of strategic bombing for this idea to become a feasible, and therefore a credible, threat. And perhaps the invention of nuclear weapons was necessary too—though after World War I quite a few people in Europe came to the conclusion that the next war might end civilization through chemical and germ bombing (see Mueller, 1989: 57–60). Before that, military deterrence (insofar as it was a conscious policy) mainly depended on the threat that an aggressor would lose the war.

It might be valid to suggest, then, that the just-war people are dealing with concepts developed when war was still seen to be a useful, necessary, and sometimes desirable method for settling disputes and putting the world right and that deterrence theorists are trying to eliminate war entirely, relying on less dramatic methods to resolve disputes. It's not clear where the burden of proof lies, but since the deterrers can argue that their policy has prevented major war entirely in recent years, it seems that the moralists will never engage them unless they can show that making war bearable will not increase its likelihood.

2. *War will never be fully abandoned if people are encouraged to believe that war can be good, moral, or just.* People who advocate using military threats to deter war are often criticized because while the goal of their policy may be to maintain peace, the policy itself perpetuates an emphasis on military considerations and this emphasis, it is feared, will eventually lead to the use of "deterrent" weapons. Thus, it is argued, deterrence (that is, military deterrence) enhances the likelihood of war (see Holmes, 1989: 256–259).

Much the same could be said about any theory that holds that war can be good, just, or moral. If war can still be meritorious, if it remains an accepted method for settling issues, it is reasonable to anticipate that eventually it will come about. And war advocates over the centuries have had little difficulty in fabricating excuses that resonate with just-war rhetoric.

Deterrence suggests that peace—general stability—is likely to be firm when the horrors of war and the benefits of peace are dramatically evident. But peace is most secure when it gravitates away from conscious rationality to become an unexamined habit of mind—to become, in a sense, irrational. An idea becomes impossible, not when it becomes reprehensible or has been renounced because it is often immoral or unjust, but when it fails to percolate into one's consciousness as a conceivable option.

Consider a man who is on the fifth floor of a building and is musing over two methods for reaching the ground floor: walking down the stairs (slow) or jumping out the window (fast). Although there are uncertainties, the decision is not a terribly difficult one to be "rational" about. If war is like a fifth-floor jump, only someone who is suicidal will start one— or even get close to one. But an important oddity in that little analogy lies in the notion that someone would spend any time at all thinking about whether walking down the stairs is preferable to jumping out the window. The alternative of jumping is not rejected after a balanced, rational decision is made, nor is it even rejected out of hand; rather, it never even comes up as a coherent possibility. Somewhere along the line we learn that jumping out of a fifth-floor window is a really terrible idea, and we live out our lives without ever reassessing the validity of that conclusion. It apparently becomes a truth so self-evident that it requires no periodic reexamination.

War could be like that. Through rational or semirational deterrence calculations, one might come to believe that war makes no sense—that it is very stupid. Such reasoned war-avoidance—such deeply conditional deterrence—could then become so habitual that war never comes up again as a serious option, even when it might have been objectively reasonable at least to consider it as a possibility. The United States refrains from attacking Canada today, but not because U.S. decision makers from time to time examine the option of invading Canada and then soberly reject it because they decide they prefer the status quo to war. Instead, the option never gets seriously considered, and by now it has slipped so far from the realm of conscious possibility that even to bring it up may seem peculiar if not downright perverse (especially to Canadians). There is also the unexamined and apparently perpetual peace that has evolved between the United States and Britain; both nations now have the technology to annihilate the other, but neither spends much time worrying about that fact. Or, even more strikingly, there is the comfortable neighbor relationship that has developed between Germany and France despite centuries of enmity and despite the fact that France's nuclear arsenal could easily devastate Germany within minutes.

This process seems to have occurred quite broadly in the developed world, and it must be admitted that a moral revulsion from war has been one of the causes of this development. As Luard suggests, a "willingness for war . . . may make war almost as inevitable, sooner or later, as a definite intention of war" (Luard, 1986: 231). That attitude, that war willingness, came under concentrated attack in the nineteenth century and has been almost universally rejected in the developed world in the twentieth. Potential combatants in the developed world have come not only to appreciate the high costs of war there but also to generally believe that war no longer is something one *does* (see Mueller, 1989). If a "willingness for war" can make war nearly inevitable, continues Luard, "a general unwillingness for war" means that "precisely the opposite is the case" (Luard, 1986: 231). The elimination of war, therefore, rests in the prospect that there will exist a "general unwillingness" for war—that war will become obsolete, that it will go out of style, that it will become literally unthinkable—not that it will become physically impossible or completely extinct.

The idea that war is a viable, accepted, and expected way of going about things is a necessary cause of war; if that idea fades (as it has, for example, with dueling and slavery), war can't happen (on these analogies, see Mueller, 1989: 9–13; Ray, 1989). But the just-war theory *does* help to maintain war as a viable, accepted, and thus expected way of doing things. To that degree, it helps to prevent a state of "general unwillingness" for war from coming about.

If war becomes as fully eradicated from the course of human events as slavery or dueling, however, it would mean that people would often find themselves tolerating what Aquinas called an "evil peace" (1990: 9). Peace is what emerges when nations abandon war as a method for dealing with one another, and, as war enthusiasts have often noted, it often seems to wallow in pettiness, materialism, crassness, small-mindedness, willfulness, and contentiousness (see Mueller, 1989: 42–43). There is nothing terribly good or ennobling about peace; it does not really seem to bring out the love, goodwill, harmony, justice, and brotherhood with which it is constantly associated by its well-meaning, if self-deluded, propagandists. In particular, living at peace means abandoning war as a method for curing the ills of the world. The chaos in Lebanon and the famine and chronic social and economic mismanagement in Africa could probably be improved by sending in troops from the enlightened developed world. Peace dictates that we send money and valentines instead. Sydney Smith recognized this fact in 1823:

> I am sorry for the Spaniards—I am sorry for the Greeks—I deplore the fate of the Jews; the people of the Sandwich Islands are groaning under the most detestable tyranny; Bagdad is oppressed; I do not like the present state of the Delta; Thibet is not comfortable. Am I to fight for all these people? The world is bursting with sin and sorrow. Am I to be champion of the Decalogue, and to be eternally raising fleets and armies to make all men good and happy? [Auden, 1956: 323]

He also recognized the ultimate futility of such efforts: "We have just done saving Europe, and I am afraid the consequence will be, that we shall cut each other's throats" (Auden, 1956: 323–324). If this perspective triumphs, we will have to live without the crusading benefits of war. As the Swiss have shown after 190 warless years, it does seem quite possible to get along without them.

3. *A moral or religious code that treats human life as sacred or paramount will, if accepted, reduce the likelihood of war, but it is logically deluded and absurd.* In the last century or two, a notion about the "sanctity of human life" (as opposed to the sanctity of the soul) appears to have gained a fair amount of currency in the developed world. If this trend suggests that human life has become more highly valued than it once was, deterrence is more likely to be firm because the costs of any given war will effectively rise.

The problem with the idea that there is nothing more important than human life is that it is effectively hypocritical. Antoine de Saint-Exupery's

1942 novel, *Night Flight*, concerns a dangerous airmail operation in which some pilots' lives are inevitably lost. The people using the service find it a convenience, but none would wish to have anyone sacrifice his life for the convenience. "Yet," observes one of the novel's characters, "even though human life may be the most precious thing on earth, we always behave as if there were something of higher value than human life. . . . But what thing?" (Saint-Exupery, 1942: 94–95).

There are many social policies in which the loss of human life is an important element; war is only one of them. Another instrument for mass destruction is the private passenger automobile. We may hold that there is nothing more important than the value of human life—indeed, a code of ethics for engineers requires them to hold the safety of the public paramount, that is, preeminent, supreme. Yet it is obvious, as Saint-Exupery points out, that we don't really believe it is that important. Getting around in cars is clearly far more important than human life, as each year for the privilege we willingly inflict upon ourselves 50,000 deaths and 2 million or so disabling injuries (concentrated, not among the weak and infirm, but among strong, young adults)—not to mention considerable death and illness because of atmospheric pollution.

It is, of course, quite possible to move people without killing them. Large commercial airlines have gone entire years without fatalities; passengers killed on railroads in a typical year are also few. The New York subway system, regularly and justly maligned for filth, inefficiency, noise, and other indignities, moves millions of people every day and sometimes goes decades without a fatality (homicides on the subway, hardly the fault of the system itself, run about a dozen a year); even taxicabs—involved in less than 1 percent of all auto accidents—may be considered comparatively safe (*Accident Facts 1985*: 77). But we tend to prefer the private automobile.

In some respects war, an important rival to the automobile as an invented method for slaughter, is surrounded by less hypocrisy. People who plan and conduct wars know lives will be lost, and they often forthrightly, if grimly, build these considerations into their calculations: they estimate how many casualties it will take to capture an objective and consider whether the objective is worth it. The automobile, by contrast, is far less frequently put into that framework; the obvious, Is having the automobile worth the cost? is too rarely asked. Can the existence of the automobile be reconciled with the principles of proportionality, discrimination, and noncombatant immunity?

It may seem strange to put war and the automobile in the same class, but the moral distinction between the two may not be as great as it seems. For example, war might seem to be worse because the probability of being killed in a war is higher than the probability of being killed in a car crash. This distinction is not terribly useful, however, because it is quite possible to have wars in which the chance of being killed is very low. Indeed, the probabilities are often within hailing distance: by one calculation, driving a car and being in the army in Vietnam reduced an American's life expectancy on the same order of magnitude (Fischhoff et al., 1981: 82). In some large wars, there may be an eerie relation between the two phenomena: World War II probably "saved" some 50,000 U.S. lives by reducing traffic casualties significantly below pre- and postwar levels because gasoline was rationed and because so many dangerous drivers were drafted (*Accident Facts, 1985*: 13).

Another popular distinction between war and the automobile stresses that using the automobile is voluntary—no one is forced to drive around in a car—while wars involve conscription. But many armies (the British in much of World War I, for example) rely entirely on volunteers, and some 15–20 percent of the people killed in traffic accidents are pedestrians (i.e., noncombatants), and it is scarcely realistic to suggest that anyone has a choice about whether to be a pedestrian.

War is most often seen to be morally inferior to other forms of destruction because death is part of its very intent. By contrast, no one intends anyone to be killed by automobiles. The distinction is an important one, and it accounts, along with the low probability of injury during a single trip, for the benign acceptance of automobile use. But suppose there existed two ways to spend $10 billion: one would prevent a war that would kill 1,000 people (by intent), the other would prevent 20,000 accidental deaths. Would it be sensible to prefer the former?

Furthermore, it is a bit disingenuous to suggest that the death and injury automobiles cause are entirely unintentional. Unlike some cancer and heart disease, they happen because, as a society, we have systematically chosen to encourage the automobile over less dangerous means of transportation. A reduction of the speed limit for private passenger automobiles to ten miles per hour in the United States would, if enforced, save nearly half a million lives by the end of the century; to oppose such a law is willingly to pay the price to get there faster by automobile. But if we are willing to pay this cost, we should also explicitly acknowledge that fact. Although the engineers' code requires that they hold the safety of the public paramount, neither they nor the country's leaders really believe in that code; getting around in cars is obviously far more important than human life.

The purpose here, of course, is not to argue that wars are good and automobiles bad but to suggest that both should be subjected to the same sort of cost-benefit analysis. One might well conclude that few wars have been worth their cost and that 50,000 lives and 2 million disabling injuries per year (plus pollution) are a small price to pay for the blessings of the automobile—the pleasure, the convenience, the personal mobility, the economic benefit, the aesthetic charm, the macho gratification.

Many other social policies involve the same sort of consideration. To take an extreme example: Every year a few thousand people die in falls from buildings that are more than one story high. Those lives could be saved by closing off all buildings at the second floor. To reject such a policy is to say that tall buildings are worth the cost in lives. As a society, we regularly and inescapably adopt policies in which human lives are part of the price, yet often we casually and opaquely gloss over the full cost consequences.

Deterrence, or at least nuclear deterrence, is often held to be fundamentally immoral because in part it threatens or appears to threaten massive, suicidal destruction to prevent a lesser evil. But the hypocritical notion that there is nothing more important than human life suffers from logical and moral defects that are also severe.

4. *Religion and religious absolutes often increase both the likelihood of war and its potential for massive destruction.* In the 1590s, a Spanish official proclaimed, "If we are defending God's cause . . . there is no reason to abandon it on grounds of impossibility" (Luard, 1986: 338). Often such remarkable absolution has been linked to war, and in those cases, deterrence theory suggests, peace is in big trouble.

In 1984, on the birthday of the Prophet Muhammad, Ayatollah Ruhollah Khomeini proclaimed that "war is a blessing for the world and for all nations." God, he explained, "incites men to fight and to kill," and war "purifies the earth," because "if one permits an infidel to continue his role as a corrupter of the earth, his moral suffering will be all the worse. If one kills the infidel and thus stops him from perpetrating his misdeeds, his death will be a blessing to him. For if he remains alive, he will become more and more corrupt" (quoted in Mueller, 1989: 255).

This pattern of thought stems rather naturally from a certain kind of religious thinking. After all, if one has found the right God, permitting unrepentant unbelievers to continue to exist carries with it the danger that they will subvert or convert believers away from the true faith, thereby plunging them into a life of sin and an afterlife of perdition. According to Moses, it was God's notion that war would have to be used to cleanse the promised land of troublesome unbelievers and infidels. If they were permitted to live, God was reported to fear, they might teach the Israelites "their abominable practices which they have done in the service of their gods" and thus cause the Israelites to sin against their God. Consequently, in victory the Israelites were ordered to "save alive nothing that breathes" and to "utterly destroy them" (Deuteronomy 20:18, 16–17). Accordingly, says the Book of Joshua, with

God's help and under His orders, the Israelites utterly annihilated the peoples of Jericho, Ai, Libnah, Lachish, Eglon, Hebron, Debir, Hazor and the areas in between (the people of Gibeon, however, cut a deal and were merely enslaved).[12] The Israelites were not unique in taking their faith to this somewhat logical extreme. In ancient times, it was rather common for victors to "consecrate" conquered cities to their gods by killing every person and animal in them and by destroying all property (Botterweck and Ringgren, 1986: 189–198).

Just-war theorists sought to modify or mellow such doctrines of the holy war or "herem" (jihad in the Islamic tradition), but that kind of thinking existed in much of the early just-war theorizing. Augustine, in fact, does not appear to have minded war's destructiveness as much as the disgusting and unruly passions it tended to unleash. "What is the evil in war?" he wrote. "Is it the death of some who will soon die in any case, that others may live in peaceful subjection? This is mere cowardly dislike, not any religious feeling. The real evils of war are love of violence, revengeful cruelty, fierce and implacable enmity, wild resistance, and the lust of power, and such like" (Holmes, 1989: 128). His objection to war, in other words, seems to have stemmed from a sort of early Puritanism: War was okay as long as it wasn't too passionate. On the other hand, a certain amount of *religious* passion was both acceptable and obligatory: "to punish these things . . . force is required to inflict the punishment, that, in obedience to God or some lawful authority, good men undertake wars" (ibid.).

A few centuries later, Thomas Aquinas quoted Augustine approvingly in phrases that anticipate Khomeini's: "When we are stripping a man of the lawlessness of sin, it is good for him to be vanquished, since nothing is more hopeless than the happiness of sinners, whence arises a guilty impunity, and an evil will, like an internal enemy" (Aquinas, 1990: 9). In 1393, a pair of Cambridge theologians assured all that it was "permitted to Christians to fight against unbelievers, pagan or others, so as to bring about their forcible conversion to the Christian faith" (Contamine, 1984: 294). It would be difficult to sort things out in a fully quantitative manner, but it seems at least possible that, on balance, wars would be less frequent and less murderous if moral and religious precepts had never been applied to them.

5. The belief in an instrumental and guiding god helps to reconcile some major difficulties in the prosecution of warfare and therefore facilitates war. In his classic book, *On War*, Carl von Clausewitz stresses that there is in warfare a colossal amount of uncertainty, which he calls "friction," analogous to the untidy forces in classical mechanics that keep its laws from being precisely true in real life. "No other human activity," Clausewitz concludes, "is so continuously or universally bound up with chance" (Clausewitz, 1976: 85). War is a lethal, improvisatory free-for-all between dedicated and often desperate contestants who are playing for extremely high stakes and who have usually never fought each other before. There are few, if any, rules and no time limits, and although each side is fighting for its own self-interest, that interest may be difficult to assess and may change as the war progresses. It is often extremely difficult at any point to know what is going on (some people, following Clausewitz, have referred to the "fog of war"), and each side will do its utmost to confuse and deceive the other. Even small wars involve the command of large, complex organizations, which are difficult to manage even in peacetime, and the course of the war can be crucially determined by such changeable and unmeasurable qualities as morale and leadership and by such imponderables as weather, evolving technology, the caprices of allies or neutrals, and dumb luck. As Livy put it earlier, "Nowhere do events correspond less to men's expectations than in war" (Linderman, 1987: ii). Or, later, Leo Tolstoy: "A countless number of free forces (for nowhere is man freer than during a battle, where it is a question of life or death) influence the course taken by the fight" (Tolstoy, 1966: 1109).[13]

It is not particularly clear whether this enormous uncertainty helps to deter war or to encourage it. In some cases (the Japanese in 1941, for example), the uncertainty has inspired a fair amount of wishful thinking about the prospects of success (see Mueller, 1968). In others (the United States and the USSR since 1945), it may well have inspired exceptional caution. But anything that appears to reduce uncertainty *and* to make a potential aggressor more confident of victory makes war more likely. Religion has often had that effect. It has also importantly facilitated the prosecution of war.

There is a fierce, even desperate, need for commanders to find coherence in the uncertainty, and many have looked to God for help. As Douglas MacArthur put it, "In war, when a commander becomes so bereft of reason and perspective that he fails to understand the dependence of arms on divine guidance, he no longer deserves victory" (Jury, 1971: 57). Prayer can be seen as an effort to manipulate luck. If a commander believes in God, has prayed, and has subsequently been lucky, it is natural to credit the luck to divine guidance rather than to chance—to conclude that one's prayers have been answered and therefore that God is on one's side.

This conclusion can lead, equally naturally, to a sense of arrogance and self-righteousness, and it can inspire a messianic self-image: it is, in fact, a reasonable inference from MacArthur's dictum that any victorious commander is being guided by God. One of the most spectacularly lucky commanders in history was William the Conqueror in 1066. A whole series of events went right for him—including some extremely freakish weather. He was quick to conclude from these events that he had become God's instrument, and he carried out his war and the destructive occupation of his conquered territory with that confidence. A commander obsessed with the notion that he is God's instrument can also be peculiarly insensitive to signs that luck has turned against him, and thus he may overconfidently carry on a senselessly destructive war when a less deluded commander would cut his losses and quit.[14]

As military observers have often noted, it is frequently—perhaps usually—true that the outcome of a battle or war is determined more by an army's fighting spirit than by anything else: few people would disagree with Napoleon's dictum that in war, moral considerations account for three-quarters and the balance of actual forces for only the other quarter. Accordingly, anything that buoys the fighting spirit facilitates the prosecution of war. Religion—in particular the notion that an instrumental and guiding God is one's ally—has very often served that purpose (see also Kaeuper, 1988). In 1466, one soldier put it this way: "I believe that God favors those who risk their lives by their readiness to make war to bring the wicked, the oppressors, the conquerors, the proud and all who deny true equity, to justice" (Vale, 1981: 30). Or, as Gerald Linderman observed of the American Civil War, "A conviction of wide currency was that God would ensure the victory of the army whose collective faith was the sturdiest" (Linderman, 1987: 10). In 1911, a British writer, Harold F. Wyatt, argued that war is the "Court of God"; "whichever people shall have in it the greater soul of righteousness will be the victor" (Wyatt, 1911: 602).

Religion and a belief in God, as John Keegan has noted, can also aid the conduct of warfare by helping soldiers to overcome their natural terror of battle—there are, as they say, no atheists in foxholes (Keegan, 1987: 197). For this reason, commanders have often used religious ritual and appeals to buck up their forces as they gird for battle. As Machiavelli observed, "Where religion exists it is easy to introduce armies and discipline" (Machiavelli, 1950: 147). Religion is not the only mechanism for accomplishing this effect—Keegan also points to drugs and patriotism—but there can be little doubt that a belief in the existence of a guiding and an instrumental God has helped to facilitate the sacrificial, uncertain, masochistic, improbable, and fundamentally absurd activity known as warfare.

Notes

1. Morgan, 1977: 9. See also Snyder, 1961: chap. 1; Singer, 1962: chap. 2; Art and Waltz, 1983: 10.

2. This discussion develops and expands some ideas presented in Mueller, 1989: 246–251. See also Mueller, 1968.

3. For an essay stressing the "anarchy" of international politics in which "statesmen are preoccupied with the use of force," "pure coercion" tends to reign, "trust is hard to come by," "statesmen are shortsighted," states "cannot afford to be moral," "all states all of the time must make provision for their defense," and "military power is necessary for survival," see Art and Waltz, 1983: 3–8. For the argument that in "anarchy" a "state of war" will exist not only if "all parties lust for power" but also "if all states seek only to ensure their own safety"; that "war is normal"; that "peace is fragile"; and that nuclear weapons are crucial and have been a "great force for peace," see Waltz, 1988: 620, 624.

4. It will be assumed that someone contemplating war does at least a modicum of rational thinking about it before taking the plunge. Although it would be foolish to suggest that in thinking about war decision makers go through an exquisite and precise numerical process, there does seem to be a fair amount of rationality in the way wars begin. Military historian Michael Howard concludes, after a life-long study of the subject, that "wars begin by conscious and reasoned decisions based on the calculation, made by *both* parties, that they can achieve more by going to war than by remaining at peace" (Howard, 1984: 133). Political scientist Bruce Bueno de Mesquita argues that "for all the emotion of the battlefield, the premeditation of war is a rational process consisting of careful, deliberate calculation," and he notes "one clear indication of the rational planning that precedes war is that only 10 percent of the wars fought since the defeat of Napoleon have been quickly and decisively lost by the nation that attacked first" (Bueno de Mesquita 1981: 19; see also Blainey, 1973: chap. 9; Luard, 1986: chap. 5; Mueller, 1989: 227–232).

5. Bernhardi, 1914: 28. He gives as an example the gains the Boers found after their defeat in the Boer War (pp. 43–45).

6. Thus, the nuclear-winter thesis—the notion that even a fairly "small" nuclear war could trigger a catastrophic climatic change because of the lofted smoke and soot from fires (see C. Sagan, 1983–84)—would be, if accepted as valid, an example of an effective doomsday machine since it would be credible and could not be set off by accident.

7. This proposition assumes, of course, that the aggressor prefers victory to defeat, certainly a reasonable assumption under most circumstances. There may be a few instances, however, where it doesn't hold true. In 1898, many Spaniards welcomed a war with the United States over Cuba because a defeat there would allow them to withdraw honorably from that highly troublesome colony. Unfortunately for them, however, the victors went on to take over more valued Spanish colonies—Puerto Rico and the Philippines. This development caused a revolution at home, exactly what Spanish politicians had sought to avoid with their Cuban policy, which was insufficiently fine-tuned as it turned out. For this case, see Lebow, 1985: 222–223, and Small, 1980: 20 and chap. 3. Another instance is a fictional one. In the 1959 film, *The Mouse That Roared*, the impoverished Duchy of Grand Fenwick, a tiny country in Europe that somehow

managed to miss being involved in World War II, decides to invade the United States so that it can then enjoy the generous aid that country gives to countries it defeats in war. Unfortunately, the Fenwickians accidentally win—had they suspected their fate in advance, they would have been deterred from their aggression. Although they never actually started a war, some Grenadians and Panamanians may be real-life Grand Fenwickians: in the view of many grateful Panamanians and Grenadians, the U.S. invasion of their countries threw out bad governments, which had somehow gained control over their lives, and replaced them with better ones and with U.S. largesse. Some French communist leaders have said that they would fight for the Soviet Union in a war with France, thus suggesting that, as Frenchmen, they would prefer defeat to victory in this case (Shulman, 1963: 58–61). However, they might be considered, from the French perspective, to be traitors or enemy agents and therefore not really speaking as true Frenchmen. The Soviet Union has had reason to believe that many of its Polish allies might find defeat in a war with the West to be preferable to victory.

8. One Egyptian diplomat reportedly argued that it was important to "destroy Israel's image of military invincibility, irrespective of whether Egypt finally won or lost" (Shevchenko, 1985: 254).

9. For a further discussion of these issues, see Mueller, 1988; for another view, see Jervis, 1988. See also Holmes, 1989: 238–248, and Bundy, 1988.

10. This is the view of analysts of widely different perspectives. Arkady Shevchenko, while stressing that "the Kremlin is committed to the ultimate vision of a world under its control," gave an "unequivocal no" to the question of whether "the Soviet Union would initiate a nuclear war against the United States"; instead, the Soviets "are patient and take the long view," believing "that eventually [they] will be supreme—not necessarily in this century but certainly in the next" (Shevchenko, 1985: 285–286). Similarly, Michael Voslensky asserted that Soviet leaders desire "external expansion," but their "aim is to win the struggle between the two systems without fighting"; he notes that Soviet military ventures before and after World War II have consistently been directed only against "weak countries" and only after the Soviets have been careful to cover themselves in advance—often withdrawing when "firm resistance" has been met (Voslensky, 1984: 320–330). Richard Pipes concluded that "Soviet interests . . . are to avoid general war with the 'imperialist camp' while inciting and exacerbating every possible conflict within it" (Pipes, 1984: 65). William Taubman says that Stalin sought "to avert war by playing off one set of capitalist powers against another and to use the same tactic to expand Soviet power and influence without war" (Taubman, 1982: 12). MacGregor Knox argues that for Hitler and Mussolini, "foreign conquest was the decisive prerequisite for a revolution at home" and in this respect, those regimes differ importantly from those of Lenin, Stalin, and Mao (Knox, 1984: 57). In his memoirs, Nikita Khrushchev was quite straightforward about the issue: "We've always considered war to be against our own interests"; he says he "never once heard Stalin say anything about preparing to commit aggression against another [major, presumably] country," and "we Communists must hasten" the "struggle" against

capitalism "by any means at our disposal, *excluding war*" (Khrushchev, 1974: 511, 531–533; emphasis in the original). The Soviets have always been concerned about wars launched against them by a decaying capitalist world, but at least since 1935 they have believed that such wars are potentially avoidable because of Soviet military strength and international working-class solidarity (see Burin, 1963: 339). See also Jervis, 1984: 156; McGwire, 1985: 122; Mueller, 1989: chaps. 4–9.

11. As James put it: "The military party denies neither the bestiality nor the horror, nor the expense; it only says that these things tell but half the story. It only says that war is *worth* them" (James, 1911: 283).

12. Dangers, however, might persist even after setting up shop in the newly devastated cities. For example, it might come to pass that "certain base fellows" in a city might subvert the inhabitants by saying, "Let us go and serve other gods." Should this "abominable thing" come about, the vengeful right thinkers were ordered to "put the inhabitants of that city to the sword, destroying it utterly, all who are in it and its cattle, with the edge of the sword." Then they were ordered to "burn the city and all its spoil with fire as a burnt offering" to the right god, after which it would become "a heap for ever, and shall not be built again" (Deuteronomy 13).

13. Apart from any moral concerns, it is probably the enormous uncertainty of war that has caused business people over the centuries to dislike it. They would tend to agree with Bernard Brodie, "Peace is better than war not only in being more agreeable but also in being very much more predictable" (Brodie, 1959: 408).

14. A formal religious belief, however, is not required for a leader to acquire a self-deluded sense of messianic mission. After a remarkable series of successes between 1933 and 1936, Adolf Hitler clearly began to imagine that he was being guided by something he called "providence" (see Kershaw, 1987: 82).

6

What Power Do Nuclear Weapons Give Their Possessors? The Basic Instability of Deterrence

Kenneth E. Boulding

The Nature of Power

Power is a very complex phenomenon, and it is important to look at this central component of international politics as a totality, that is, as a total system. Power can be divided roughly into three parts: power in threat systems, power in economic systems, and power in what I call "integrative systems," involving such relationships as legitimacy, loyalty, respect, and love.

A threat system may originate when A says to B, "You do something I want or I'll do something you don't want." What happens then, of course, depends on B's reaction. There are at least five possible responses. One is compliance, in which B says, "OK, I'll do what you want." This reaction is mainly why we pay our income taxes, why we pull over when the police officer says "Pull over," and so on.

The second response is defiance. In this case, B says to A, "I won't do what you want." This answer throws the system back to A, who has to decide whether to carry out the threat or not, often a very difficult decision, as carrying out the threat is frequently costly to the threatener and may erode other sources of power such as legitimacy.

The third possibility is flight, in cases in which A's power to carry out the threat diminishes with distance, as do almost all forms of power, from the force of gravity to economic competition. Flight has been very important in human history—for the Pilgrims to New England, for the Quakers in Pennsylvania, and for refugees everywhere.

The fourth reaction is counterthreat. B says to A, "If you do something nasty to me, I'll do something nasty to you!" This response may lead to deterrence—or to its breakdown and the carrying out of both threats. Deterrence, as we shall see later, cannot be ultimately stable.

The fifth response might be described as "disarming behavior." B says to A, "You don't really mean that, do you? Let's get together and have a good time." This response is also historically very important and suggests why human communities have almost continually increased in size.

Power is a word with many definitions, as any good dictionary will show. From the point of view of human and social systems, perhaps the simplest definition is that power is the ability to get what we want. If we want the wrong things, however, the power to get them may actually do us harm. We might perhaps define rational power as the ability to get what we really want, or perhaps what we ought to want. Societies have surprisingly neglected the problem of the formation of preferences and valuations. Economists simply assume that people have indifference curves without asking how they get that way. Political scientists tend to assume that there is something called the "national interest," which is what the people who run a nation want, without regard to the fact that it is highly variable and is largely learned, and has very little objective reality. National interest is what a nation is interested in.

The power of individual actors, whether individual persons, firms, organizations, nation-states, or military establishments, depends not only on their own situation and possessions but also on what other people own or control, that is, the power of individuals depends on the nature of the total system. It cannot be defined simply by the individual actors themselves. The total system consists of individual persons and organizations who visualize themselves as exercising power, and it also includes the "instruments of power," which individuals can control or command. These instruments can be divided roughly into the means of destruction, the means of production, and the means of communication. Threat power tends to concentrate on the means of destruction; economic power, on the means of production; and integrative power, on the means of communication.

Actually, however, all three forms of power involve all three instruments in different proportions. A military organization is helpless unless it has some economic power to purchase things, pay wages, and so on. It is also helpless if it has no integrative power: if it cannot command respect, legitimacy, and morale among its members and its clientele. Economic power rests to a considerable degree on the possession of or access to instruments of production—tools, machines, human bodies and minds, and so on—but it also involves certain means of destruction like bulldozers and chain saws. It depends also on the capacity to find people to exchange with, and thus on instruments of communication. Integrative power rests very heavily on the means and instruments of communication—persuasion, symbolism, and so on—but it also rests on a capacity to use instruments of production—such as television stations, printing machines, pens and paper, and art works. The integrative power of a church may be enhanced by building cathedrals, that of a state may be enhanced by building beautiful capital cities. Instruments of destruction play a minor, and a very complex, role in the development of integrative power, sometimes enhancing, often destroying it.

The Technology of Destructive Power

Changes in the instruments of power and its technology can have very profound effects on the distribution of power among individuals and institutions. Likewise, changes in the nature of individuals and insti-tutions—new ideas, ideologies, and so on—can also have a profound effect on the distribution of power. The system of power is very much like an ecosystem in which everything depends on everything else and in which, therefore, single relations like threat, an offer to trade, or a friendly gesture cannot be understood with regard to their effects without looking at the system as a whole. Even bilateral relationships like trade or fights or debates have outcomes that cannot be determined by simply looking at the two parties concerned because they are profoundly affected by the total environment of the system.

Many examples of these principles can be given. One is the collapse of feudal power and the feudal system with the introduction of the effective cannon, especially in Europe in the fifteenth and sixteenth centuries. As long as the instruments of destruction were spears and arrows, and even an occasional catapult, it made some kind of sense to have castles and city walls, what might be called "destructive power reducing structures" (DPRS)—of which, incidentally, diapers are an in-teresting example on the personal level; so are suits of armor and bulletproof vests. The development of an effective cannon destroyed feudal baronies and most city states and led to the rise of the modern nation-state. Castles became tourist attractions, and city walls became boulevards, simply because if you stayed in your castle or inside the city wall, you got blown up with it. Attempts were made to improve this DPRS technology, such as constructing city walls with triangular points from which an invading cannon itself might be attacked, but these turned out to be ineffective. It seems to be a general principle indeed that improvements in the technology of the means of destruction are never adequately offset by improvements in the technology of DPRS systems.

Another example of the impact of the total system of power on particular forms of it is the erosion of economic power by military threat. Paul Kennedy's *The Rise and Fall of the Great Powers* (1987) has indeed called attention to this type of impact, and there are many historical examples of it. Empire, which is largely achieved through the often apparently successful use of military threat, time and again has eroded the economic and often the cultural foundations of the imperial power. Thus, in the nineteenth and early twentieth centuries, the imperial powers in Europe—Britain, France, to a lesser extent the Netherlands, Belgium, and Portugal, and later Germany and Italy—paid a very heavy price for their empires in terms of slow economic development, and earlier, the great Spanish Empire crippled Spain economically and culturally for 400 years. The nonimperial countries like Sweden, Denmark, and Switzerland passed from being among the poorest countries in Europe to being among the richest in little over a hundred years, largely by staying home and minding their own business well. The extraordinary economic rise of the United States had something to do with the fact that for a long time it exercised very little military power. Even in 1929 the proportion of the U.S. economy going to the war industry was only half of 1 percent. And apart from the Civil War, from which the United States fairly rapidly recovered, the wars of the United States were relatively minor until World War II. Now it is very clear that the roughly 6.5 percent of the economy that has gone to the war industry in the last forty years has had a very deleterious effect on the U.S. economy. That industry is an internal brain drain, and it has drawn needed resources away from what might be called the "public infrastructure," things like roads and bridges, education, and crime prevention.

A third aspect of the intricacy of the total power structure, one that has been much neglected by historians, is the benign consequences of military defeat. There are very many examples of this factor. The defeat of the Roman Empire in Europe, even by "barbarians," was followed after a century of adjustment by a steady rise and improvement of technology. The conquest of Byzantium by the Turks in 1453 set off an extraordinary explosion of economic and scientific development in Europe. It is perhaps significant that both Columbus and Copernicus were born fairly close to 1453, after which date the Turkish Empire stagnated both economically and culturally for 400 years. The great cultural contributions of Islam in its early years—in science, the humanities, and the preservation of Greek thought, for instance—came to an end after 1453.

Another example is the total military defeat of the German-speaking part of Europe in the Thirty Years War. The absence of German military power was accompanied by an extraordinary cultural expansion—Bach, Beethoven, Mozart, Schubert, Brahms, Kant, Leibnitz, Goethe, Hegel, Schiller—and it was the militarily weak Germany that was the cultural core of Europe from about 1700 to 1871. Then, after the defeat of France by Germany in 1871, Paris became the cultural capital of the world—in art, the impressionists; in music, Claude Debussy, Léo Delibes, César Franck—and the militarily powerful Berlin stagnated. It is interesting that Berlin after the German defeat in 1919 produced the Bauhaus and modern architecture, Bertolt Brecht and a great upsurge in literature and the arts, all of which Hitler stopped abruptly in 1932 because of his belief in military power and the power of threat.

A fourth example of the impact of changes in the technology of the instruments of power on the power structure itself is, of course, the development of aerial warfare and the nuclear weapon. These changes are having the same impact on national defense that the cannon had on the feudal baron, and they have really made militarily defended national states obsolete. This fact does not necessarily mean that the national state itself is obsolete. On the civilian level, there is much to be said for it, and there is some evidence that the optimum size of the national state from an internal point of view is fairly small. Denmark is a good example, although one might put El Salvador as a counter-example. Much of the success of the United States rests on the relative insignificance of its federal government. Outside of national defense, the U.S. federal government absorbs only some 3 percent of the total economy, whereas state and local governments absorb something like 16 percent, and most of the ordinary functions of civilian government are carried on at the state and local levels in the United States. One could argue that there is a role for the federal government, for instance, in managing the overall economy to prevent unemployment and inflation, but it has had many dramatic failures in achieving these objectives, like the Great Depression, the long inflation, and the failure to deal with poverty and poverty-related problems like drugs. Since World War II, the military establishment has dominated the federal government quantitatively, which has had some disastrous effects on the civilian economy, though qualitatively it is ironic that the military leaders are probably less prone to war than are civilian politicians and large parts of the general public.

Militarization and Deterrence

The military could be said to derive its legitimacy from two major functions historically: conquest and deterrence. Conquest is effective only when a society with high technology, especially in the means of destruction, faces a society without this technology. The conquests of the Americas, Australia, New Zealand, and Siberia by Europeans in the last 500 years are good examples. The conquests by Islam are a little more ambiguous, especially in the early days when the powers of persuasion such as integrative power may have been more significant in many places than military power. But the capture of Constantinople was a result of improved weaponry on the part of the Turks, especially cannon, which knocked down the old city walls.

The other function that legitimizes the military is deterrence, that is, the prevention of another military power conquering or dominating a society that supports its own military. There is a widespread belief, particularly in the United States, that deterrence can be stable, but all the historical evidence denies this proposition. It can be shown logically that deterrence can be stable only in the short run, at the cost of being unstable in the long run. We can see this point dramatically in the case of nuclear deterrence. If the probability of nuclear weapons going off were zero, then they would not deter. It would be the same as not having them. If the probability of nuclear weapons going off is not zero, then if we wait long enough, they will go off. It is a very fundamental principle that any event that has a positive probability must eventually happen. A good example of this principle is flooding. A 100-year flood in any particular place is a flood with a 1-percent-per-annum probability of happening. It can easily be calculated that the probability of such a flood happening within 100 years is about 63 percent, in 400 years over 98 percent, and in 1,000 years, 99.996 percent.

There is some evidence (Singer and Small, 1972) that nonnuclear deterrence, say from the early nineteenth century on, has had about a 4-percent-per-annum probability of breaking down, rather like a 25-year flood. The breakdown of nuclear deterrence, because of the total disaster that a nuclear war would cause for all parties, is almost certainly less probable than that of nonnuclear deterrence, but it is still a positive number, and nobody knows what it is. It could easily be 1 or 2 percent. The probability of an accidental and unintended firing of nuclear weapons, leading to a nuclear exchange, may be even greater than the probability of an intended nuclear attack. Chernobyl, after all, was designed not to "go off," and nuclear weapons *are* designed to go off. What national defense has done in the modern world is to create societies under an indeterminate sentence of death. The stability of nuclear deterrence over the last 40 years is no proof whatever that it will be stable in the future. The geological faults under San Francisco were stable for 83 years, and the system of nuclear deterrence has some similarities to the San Andreas Fault.

The Power Illusion

How, then, do we get out of this situation? The first thing to look at perhaps is what causes illusions of power, which can be very destructive to the people who hold them. One of the principal sources of these illusions is the development of what might be called "self-defending images" of the world. These images are in and of themselves untrue and do not correspond to reality, but they defend themselves against change by rejecting any information that comes in which suggests they are false. It is because these images are a source of self-identity that people are unwilling to give them up. Nevertheless, one principle which makes for optimism is that of the ultimate instability of error; that is, if we believe something that is not true, we are a little more likely to change it than if we believe something that is true. A self-defending image is a little like an imposing iceberg. It sails on unperturbed by the air around, but underneath it is melting and eventually, it will become unstable and overturn. Many historical examples could be given of this phenomenon.

The extraordinary events in 1989 and 1990 in the communist countries are a good example of the instability of error. Marxism might perhaps be considered a set of wrong answers to some quite legitimate questions about the nature of capitalism. The extraordinary collapse of what we might call "fundamentalist Marxism" is a good example of the principle that nothing destroys legitimacy like a dramatic failure to fulfill expectations. It is ironic that "other-worldly" ideologies, to be found in the great world religions, seem to be much more stable than "this-worldly" ideologies. "Pie in the sky" is very hard to check up on; promising pie for the grandchildren is very dangerous because the grandchildren turn up—some of them are called Solidarity!

The abolition of private property and the market did not produce societies in which everybody did everything for love, but societies in which people did most things out of fear. Fear can produce temporary conformity, but it nearly always has the effect of destroying the underlying legitimacy of the exerciser of the threat. There is something ultimately unstable about tyranny. Even when a tyrant dies or is overthrown by another, the successor inherits the loss of legitimacy and respect that the tyrant caused. It is one of the virtues of democratic societies that elections may be substitutes for funerals as a source of social change— and they can take place at more frequent intervals. But even in non-democratic societies, funerals of dictators are very powerful agents of social change, as we saw with Stalin.

Military Power After the Cold War

Now that communism has collapsed, the next candidate for the loss of legitimacy is the military. The military achieves legitimacy partly through promises that are not fulfilled but partly also because armed forces create a subculture of heroism, courage, and self-sacrifice, which commands a certain respect and admiration. One of the sources of legitimacy, ironically enough, is what I have called the "sacrifice trap" (Boulding, 1964). If we make sacrifices for something, our identity gets bound up with those sacrifices, and it is very hard for us to admit that the sacrifices have been in vain. The Aztecs are a good example of this situation. It is not surprising, therefore, that the blood of the martyrs is the seed of the church, and the blood of a country's own soldiers is the seed of the state, as war memorials all over the world testify.

Nevertheless, sacrifice, again, is a bit like the iceberg mentioned earlier. If it becomes too great, the legitimacy it creates may suddenly erode. We saw something of this process in Vietnam, we have certainly seen it in the collapse of empires, and we have seen it in the collapse of communism. Are we now going to see it in the collapse of national defense organizations, which are implicitly creating the probability of a sacrifice that is too great even by their own standards? It was Anatol Rapoport, I think, who once said that the major conflict in the world today is between the united national defense organizations of the world, which form a single cooperative system, and the human race.

In a system of deterrence that is supposed to be stable, the military systems are in a very strange psychological position. They are useful only as long as they are not being used, which is rather like a football team that practices and practices and is never allowed to play. One could perhaps interpret the invasions of Grenada and Panama, the attack on Libya by the United States, the Falkland/Malvinas War, and on a larger scale, even the Vietnam War for the United States and the Afghanistan war for the Soviet Union as what might be called "ritual wars," designed essentially to give the military something to do. Such wars, however, are very dangerous, because in the past, many wars that may have started as ritual wars have escalated.

One reason why the military establishment and the people who support it are highly subject to self-defending images is that they have to have an enemy in order to justify the military budgets. This need makes them very inefficient sources of genuine power, which involves the development of skills of conflict management and a much greater reliance on integrative power than on threat. There is an inescapable pathology in the very concept of national defense, rather similar to the pathology involved in the concept of centrally planned economies. It is ironic indeed that the United States Department of Defense, at least in the pre-Gorbachev era, was about the third-largest centrally planned economy in the world, after the Soviet Union and China, in terms of its GNP—at least in terms of its costs, its product is never mentioned.

Stable Peace

The obsolescence of national defense and the substitution of integrative structures for threat systems are processes that have actually been going on for a very long time, long before the development of the nuclear weapon made them so urgent. One sign of these changes has been the development of an increasing area of stable peace among independent nations. Stable peace may be defined as a situation between two independent nations in which neither has any plans whatever to go to war with the other, even though each may still maintain something of a military capability. Such a peace seems to have first appeared in Scandinavia about the middle of the nineteenth century, when the Swedes and the Danes, after hundreds of years of war, stopped fighting each other. It came to North America, and, one might say, to the whole British-American complex, by about 1870 as a result perhaps of three lucky events: the Rush-Bagot agreement of 1817, which disarmed the Great Lakes, the "54–40 and we didn't fight" episode, and the abstention of the British from intervening in the American Civil War. It came to Western Europe after World War II, and now there are strong signs of this type of peace expanding to Eastern Europe and to the Soviet Union.

There are areas in the tropics where international war may still be possible, and indeed still exists, and the Middle East is certainly a profoundly dangerous area of what might almost be called "stable war" broken by interludes of unstable peace. There is, however, increasing recognition that international war is too destructive to be tolerated. The war between Iran and Iraq, for example, had only trivial conflicts behind it and was a result essentially of the dynamics of national defense organizations. The most serious conflict, which has centered on Israel, which itself is a result perhaps of the last war of conquest, has led to surprisingly little international war. What deterrence has been achieved, for instance, between Israel and Syria, has been at terrible economic and cultural costs. It is ironic indeed that the Jews, who had survived for 2,000 years without a national state and have made enormous contributions to the human race, should have founded a national state just at the moment when national states of this kind were becoming obsolete.

The Instability of Deterrence:
The 1990s and Beyond

As we look at the twenty-first century, it is tempting to think of the number twenty-one as the magic symbol of maturity, a kind of coming of age of the human race. We must not carry the metaphor too far—

indeed, by this standard Islam is still a teenager!—but the environmental crisis that the human race is producing suggests that in the twenty-first century, we will have to come to terms with population control, move toward a technology that is much less dependent on fossil fuels and on mines, and be more concerned with recycling. An essential condition for human survival is the movement toward a more stable world society, in which we preserve diversity and a variety of cultures and organizations and at the same time develop what might be called a "world political ecology," which will prevent this diversity from becoming destructive. The abolition of international war is a first step toward this goal. We seem well on the way to achieving this first step, but the problem of noninternational violence, both internal war and violence in the family and in the streets, may be more difficult to manage.

Nevertheless, the world as seen from outer space is an incredibly beautiful planet and the homeland of us all. This picture is perhaps the greatest symbol to emerge from the twentieth century. At a conference in Israel not long ago, a Palestinian spoke of "two nations in one homeland"—surely the only concept that can bring peace and humanity to that agonizing nonsociety. For South Africa, perhaps up to twelve nations in one homeland is the answer. I daydream about a world of 500 nations in the one homeland of this lovely earth, in stable peace, each preserving a distinctive culture and identity, each able to solve its local problems, yet at the same time feeding into the "invisible hand" of a world ecological system which favors those social species that make for a world we judge to be better and does not favor those that make for a world we judge to be worse.

This vision does not necessarily mean that we would abandon threat as an element in the total world power system. It is hard to raise children without some of it, it is hard to establish a legal system without some of it, and a legitimate threat system may be necessary to deal with certain social pathologies. But perhaps the greatest obstacle to maturity is the idea that threat is the ultimate power, which the unrealistic "realists" of political theory tend to believe. Actually, threat is probably the weakest of the three elements in the overall power system. It is very hard to get rich by mugging. Even the Mafia get rich only up to a certain point and at the cost of personal insecurity; the grandchildren of Mafia members tend to become respected professionals such as doctors and lawyers. Neither threat power nor economic power is really very effective without integrative power. Without legitimacy, even riches are unstable and do not command respect.

An important question is, What are the characteristics of a transition from a less mature to a more mature world? We face this problem now very immediately in the transition from fundamentalist communism to something more relaxed, more market oriented and democratic. We also face this problem in the transition from an immature military to what might be thought of as a mature, organized threat system, which will inevitably involve some radical transformations in the military ethos. The traditional military ethos, however, of courage and sacrifice and "fighting," has been so destroyed by the development of aerial warfare and the bombing of cities and the nuclear weapon that war has been transformed from fighting into genocide, with no moral appeal whatever. One wonders whether there are stages in this transformation of the military. The first stage should perhaps be to abandon the idea of victory as an ideal, acknowledging that if you have a war, a "drawn" war is better than a "won" war. Sometimes, as we have seen, even a "lost" war is better under many circumstances.

Another question is, Can we look to a more "defensive defense," that is, the development of defense institutions that do not threaten anybody else but reduce the threats of others? Ironically enough, the whole Star Wars fiasco is a symbol of the obsolescence of national defense. It pretends to be a bulletproof vest. What it really is, is a device for shooting down bullets, which is very unlikely, can easily increase the overall dangers, and may make the deterrence system even less stable than the existing one. The SDI is, however, a strange implicit acknowledgment of the obsolescence of national defense in a world of nuclear weapons.

Another interesting question is whether the military could be persuaded to develop what might be called a system of "limited response." The work of Robert Axelrod (1984) on prisoners' dilemma games suggests that a tit-for-tat strategy is the most effective response. Suppose, for instance, after Pearl Harbor that the United States had said to the Japanese, "We will bomb one of your naval bases and no more unless you do something else to us." One of the whole problems of the obsolescence of national defense by comparison, for instance, with the law is that the law is a specific threat system that says, "If you don't pay your income tax, such and such will happen to you." National defense is an unspecific threat system that says, in effect, "If you do something unspecifiedly nasty to me, I'll do something else unspecifiedly nasty to you." This type of system is much less likely to operate as a deterrent than a more specific threat system, though even the deterrence of the law is in many respects rather dubious. There is very little evidence, for instance, that capital punishment diminishes murder or that heavy sanctions discourage drug use. Little threats that are fairly sure to be carried out are much more effective in deterring adverse human behavior than large threats that are unlikely to be carried out. One would certainly like to see these kinds of questions discussed in the military academies.

Underlying all the problems, however, is the question of individuals' and nations' images of their own identity. Statistically, a 100 percent American is only about 5 percent human, Americans being about 5 percent of the human population, but statistics, of course, are not the whole story. There is a legitimate identification with the "local," and a love of self, family, and country is better than the hatred of these things. Perhaps the greatest question is whether we can steer the human race toward what might be called a "positive identity" of approaching what we want rather than a "negative identity" of going away from what we do not want and what we do not like. A negative identity, which creates the need for an enemy, ironically enough, is apt to be characteristic both of the military and of the radicals. It is the positive identity, however, that resolves problems and manages conflicts and becomes mature. The negative identity is essentially childish, and as St. Paul says, at some point or other, we have to learn to "put away childish things." As one who became an American out of a deep affection for this unique society, I yearn that we may fulfill the great potential of our culture for simple decency and become a "good" power rather than a "great" power.

7

MAD (Minimum Assured Deterrence) Is *Still* the Moral Position

Paul M. Kattenburg

The Morality of Mutual Assured Destruction

When I wrote "MAD Is the Moral Position" (Kattenburg, 1985), the whole premise of nuclear deterrence between the superpowers had come under increasing attack. From one side, a group of think-tank nuclear strategists and pseudomoralists had combined with high-tech weapons technologists to convince both the late-Carter and the early-Reagan defense establishments of the virtues of various counterforce doctrines leading to nuclear war-waging and even nuclear war-prevailing strategies. From the other side, peaceniks and nuclear disarmers both in the United States and in Europe seriously reexamined mutual assured destruction (MAD) doctrine and found it leading not only to an inevitable but also to an imminent doomsday.

In the first group, Colin Gray (1984) and Albert Wohlstetter (1983) stood out. Literally and perhaps willfully misinterpreting Soviet strategic doctrine as being represented by nuclear war-waging theorists in Soviet military journals (rather than by the pronouncements of more responsible Soviet political and foreign policy leaders), this group of U.S. think-tank analysts had previously claimed credit for their instrumental role in helping to sink the 1979 SALT II Treaty's ratification in the U.S. Senate. They convinced high Reagan administration officials of a viewpoint expressed years earlier by Fred Charles Iklé (1973), who had by 1981 become undersecretary of defense for policy, that it was fundamentally unethical for the United States, under MAD doctrine, to threaten that which, presumably, it could never have any real intention of carrying out.

Such an assertion threatened the very foundations of mutual assured destruction, which rested on the existence, not only of an invulnerable second-strike retaliatory force (which the United States still possessed in its submarines at the very minimum), but also of the credible threat of its use to inflict unacceptable damage in order to deter a first strike by a nuclear-armed enemy. The arguments advanced about MAD's alleged immorality undermined the credibility of the U.S. threat. These were essentially technology-driven arguments, meant to justify the possession in superpower nuclear arsenals of "small," "refined," so-called tactical nuclear weapons, as well as their employment in an allegedly counterforce mode in "limited" nuclear wars. The argument was further refined in Albert Wohlstetter's (1983) article in the influential journal *Commentary*. This new thinking, in turn, fundamentally contributed to the U.S. National Conference of Catholic Bishops' (1983) newly emerging focus on the ethics of the balance of terror.

It is an interesting question why the ethic of a "prevailing" MAD doctrine had not been examined more closely in the glare of mass media publicity somewhat earlier in the nuclear age (the latter being more than three-and-a-half decades old by the time the bishops got around to pondering the question). The answer, in my view, lies in factors quite similar to those that had prevented West European parliaments and publics from debating the fundamental bases on which NATO strategic and tactical doctrine had rested since the early sixties. First, memories of the horrors of World War II and aversion to the known excesses of Stalinism in the earlier postwar period added to the impulse to leave matters to the United States alone—at least until Gens. Charles de Gaulle and Pierre Gallois demonstrated in the early 1960s "the relative equality of states before the law of missiles" (Gallois, 1961). Second, and more important, there appears to have been a virtually universal aversion to the elaboration and clarification of strategic doctrines governing the employment or use of armaments as horrendous as nuclear weapons. Media and publics in both Europe and the United States tended to leave the problem to the military analysts in governments and to the Strangelovian characters inhabiting secluded think tanks and laboratories.

Third, a well-founded desire of governments to leave such esoteric and logically convoluted questions to the relatively mysterious recesses of national strategy centers contributed to the continued relative absence of public debate. Even long after Herman Kahn (1966) had published his disturbing *Thinking About the Unthinkable*, after Secretary of Defense Robert S. McNamara had publicly exposed the limitations of nuclear strategy in his commencement speech at the University of Michigan in

1962, and even after the debates over SALT I in the early 1970s and SALT II later in the decade, the doubts remained.

The net result of the mystery about MAD was that publics in virtually all the Western democracies by the early 1980s were grossly uninformed about the nature of the war-waging strategies that were being proposed (Scheer, 1982). Thus, leaders were left in a poor position to make doctrinal, strategic, and moral decisions backed by informed and enlightened public judgments.

My view was then (Kattenburg, 1985) and still is that Wohlstetter's (and earlier Iklé's) arguments were pernicious in the extreme because their thrust favored replacing the known parameters of MAD with the unknown but almost certainly fatal precepts of nuclear war-waging strategies founded on counterforce doctrine. Let us leave aside the probably insuperable issue of inevitable collateral damage in a tactical nuclear war. Even so, given the unwillingness by any known or conceivable national leader anywhere in the world to state in advance an acceptable damage limit beyond which the destructiveness of a tactical nuclear war would presumably not be allowed to proceed, there seems really no possibility at all that a tactical nuclear war could or would be limited. These proposals, in former Secretary of Defense Robert S. McNamara's (1987) phrase, prepared the way for the superpowers' *Blundering Into Disaster*.

In fact, the logic of the tactical nuclear warriors was inverted: If damage limits could not be stated in advance, there was no rationality whatever in believing that they would be established after the immense destruction and furies of a tactical nuclear war had been unleashed. Accordingly, given the realities of the political conditions under which a tactical nuclear war would be fought, it would almost certainly escalate to wholly unacceptable levels of destructiveness. George Kennan's (1983) view that escalation of nuclear war-waging is politically inescapable remains entirely correct. And it is far preferable to remain under the relatively tried and true general conditions of MAD doctrine, or of the balance of terror as it has been popularly called, under which superpower nuclear war has been avoided since 1945 and (even more significant) since the emergence of substantial nuclear parity between the superpowers in the early 1960s.

MAD was also moral because if one rejects an absolutist ethical position, and takes account of humanity's tendencies to imperfections in its striving toward progress and adaptation, it was simply the best that could be achieved under existing circumstances. The world is not immediately perfectible; humankind may not do better rather than worse. But even given this pessimistic predisposition, it is undeniable that in 1990, after roughly some forty years of MAD, large-scale destructive war has been avoided, superpower peace has been preserved, and the prospects for its continuation are greatly improved despite the existence on both sides of massive arsenals of the most destructive weapons ever possessed.

This situation bodes well for the continued maintenance of superpower peace. Stability appears contingent on two basic operational assumptions of the MAD doctrine: first, mutual possession of invulnerable second-strike retaliatory forces; second, their unquestioned credibility. If these factors are not abused by unbridled technologism (the development of even more precise delivery systems) or by a fatuous moralism eating away at the essential notion of the retaliatory forces' employment in a deadly responsive mode, then a continuation of the prolonged great-power peace (Gaddis, 1987b) seems more than a mere wishful aspiration.

It is a way from that to argue that MAD or the conditions of MAD themselves *caused* superpower peace in the years since World War II. Given the prevailing conditions of stability and peaceful coexistence between the superpowers, MAD can be viewed as a condition empirically producing a moral or an ethical outcome, regardless of its abhorrent logic. It remains true that "in this case, the morality of the ends justifies the apparent immorality of the means" (Kattenburg, 1985: 83), which is not at all the same as arguing that nuclear deterrence caused superpower peace (see Mueller, 1988), though perhaps a case might be made for that argument. I suppose that those who cannot accept that a second-strike retaliatory force would operate once significant damage had been sustained in a first strike also cannot understand what the furies of war and the irrationality of people at war are all about. Like the tactical nuclear war-wagers who believe in the limitability of such a war once it has been initiated, the strategists who perceive nuclear weapons as merely another usable instrument ignore the purely psychological factors involved in favor of some sort of inverted rationality. Some people will consequently never concur in the fundamental morality, or moral acceptability, of the MAD doctrine.

Since the early 1980s, MAD has had to undergo yet another assault: that of the advocates of "strategic defense," initiated by President Reagan's Star Wars proposal in March 1983. The technology-driven advocates had been stymied in their efforts to establish the predominance or at least operational viability of nuclear war-waging strategies, primarily by the successful efforts and demonstrations of the European peace movements of the early 1980s—movements that arose rather suddenly as a response to what had been the realities of NATO strategic doctrine for thirty years. The same group that had earlier conceived and popularized counterforce nuclear war-waging doctrine now renewed its anti-MAD offensive by strongly advocating strategic defense as the moral alternative and appropriate answer to the balance of terror. Its doctrines and concepts, by perfecting defense, would clearly and unequivocally degrade the precepts of MAD and, by giving the advantage to the technologically superior superpower, wholly destabilize Soviet-U.S. relations and super-power peace.

The United States had gone through virtually all these arguments before, in the late 1960s and early 1970s, but with the roles reversed: the United States had then argued against the ballistic-missile defense systems, which both superpowers had started to develop in earnest. Ultimately, in the debate of that time, both superpowers had banned ABMs in the 1972 SALT I Treaty, owing largely to successful U.S. persuasion of the Russians that deterrence based on defense was too uncertain, given its technical complexity, and accordingly too expensive; and that offense had in the past and would continue in the proximate future to deter superpower war effectively (Garthoff, 1985). The result of this persuasion had been the successful seven-year effort to negiotiate an appropriate arms-limitation treaty, the SALT II Treaty of 1979, comfortably rooted in offensive doctrine and effective to this day in terms of the framework it set toward the achievement of mutual systems reductions, despite the failure of the U.S. Senate to ratify it.

The Strategic Defense Initiative of the mid- and late-1980s has remained as basically ineffective as the tactical nuclear war-waging initiative of the earlier years in dislodging MAD from its position as the principal condition under which the strategic relationship of the superpowers continues to be peacefully conducted. But in the interim of the 1980s, as if to give MAD its ultimate moral sanction, the realities of politics (which tend always to determine those of weapon systems) have brought both superpowers much closer to major decreases in their offensive nuclear arsenals. In keeping with both realistic and ethical politics, this fact points the way to the ultimate and, to my mind, highly desirable goal of a new MAD—that of "minimum assured deterrence" between the superpowers.

The Ethics of Minimum Assured Deterrence

In early 1990, the question is, What further is there to argue about in this relatively arcane area? Soviet-U.S. relations have moved from the high tension of the 1950s and 1960s, through the fizzled détente of the 1970s and the renewed confrontation of the early 1980s, to the peace offensive of the late 1980s and the early 1990s. Both superpowers seem inexorably drawn in this direction, driven by similar sets of influences. And MAD is still with us, although both the numbers and the types of launchers and warheads have been diminished, with the propitious prospect of even more substantial mutual reductions at hand. This situation will lead us, sooner rather than later, to what should become the universally desirable condition of minimum assured deterrence and the equally desirable restraint in nuclear weapons "technologism."

We should remind ourselves of Theodore Draper's (1983) observation that it is not "deterrence"—an abstraction of strategists and policy analysts—that can fail or could have failed, only Soviet-U.S. relations. Fortunately, those relations have not failed but instead improved. Accordingly, the abstration of deterrence has held firm. Conversely, it is not that MAD has succeeded but, through all the pronounced vicissitudes, that Soviet-U.S. relations have remained stable and nonviolent through the forty-five years of the post–World War II period.

But what is the prudent moral course in the area of nuclear weaponry for the 1990s? Assuming once more a nonutopian, nonabsolutist ethic, is it more moral to go to a mutually verifiable 0-0 formula in superpower nuclear arsenals than to achieve and then preserve a condition of superpower minimum assured deterrence, achievable under the tried and proven rules of mutually invulnerable and credible second-strike retaliatory forces, minimal in warheads and launchers though these may be? In other words, is a condition under which the two superpowers have no nuclear weapons arsenals ethically more beneficial to the world, if achievable, than reaching a new condition of minimum assured deterrence?

There is a legitimate argument here, since the harmony and peacefulness of superpower relations that would make minimum assured deterrence possible might also be used to justify both superpowers totally disarming their nuclear weapons arsenals. As I understand it, this is the essential argument of the total nuclear disarmers, whether they find themselves in the West, the East, or the so-called Third World. But is this argument well founded? Would a world in which both superpowers were nonnuclear be not only more peaceful but also a better, more just world?

The Path to Security After the Cold War

In my view, there is very little to support that thesis. Some people have averred that a 0-0 nuclear formula would only tend to make the world safer for large-scale and increasingly destructive superpower conventional warfare. This argument contradicts the prospect that large-scale conventional warfare between the superpowers has become virtually inconceivable. It seems more likely that minimally nuclear-armed superpowers have a potentially important and ethical role to fulfill in the world of the 1990s and beyond, given (1) the current nature of politics and conflicts in the real world, (2) the issue of nuclear proliferation, and (3) the potential capacity of minimally nuclear-armed super- and major world powers to exercise jointly, during an emergent entente period in the 1990s, some real-world policing functions on behalf of the peace, justice, and order of humankind as a whole—a rudimentary but nonetheless real form of world authority.

Future conflicts in the world may well fall into primarily three categories. First, ethnic-secessionist conflicts within existing states are likely to be the most frequent and intense conflicts, as is already clearly visible today in the Soviet Union, China, the Near East, southern Africa, southern Asia, Latin America, and eastern Europe.

The second major category of conflicts is likely to consist of regional power and territorial conflicts, some of them (like the Arab-Israeli, Gulf states, or Indo-Pakistani) of very long standing. New conflicts are likely to emerge in this category, and some of these might be extensions of what could best be described as ideological conflicts with nationalist or racial overtones, such as in Indochina and Korea as well as in Africa and South America.

Third, interstate conflicts of predominantly socio-economic character will occur. Some of these will be purely economic, such as those opposing major economic powers within the advanced world, but the majority are likely in some way to involve social issues (whether immigration, drugs, or other problems) and will reflect controversies between rich and poor countries. This category by no means excludes the possibility of violent or virulent explosions between or among most of the rich countries in the North, including the USSR or a potential successor Russian state as well as European countries and Japan. Nor does it exclude conflicts involving most of the poor countries in the South, such as China, India, Africa, most of the Middle East, and South America. But some conflicts might be generated primarily as a result of overwhelming population pressures in the South leading to intolerable patterns of immigration into the North, which the latter would in all probability seek forcibly to resist, impair, or arrest (Head, 1989).

Although seemingly remote, worldwide proliferation of nuclear technology and materials in recent decades has made it possible to envision the threat or even the actual use of nuclear as well as chemical weapons by some party in any of the three categories of future conflict identified above. In the first category, nuclear resort would be related to what has heretofore tended to be called the "terrorist nuclear threat" (Beres, 1990). Believing itself faced with imminent extinction by a powerful revolutionary group (say, the Palestine Liberation Organization or the African National Congress), a nuclear-armed central authority might at least conceivably threaten to use a weapon of such destructive potential as to make the risk to the other party greater than the benefit it sought.

Or such a central authority might in fact explode such a weapon out of what under these circumstances might be regarded as a rational belief that its hold on power would then be assured, regardless of the ruin and damage caused. Conversely, of course, a similar resort to nuclear weapons might be sought by the revolutionary groups opposing the status quo.

In the second category, that of regional conflicts, the threat of use or the actual use of nuclear weapons is equally reasonable to consider. For example, Israel, which may intensify its drives of annexing the territories conquered in 1967 and of expelling the Palestinians, might seek to attain these goals by either threatening to use or actually using its nuclear arsenals. Such behavior would not be out of keeping with the often-held view of the Palestinians as a sort of human sub-species. Conversely, even under rational leadership, if Israel believed that it was threatened with extinction or destruction as a state by a PLO-Arab combination, it might resort to a preventive use of nuclear power regardless of the utimately suicidal nature of such an action. Similar scenarios could be drawn for the southern Asian, Korean, Middle Eastern, and other conflict areas, particularly those in which irrational, dynastically oriented leaders tend to equate their fate with that of the world. Finally, in the third category, it is not at all inconceivable that leadership elements in the industrial North could at some point feel themselves so besieged or racially threatened that it would seem to them only the use of nuclear weapons would stem the advancing horde of invaders from the South (Raspail, 1974).

Such scenarios tend to illustrate the principal point, that a world without nukes in the hands of the present superpowers does not necessarily mean a world in which the menace of nuclear threat or use has been eliminated, even if one argues that a 0-0 formula resulting from scheduled Strategic Arms Reduction Talks (START) between the United States and the Soviet Union might greatly diminish, if not altogether abolish, the threat of nuclear use in Europe. One could dream of a world in which the threat or use of nuclear weapons no longer exists only if proliferation ceases and nuclear capacity is confined exclusively in the hands of the UN Security Council's five permanent members (plus, conceivably, India).

However, this is an idle dream. Despite all the professed goodwill in the world, proliferation is not at all likely to cease in the proximate future. There are at present any number of imminent nuclear-capable states in the world (G. Smith and Cobban, 1989). Moreover, many more such states can and are in fact likely to emerge because nuclear technology is widely known and is being constantly disseminated, despite the 1968 Non-Proliferation Treaty and other more recent safeguards. It does not appear at all likely, therefore, that the genie of nuclear weapons-making, out of the bottle since 1945, will reenter it anytime soon. This probability leaves humankind exposed to the escalating dangers of nuclear warfare regardless of the possession or nonpossession of nuclear arsenals by the superpowers themselves. Even the latter, if they were to stuff the genie back into the bottle in Europe, would be quite capable, given their technological knowledge, of letting it out again.

As a consequence, the moral possibilities of a condition of minimum assured deterrence between the superpowers reenter the picture. One must first accept the premise that if such a condition is in fact reached, a period of serious entente is likely to prevail and joint endeavors on the part of the present superpowers toward the ensuring of universal peace become more readily conceivable. A new MAD in a persistently conflictual world would thus no longer oppose but rather aid the superpowers in their task of ensuring global order under the specific conditions of "justice," which they themselves (along with the other major powers) would largely determine. Clearly, the size of the nuclear arsenals required of the superpowers in such a future condominium would be only a small fraction of their present size, as they would consist of only the absolute minimum number of launchers and warheads required to ensure worldwide deterrence of threat or use by new nuclear-capable powers or by themselves.

In such a case, the superpowers would possess no defensive systems; no first-strike tactical systems, including nuclear-tipped cruise missile systems from whatever platform launched; and no triad systems of launchers. Superpower monad systems, conceivably consisting only of missile submarines based in remote, inland water basins (such as the Great Lakes of the United States or Lake Baikal in the Soviet Union) could possibly do the job of worldwide deterrence. From these invulnerable locations, and assuming credible political direction by the UN Security Council, these submarines—perhaps armed with Trident D-5 or equivalent missiles—would threaten and if required perform horrendous countervalue retaliation on any nuclear transgressor anywhere in the world or in any conflict situation demanding such a scale of response. The potentially nefarious effects of nuclear proliferation might thereby be averted, and nuclear weapons under such circumstances might therefore continue to play the principal role they have played heretofore: to prevent their own use.

Is it really too visionary to project a superpower entente that would actually enforce worldwide deterrence of the type of potential future nuclear conflict discussed earlier? Conversely, could the superpowers, assisted or at least not hindered by the other large nuclear-capable states that are members of the UN Security Council, enforce deterrence of such conflicts through their continued possession of only minimal nuclear forces? And, most important perhaps, could they do so through their understanding and application of a strategic doctrine in which a credible threat of unacceptable (necessarily countervalue) damage inflicted by an invulnerable second-strike nuclear force held back the potential nuclear warriors of tomorrow?

Such a projection is not, in my view, too visionary in theory, but it would require the establishment of a common ethos on the part of the world's major powers that is not yet extant (especially not in the United States). Assuming that the conditions emerging in 1989 and 1990 stabilize in the USSR and in Europe, there could emerge an opportunity for Western leaders of vision to seize the moment. Together, they could construct a new global regime, a new concert of the great powers, backed by the possession of "ultimate weapons" and a judicious doctrine for the threat of their use. Only when a common ethos as to the desirability and essential nature of such an authority arises will it be possible to consider further such ambitious visions. We would stand, then, on the threshold of a rudimentary world government.

If sufficient wisdom prevails, we might thus be able to share the modest conviction that humankind, having conceived these weapons of total destruction, can also be capable, if not of destroying them all, at least of harnessing their power to prevent their own use. We may thus have reached, in world affairs, an extraordinary stage where nuclear weapons might actually offer the best hope for dissuading and preventing world destruction, and thus for enforcing and/or preserving humanity's peace. In the sense of a nonabsolutist ethic based on a realistic acceptance of the flawed nature of humans (of which we have had sufficient testimony in the course of the twentieth century), there is therefore nothing unethical or immoral about a continued—though minimized—balance of terror among the superpowers. On the contrary, such a balance could instead be viewed as the most moral means of enhancing humanity's self-preservation.

In acknowledging this possibility, we should not jump to the fallacious conclusions that conflicts and wars will disappear overnight or that eternal peace can be established by humans. Recognizing that wars are likely to continue, however, should not imply that they be nuclear and therefore wars of annihilation. The superpowers can play a major role in bringing about a moral alternative.

8

An Acceptable Role
for Nuclear Weapons?

Bruce Martin Russett

The U.S. Catholic bishops' 1983 pastoral letter on war and peace drew on the teachings of the church about civic obligations and the acceptable use of lethal force as those teachings have evolved over almost 2,000 years. In doing so, the bishops restated and developed lines of reasoning about pacifism and the just-war tradition in a manner that was meant to be broadly applicable across ages and nations, appropriate to a church with a long-standing and universal teaching claim.

Whereas the letter remains in many ways a statement of enduring value, some of its conclusions have been overtaken by more-recent dramatic events because it was prepared in the particular historical context of 1982 and 1983. The context was that of a nuclear superpower with global alliance commitments, a democracy populated by a Catholic minority (many of whom were well-informed and intensely involved in policy issues concerning nuclear weaponry), intense fears of both the Soviet Union and nuclear war (Russett and DeLuca, 1983), and bitter public controversy for and against further escalation of the nuclear arms race. Therefore, it was neither intended nor possible for the letter to be, in its details, a document for the ages.

The main body of this chapter, which draws on a previous assessment (Russett, 1988), discusses applications of the letter to the international situation that existed into 1988; as such, it addresses perceptions of strategic reality that had not changed fundamentally for several decades. In presenting these applications, I reveal my own reasoning as I helped to write the letter, and some of what I say here was not appropriate for explicit articulation in the letter. Parts, notably those elaborating circumstances for the possible use of nuclear weapons, were unsuited for statement by men whose function was to serve as spiritual leaders rather than as military strategists; others clarify passages deliberately left ambiguous so as allow the document to be widely acceptable; still others reflect my own views and, even more than the chapter as a whole, should not be attributed to any ecclesiastical group or individual. Yet what I say here is consistent with the letter and explains why I was then comfortable with it as a Catholic and as a political scientist. I hope this chapter will show that a coherent political-strategic vision could indeed underlie the document.

The main analysis proposes a limited role for nuclear deterrence in the form of a sharply restricted "countercombatant" strategy. It is followed by a new epilogue, which considers how the analysis should be adapted to current conditions and suggests that recent events call the acceptability of even that limited role into question.

The Evolution of Deterrence Policy

Extended deterrence, also known as third-party deterrence, continues to pose some of the most vexing problems of modern strategic policy. Deterrence in general means dissuading someone, by means of a threat, from taking an action one deems undesirable. The general concept raises many questions. When is it needed? What makes a deterrent threat credible? Under what conditions are such threats instead likely to provoke an adversary? How might deterrence be transcended so that threats of punishment become unnecessary?

Most of these questions seem even more difficult when applied to situations of *extended* deterrence to protect allies than to situations of merely deterring a direct attack on oneself. It should be no surprise, therefore, that the central problem of NATO security—how, with the assistance of American military capabilities, to deter Soviet attack on the states of Western Europe—has been so contentious and evasive of satisfactory resolution. In this chapter, I shall (1) briefly review the history and emerging contradictions of Western deterrent strategy; (2) point up the political and especially normative conflicts over strategy epitomized by recent German and U.S. Catholic bishops' statements; (3) attempt to clarify, by historical study and logical analysis, reasoning on just what restricted role nuclear weapons need play; (4) review the possible means of deterring conventional attack and from them propose a solution of sorts; and (5) modify these conclusions in light of the changes that have occurred since the end of the Cold War.

The Western response to the problems of extended deterrence has basically been to rely on nuclear weapons. The chief and perhaps sole purpose of U.S. atomic weapons in the first years of the nuclear era was to coerce or deter Soviet actions around the periphery, not to deter immediate attack on the United States itself. The number of atomic bombs in the U.S. arsenal had reached 300 by the end of 1950, yet only in 1952 did Soviet military forces first receive operational atomic weapons. Although the United States might well have worried about future Soviet intentions and capabilities, in the first years of the Cold War the U.S. nuclear arsenal was not needed to deter the Soviet leadership from unleashing nuclear weapons on U.S. soil. Nor, realistically, could it have been needed to deter a Soviet conventional invasion of the United States (that prospect is logistically absurd, fully as fanciful as the idea of the United States invading and occupying the Soviet Union). Rather, nuclear weapons were seen as instrumental in the global diplomatic competition and as a means to protect and further U.S. interests abroad. The atom bomb was to be, as one excellent history of the era characterizes it, "the winning weapon" (Herken, 1980).

To identify the early purpose of U.S. nuclear weapons in this way implies no normative judgment on that purpose. Such weapons seemed an attractive, feasible, and relatively cheap instrument. They represented the embodiment of U.S. technological superiority and offered plausible compensation for Soviet advantages in geopolitical location (Europe was adjacent to the USSR and far across the ocean from the United States) and population (especially if one thought, as most people did then, of the hordes of the "Sino-Soviet bloc"). Furthermore, strategic nuclear systems were relatively cheap, never accounting for more than 15–20 percent of the U.S. military budget. And in the early years at least, their use could be threatened without fear of effective Soviet retaliation against the United States.

The initial one-sidedness of this equation shifted as time passed. By the mid-1950s, the Soviet Union had its own atomic and hydrogen bombs and a bomber force of sorts. A Soviet nuclear attack on the United States had become at least feasible and needed to be deterred, though it has never been very plausible so long as the United States retains its assured second-strike capability. More important for our purposes here, the U.S. threat to respond to a Soviet conventional attack on Europe with a deliberate use of nuclear weapons came to seem hardly more plausible. As Soviet nuclear retaliation against the United States became a possibility to reckon with, the U.S. strategy had to enter other phases.

First came an emphasis on using tactical nuclear weapons to contain an anticipated massive Soviet conventional attack; later, as Soviet forces also acquired large numbers of tactical nuclear weapons, Defense Secretary McNamara and others in the Kennedy-Johnson administrations urged greater reliance on building up conventional deterrence and using nuclear weapons only as a last resort. As is well known, the European allies vigorously resisted that shift in emphasis, preferring the deterrent effect of reliance on nuclear weapons to the risk that non-nuclear deterrence would fail and result in the massive destruction of another conventional war on European soil.

Conflicting Perspectives

As extended nuclear deterrence has declined in credibility with the rise of Soviet retaliatory capabilities, contradictions within strategic doctrines, and among different perspectives, have become salient. Most notably, perspectives of self-interest on the two sides of the Atlantic have become irreconcilable on a fundamental level. Most Europeans, in their exposed position, prefer a strategy of deterrence by a credible threat of intercontinental punishment (retaliation); Americans, knowing that any use of nuclear weapons in retaliation now would likely bring Soviet counterretaliation with nuclear weapons against the American homeland, often prefer deterrence by a capacity for denial (defense) in Europe.[1]

Both parties of course hope, intensely and perhaps confidently, to prevent war. But bluntly, if war should come, each prefers that it be fought largely on the other's territory. These preferences are humanly understandable, and again I do not subject them to any normative judgment. But they illustrate the fundamental differences that underlie the continuing debate, from flexible response to the French *force de frappe* ("striking force") to no first use to deployments for securely coupling American and European fates. Given each others' understanding of their interests and capabilities, the differences in policy preference can never be fully resolved, and these differences continue to be the subject of anguish in the differing conclusions of the 1983 pastoral letters of the West German and U.S. Catholic bishops. The Americans urge adopting a policy of no first use of nuclear weapons; the Germans place their emphasis on ensuring that nuclear deterrence does not fail.[2]

The differences between the U.S. and German bishops' letters do not stem fundamentally from differences in basic normative criteria, though there are such differences. The Americans flatly affirm the principle of discrimination (no deliberate, direct killing of civilians), but the Germans do not. Both sides give heavy emphisis to the principle of proportionality, and German analysts admit that in practice, given the horrific potentials of nuclear weapons, the effect is the same: any significant use of nuclear weapons in an undiscriminating fashion would surely violate the principle of proportionality and so be unacceptable.

Any assessment of whether an act will be proportional to the good one hopes to achieve, or the evil one hopes to avoid, is necessarily an assessment of the *probability* and the *utility* of various outcomes and also of the *certainty* with which one makes such assessments. How likely is it that the Soviet Union will win a war and impose its political will upon other peoples? How likely is it that a given deterrent threat will actually prevent, and not provoke, that war? How harmful would a Soviet victory be, and how does one weigh loss of liberties and freedoms? How destructive would a nuclear war be? What are the chances that casualties could be held to some proportionate, and therefore acceptable, level? How confident are we in our uncertain judgment, given the speculative nature of deterrence theory and the lack of any experience with nuclear war, of those probabilities and utilities? The search for a morally acceptable deterrent requires judgments about these matters, judgments about which conscientious individuals will unavoidably differ. Both the U.S. and the German letters agree, in practice, on extreme skepticism that any significant use of nuclear weapons could be proportionate and/or discriminating.[3]

As is generally acknowledged, the U.S. bishops did not definitively rule out the use of any nuclear weapon under any circumstances, though they went through periods of different emphases in various drafts of their letter and left some degree of deliberate ambiguity even in the final version.[4] Ambiguity was virtually unavoidable, given the various constraints under which the bishops worked. On the one hand, they could not reject nuclear deterrence entirely, because of the famous statement by Pope John Paul II to the UN Second Special Session on Disarmament in June 1982 that deterrence in some form "can be judged morally acceptable." On the other hand, they felt bound to the principle of discrimination, and so could not acquiesce in any counterpopulation strategy, and they had to avoid the consequentialist trap of tolerating, for a good purpose, an evil that they might themselves perpetrate. Thus, the logical space within which they could maneuver was narrow indeed. Finally, for reasons identified nicely by Bryan Hehir, they also could not accept the idea of a bluff deterrent—threatening to use nuclear weapons but having no intention actually of carrying out the threat. They thus were constrained to leave open the possibility, however remote, that some very limited use of nuclear weapons, to avert a grave evil, could be morally acceptable. Perhaps an individual could licitly make a threat without the intent to carry it out; a modern national security bureaucracy, especially one in a democratic state, cannot.[5]

It may be, however, that some fundamental assumptions on each side of the debate are more subject to challenge than has customarily been thought. If so, the Gordian knot of apparently irreconcilable interests and norms might be cut. Specifically, the necessity for nuclear deterrence may be exaggerated on the German side (and, of course, by many Americans as well), and even assuming the necessity for some nuclear deterrent, both sides may be exaggerating the difficulties of retreating

Table 8.1.   Possible Uses of U.S. Nuclear Weapons

Mode of Attack	To Deter Attack Against	
	U.S.	Allies
Nuclear	Probably necessary, and useful	Probably necessary, and useful in a tight alliance like NATO
Conventional	Irrelevant—not a plausible threat	Perhaps not necessary, useful only under some conditions

from a deterrent threat that would almost inevitably result in the death of many millions of innocent civilians. In this chapter, I explore some reasons why both assumptions are exaggerated, but first we need to look at the possible roles of nuclear weapons in different forms of deterrence.

The Various Purposes of Nuclear Deterrence

As indicated above, U.S. nuclear weapons may be intended to deter an attack on the United States itself or on its allies, and either kind of attack could be carried out with either nuclear or conventional weapons. Table 8.1 identifies the logical contingencies and makes some comments on the apparent necessity and possible utility of nuclear weapons for each contingency.

The judgments in the lower right-hand corner, about the role of nuclear weapons in deterring a conventional attack on allies, need to be explained in some detail. First, however, let me dispose of the other judgments in the table.

"Probably necessary" in the two sections for deterring *nuclear* attack of course assumes that the Soviet adversary has not only substantial nuclear forces but some incentive to use them offensively. Some Western observers would say the latter was obviously true. Soviet participants, by contrast, would doubtless contend that Soviet motives are entirely defensive and that Western states without nuclear forces would have nothing to fear. Western advocates of unilateral nuclear disarmament at least hope that is the case, but while observers like myself consider Soviet motives mixed and far from self-evident, few of us are prepared to subject the matter to empirical test. For us, prudence dictates reliance on some kind of nuclear deterrent so long as the Soviet Union seems likely to have any significant number of such weapons. Just what form that deterrence can and should take is a more difficult question.

Assuming that nuclear weapons are needed in principle to deter nuclear attack, they require certain conditions to be effective or useful. Currently, those conditions seem to apply to the threat of Soviet attack on the United States: there would be some significant probability, not certainty, that nuclear weapons would be used in retaliation for a nuclear attack. Anger, vengeance, denial of gains, etc., could provide motive enough. So long as nuclear retaliatory forces can survive attack, their subsequent use is plausible. The U.S. National Command Authority might decide to withhold any response to a nuclear attack on the United States, but most observers agree the Soviets could hardly count on that.

There remains greater concern about whether the nuclear deterrent is useful for the cases in the right-hand column; that is, whether the United States could be relied upon to reply with nuclear weapons to a nuclear attack on its European allies. But again, the consensus is that confidence is basically high enough. Given the close economic, cultural, and political ties between the United States and Western Europe, and the tight integration of their military deployments, a U.S. nuclear response to nuclear attack, whether a deliberate response or one embodying some sort of near-automaticity, seems plausible enough. Whether the use of nuclear weapons even in retaliation would be morally acceptable by some version of just-war criteria is, however, not yet self-evident. I shall return to this problem later.

By contrast with the two sections in the top row, the most plausible assumption about the need for nuclear weapons in the lower left-hand corner is that they are *not* necessary. Despite *Amerika, Red Dawn,* and other paranoid or pandering fancies, the combination of the United States' potential or actual conventional forces and the country's geographical location seems more than sufficient to deter Soviet conventional attack.[6] The interesting questions concern the lower right-hand corner. What really is the role of nuclear weapons in deterring a conventional attack against allies? First, there is the question of necessity. If some military deterrent is necessary, need it be nuclear?

That question can never be settled so long as deterrence does not fail in any specific instance. If deterrence fails, we will know that some necessary condition was absent; if deterrence succeeds, we can never be certain that any military means of deterrence were actually necessary (again, really what the adversary's true motives and incentives were) or, for that matter, which specific military capabilities made the difference. Lacking information on the deliberations in the adversary's councils, we can only reason from logic and experience, perhaps allowing a substantial margin for error on the grounds that when a catastrophic failure is possible, it may be better to have too much of a deterrent than too little. Nevertheless, there may be something to be learned or surmised from a systematic examination of international history.

Some Lessons from History About Deterring Conventional Attack

To try to throw some light on this matter, a colleague and I undertook a large-scale investigation of previous instances of extended deterrence (Huth and Russett, 1988; Huth, 1988 and 1990; Russett, 1989).[7] We identified what we believe to be the universe of fifty-eight cases, over the past century, of "immediate" extended deterrence. By immediate, we mean situations of overt threat and counterthreat in crisis, not longer-term conditions of implicit threat that might lead reasonable observers to argue whether anyone really had a serious intention of attacking. For these cases we asked whether deterrence succeeded or failed and what military and political conditions and behaviors were associated with success or failure. By a combination of intensive analysis of the diplomatic record of particular cases and multivariate statistical analysis of the whole set, we were able to reach some tentative conclusions.

For the purposes of this discussion, the key dimension concerns different elements of military capability. We looked at three aspects of the military balance between the attacker's side and the defender's, characterized as the immediate, short-term, and long-term military balances. The immediate balance consists of forces present in the immediate area of the conflict, typically the vicinity of the state being threatened and any border area shared by the major adversaries; at issue is the attacker's ability to achieve a quick fait accompli, requiring the defender to undertake a difficult and costly effort to reverse the situation. If the attacker can strike and win quickly, it may be able to dissuade the major defender from resisting at all.

The short-term military balance consists of all active-duty forces and readily mobilizable reserves. This balance largely determines whether, if the defender should choose to fight, the attacker can nevertheless win the war in a reasonably short time without having to engage in a protracted war of attrition. If the balance favors the attacker, at worst it can expect to win a relatively low-cost war; at best it can, as with a favorable immediate balance, deter the defender from entering the fray at all. The third part of the key dimension is the long-term military balance, defined as all existing military forces and national mobilization capabilities (economic, industrial, demographic) for fighting a protracted war—an eventuality any attacker presumably wants to avoid, except possibly for the most extreme prospects of gain or loss.

Our results strongly supported arguments that defenders should maintain a favorable, or at least a not too unfavorable, military balance in the local area of potential conflict and readily mobilizable reserves. Long-term capabilities did not significantly improve the chances of achieving successful deterrence. The implications for maintaining strong forces in Western Europe are clear, if not always welcome.

One final aspect of military capability involves nuclear weapons. There is of course a vast, and largely abstract or speculative, literature on whether nuclear weapons have enhanced or diminished extended deterrence in the contemporary world. To gain some empirical evidence on the matter, we included one variable for whether the defender possessed nuclear weapons, and another for whether the defender made an overt threat to use those weapons in a particular confrontation.

Somewhat to our surprise, both possession and threat to use nuclear weapons proved to be almost irrelevant to deterrence outcome, especially after the consolidation of mutual assured destruction capabilities by both superpowers in the middle 1960s. Once a deterrence crisis had erupted, the presence of nuclear weapons seemed not to tip the balance much; existing and local conventional forces were much more important. Our result is in contrast to much of the conventional wisdom about the utility of nuclear weapons for extended deterrence, as it generalizes the view that in the Cuban missile crisis U.S. decision makers were not reassured by their overwhelming strategic nuclear superiority (Bundy, 1984). They instead relied on careful diplomacy and their local conventional superiority for success. Other systematic research (Kugler, 1984; Blechman and Kaplan, 1978) generally supports our conclusion: the role of nuclear weapons in deterrence is commonly overrated.[8]

How can the conventional wisdom be wrong? Remember that we have not questioned the view that nuclear weapons can prevent direct attack, nuclear or otherwise, on one's home territory, nor even nuclear attack on a protégé state; the problem under consideration is deterrence of nonnuclear attack on a protégé. In a majority of the cases we investigated, the destruction that would be engendered by nuclear weapons was far out of proportion to the military threat posed by the potential attacker or the immediate issues at stake in the crisis, especially in cases when a nuclear defender confronts a nonnuclear attacker. In such confrontations the risk that nuclear weapons will be used is heavily discounted, and implicit or explicit nuclear threats are largely inhibited by the disproportionate destructive capability of nuclear weapons. That is, the threat to oneself that could legitimate the use of nuclear weapons to repel a direct attack simply is not present in an extended deterrence crisis with a nonnuclear power. Hence, a normative restraint applies, particularly if the defender also possesses immediate or short-term military superiority. Whereas some nuclear threats were made against nonnuclear powers in the first decade or so of the nuclear era, nuclear weapons in such cases are now seen as "overkill." This inhibition made it absurd to consider the use of nuclear weapons a real possibility in, for example, the Indonesian confrontation with Britain in 1963–1964, Britain's conflicts with Guatemala over Belize in the 1970s, or the French-Libyan confrontation of 1983.

Furthermore, in a majority of cases the nuclear power also possessed sufficiently strong conventional forces to impose high costs on the potential attacker in the event of an armed conflict; when the immediate balance did not favor the defender (e.g., the British-Indonesian confrontation in 1963–1964), deterrence failed. The use of nuclear weapons is now rarely contemplated against nonnuclear states,[9] and primarily the conventional-force balances are considered.

In crises between two nuclear powers, the result is likely to be the same but for somewhat different reasons. If both sides possess nuclear weapons, and especially if each has a credible second-strike capability, the defender will want to avoid the kind of war that would require escalation to nuclear weapons. The immediate and short-term balance of forces, with their implications for a quick end to the war, will matter much more. Soviet doctrine and deployments in Eastern Europe were designed for just such a blitzkrieg conventional thrust (McGwire, 1987).[10]

Two cautions about these interpretations are necessary. First, the Quemoy-Matsu crisis of 1954 may be an exception to the principle that nuclear threats do not work against nonnuclear powers. The immediate balance of forces probably favored the United States, though marginally; the United States not only possessed nuclear weapons but it made overt nuclear threats; and deterrence worked. We do not know enough about Chinese decision making to know precisely why.

Second, our study generalized from a fairly small number of cases involving nuclear-capable defenders (sixteen). Of these, only two were marked by overt nuclear threats—the first Berlin and Quemoy-Matsu crises (the second Berlin and Quemoy-Matsu crises are more ambiguous cases as it can plausibly be argued that the "attacker" had no real intention or expectation of actually occupying territory). In only one case did both major adversaries possess nuclear weapons (the Soviet Union's failure to deter China's attack on Vietnam in 1979). We have limited confidence in the statistical analysis of only sixteen cases, which with only two exceptions (China in 1979 and Chinese deterrence of a U.S. strike into North Vietnam in 1964–1965) apply only to nonnuclear attackers. Our results cannot say anything definitive about conflicts between two nuclear-capable states operating with very large numbers of weapons. We would especially hesitate to declare that the possibility of nuclear war is irrelevant to deterrence under those conditions. But we do suggest that the utility of the nuclear threat is sharply circumscribed. Thus, the search for effective means to prevent conventional attack must be intensified.

Means of Deterrence

Assuming that *some* sort of deterrent is necessary to prevent conventional attack, what are the options? Five, with some significant variation possible within one of the five categories, seem possible. As general categories they are, I believe, exhaustive but not necessarily mutually exclusive. Some version of at least one of them, and possibly more than one, must be chosen. Most allow for varying degrees of U.S. participation, withdrawal, or exclusion.

Option 1: Conventional Defense

The first is some variant of conventional defense, the importance of which was stressed by the comparative case analysis discussed in the preceding section. The literature on conventional defense possibilities in Europe is immense and includes a wide range of possibilities from territorial defense by small, mobile, lightly equipped units for defense-in-depth through heavily fortified defenses on the East-West frontier to deep-strike conventional counterattacks against Eastern Europe, in the form recently christened Air-Land Battle 2000. All possibilities share a commitment to avoiding the first use of nuclear weapons, or at least to postponing any use of nuclear weapons until the conflict has become protracted and no alternative means of holding vital territory seems available. No first use in some form has been vigorously endorsed by the U.S. "gang of four" (McGeorge Bundy, George Kennan, Robert McNamara, and Gerard Smith) and by Paul Warnke in Chapter 4. In principle this concept is preferable to many Americans, including me, but we must recognize the difference of European perspectives, as noted earlier, and the difficulty of achieving a satisfactory level of conventional capability given current Soviet advantages and Western reluctance to pay the price. No first use is not yet fully convincing as a practical policy, but neither is it silly.

Territorial defense is associated with some German strategists, such as Horst Afeldt; a deep-strike strategy against Eastern Europe is associated strongly with Samuel Huntington; fortification of the border was especially advocated by some Americans. Territorial defense is widely regarded as surrendering too much of Germany's territory and population to constitute either a politically tolerable situation or a sufficiently extensive form of defense by denial. Deep-strike embodies major elements of defense by punishment and puts at immediate risk the Soviet Union's control of Eastern Europe; that very potential, however, might serve as a provocation to the Soviets and under some imaginable conditions, not deter, but make a Soviet preventive or preemptive strike more likely. Most West German commentators found heavy fortification of the border politically unacceptable, as it would have affirmed the permanent division of Germany.

No early first use has been endorsed by many NATO strategists, including General Bernard Rogers. It has perhaps been made slightly more feasible by the recent East-West agreements on monitoring troop maneuvers to prevent surprise attack, since first use would be most necessary against an unreinforced surprise attack mounted by the Warsaw Treaty Organization forces already in position. NATO has seemed to move toward a policy of no early first use, with modest improvements in conventional capabilities, the unilateral withdrawal of over 2,000 nuclear weapons from Europe in the past few years, and the intermediate-range nuclear force (INF) agreement. But this posture, by allowing nuclear first use if conditions require it and retaining substantial nuclear capabilities, preserves some nuclear deterrent, at least against deep and massive Soviet attack.

The U.S. bishops strongly disapproved of first use but did not categorically condemn it; they urged rapid efforts to move away from reliance on nuclear weapons in Europe.[11] Their position may be compatible with a strong and well-controlled posture of no early first use, though it would be a difficult reconciliation. The West German bishops avoided any kind of endorsement of no first use, in accord with their greater sense of the danger of invasion and their consistent acceptance of nuclear deterrent threats in the strong hope, and expectation, that the threats would never have to be executed in practice—that deterrence essentially can be relied upon.

Option 2: Nonviolent Defense

A second possible defensive strategy is known as nonviolent or civilian-based defense. It is associated in the United States with the work of Gene Sharp (1973) and in Europe particularly with some Scandinavian scholars.[12] It is not to be equated with either simple surrender or passive defense; at its best, it is active and complex, requiring both substantial preparation and a cohesive, determined population. Most strategic analysts reject this strategy as not sufficiently deterring; it nevertheless remains the only option for one determined to resist yet committed to nonviolence. The U.S. bishops commended it as a possibility but fell far short of endorsing it as a truly feasible alternative.

Option 3: Improved Relations

A third option involves steps to improve East-West relations to the point where substantial military deterrence is no longer needed. Long-term hopes for an evolution of both Soviet and Western attitudes are not necessarily naive; other intense rivalries have softened over the centuries, and really nothing is permanent. Both of the bishops' letters urge such efforts, the Germans' especially eloquently. Some such efforts are essential to any positive vision of peace and are compatible with at least some other options that rely on forms of military deterrence. Yet rhetoric about the pursuit of such efforts, while relying on deterrence merely "as a step on the way toward a progressive disarmament," carries an aura of pious wishful thinking that is not easily dispelled. Few people would anticipate the early realization of such hopes.

Option 4: Inadvertent Nuclear Response

A fourth option is the likelihood of an "inadvertent" nuclear response, modeled on Thomas Schelling's "threat that leaves something to chance" (Schelling, 1966: 99). This "strategy" is in fact what the NATO nuclear deterrent has become, partly by design and partly without intent or general awareness. Since the deliberate use of nuclear weapons being ordered by the National Command Authority or the Supreme Allied Commander, Europe (SACEUR) has become dubious, current deployments and dual-purpose systems have produced a "tight coupling" from conventional war to tactical nuclear war to central strategic nuclear war. Short-range weapons in Western Europe invoke the real possibility of quick "use them or lose them" decisions. Tactical nuclear weapons might have to be deployed rapidly out of their storage "igloos," short-circuiting the normal peacetime permissive action link (PAL) codes and procedures. Decisions to use such weapons might devolve to low-level military officers who are highly decentralized and subjected to an immediate threat of being overrun by hostile forces. Even if someone on "our" side did not initiate the use of nuclear weapons and subsequent "progress" up the escalation ladder, the threat of such a decentralized and largely inadvertent escalation might well produce a supposedly preemptive strike by the Soviet side (Bracken, 1983: chap. 5; Charles, 1987).

Very plausibly this risk—that we would go to nuclear war even though we did not intend to do so—poses the currently most credible deterrent threat to a Soviet conventional attack in Western Europe. For those who perceive that the greatest risk of war stems from a deliberate Soviet decision to launch an aggressive attack (analogous to Hitler in 1939), this possibility may seem an acceptable deterrent. But for those who perceive that the greatest risk of war stems from an inadvertent escalation of an unintended political conflict (analogous to events in 1914, perhaps beginning with a popular revolt somewhere in Eastern Europe), the risk of losing military control over such an initially uncontrollable incident is not acceptable. Nor does a strategy of threat by leaving something to chance deal effectively with the normative concerns about proportionate or discriminating nuclear deterrence that are so heavily emphasized in both of the bishops' letters. It implies that we will deliberately accept the risk that we will inadvertently do something that is morally unacceptable (use nuclear weapons in an undiscriminating and disproportionate manner). And the more implausible any deliberate use of nuclear weapons becomes, the more NATO will be forced to rely on a strategy that leaves such use subject to the whims of chance.

Option 5: Deliberate Nuclear Response

We turn then to the fifth option, which involves some form of deliberate nuclear response to conventional attack. Plans for using strategic or other weapons against Soviet territory require plausible means of limiting the damage the Soviet Union could or would inflict on the United States or its allies in return. It has often been assumed that no rational U.S. president would deliberately take a course of action, in response to an invasion of Europe, that would result in the destruction of U.S. cities. The argument for the French *force de frappe* is premised on this assumption, and we should acknowledge the force of the argument, despite the close affinity of the United States and Western Europe. It is imaginable that a U.S. president, out of fear, anger, or some "irrational" impulse, would order such an act, and that residual possibility does have some deterrent capacity. That chance might conceivably be enough to satisfy some analysts, but most would regard it as unacceptably risky. Any strategy for a "rational" nuclear response by the United States would require some form of damage-limiting capability (to deny the Soviets the ability to destroy U.S. cities) and/or some form of limited, controllable response and the expectation that the Soviets could and would restrain their own military response.

Damage-limiting nuclear forces typically entail prompt hard-target-kill weapons. They must be able to destroy the adversary's strategic delivery vehicles, and/or the adversary's command and control centers, so as to prevent substantial retaliation. Great accuracy alone does not suffice; they must be able to hit with rapidity as well. Only certain kinds of weapons have such a capability. They include land-based ICBMs, the soon-to-be-eliminated intermediate-range ballistic missiles like the Pershing II and SS-20, and sea-launched ballistic missiles, especially those fired in low trajectory from offshore locations only five to ten minutes away from their targets. To the degree they are MIRVed (increasing the ratio of warheads to targets), their capabilities are increased. These weapons put the adversary's retaliatory capability at risk, thus endangering crisis stability by encouraging launch under (apparent) attack, launch on warning, or even preemption. A strategy of extended deterrence that depends on such capabilities will always carry serious risks in times of crisis.

Arms control advocates typically object most vigorously to these weapons, and some therefore supported President Reagan's abortive effort at Reykjavik to abolish ICBMs. The Federation of American scientists endorsed the idea, as did former CIA Director Stansfield Turner (1986). Manned bombers and cruise missiles would not be affected. Other kinds of weapons become marginal cases, depending partly on modes of testing and deployment. Relatively invulnerable delivery vehicles like mobile land-based missiles and submarine-launched missiles such as the Trident D-5, have prompt hard-target-kill capabilities but are less destabilizing because they need not be fired on ambiguous warning in a "use it or lose it" situation. Submarine-launched ballistic missiles (SLBMs) at "normal" long-range distances and high trajectories at least take about thirty minutes from launch to impact. International agreements not to station ballistic-missile submarines off each others' shores, or not to test the missiles in low-trajectory modes, would help to reduce the risks. So too would placing an electronic twenty-four-hour delay on SLBM launchings (not now inhibited by PALs).

A different kind of damage-limiting capability is represented by "passive" civil defense (fallout or blast shelters), and the expansive active defense envisaged by advocates of the Strategic Defense Initiative (SDI).[13] In a form equivalent to the penetration-proof bubble, active population defense might not be dangerous. But in that form active defense is even more of a pipe dream than is the notion that passive civil defense can truly protect the majority of a population against an adversary determined to exterminate it. A less-effective SDI would do little good against an adversary's first strike but might be useful against the kind of only limited and ragged retaliatory strike that could be mounted by the victim of an attack by good hard-target-kill forces. This form of strategic defense would constitute a destabilizing influence in crisis.

Proposals and plans have been made to try to be able to wipe out Soviet command and control centers, thus denying that country the ability to launch retaliatory forces even though the forces themselves might continue to exist. A fully effective capacity to wipe out Soviet command and control similarly seems beyond attainment; anything less would produce the same kind of instabilities (encouraging preemption) as would other means of damage-limitation. Moreover, "decapitation" of an adversary's command and control raises the risk of decentralized and uncontrollable retaliation by a fragmented adversary no longer able to negotiate or effectuate termination of the war. Thus, all efforts to achieve damage limitation by denying an adversary the *capability* to inflict damage are either undesirable or in practice unattainable.

There remains the possibility of some form of limited, controllable nuclear strike, in response to a Soviet conventional attack on an ally, that depends on invoking the adversary's *willingness* to limit the damage that he in return will inflict. Here, we are in the realm of theories of limited war and controlled tit-for-tat retaliation, ranging from ideas of tactical nuclear warfare to those of limited strategic warfare waged against counterforce targets. Although these ideas have long been embodied in U.S. war plans, both for Europe and in the Single Integrated Operational Plan (SIOP), analysts in the liberal arms control community largely regard them as a fantasy, dangerously removed from the physical and psychological realities of decision making.[14]

To succeed, such efforts would require highly accurate and low-yield weapons capable of limiting collateral damage to civilians, tightly centralized command and control facilities able to restrict weapons use on both sides, excellent information-gathering and -processing capacities by an adversary able to ascertain that only such limited usage was occurring, and an adversary's continued willingness to limit its reply to some form of tit for tat. All this action has to occur under the pressures of fear and ignorance implied by the term "the fog of war." These conditions constitute a very tall order indeed and are not met in contemporary U.S. war plans. Many experts concur with John Steinbruner that

> once the use of as many as 10 or more nuclear weapons directly against the USSR is seriously contemplated, U.S. strategic commanders will likely insist on attacking the full array of Soviet military targets. . . . The more likely result would be the collapse of U.S. forces into isolated units undertaking retaliation against a wide variety of targets at unpredictable moments. [Steinbruner, 1981–1982: 22–23]

Most notions of limited war probably deserve the bad name they have acquired among arms controllers; they survive only because all the alternatives also seem so implausible.

Countercombatant Deterrence

There may be one form of very limited nuclear retaliation that minimizes the problems just identified. I have over the years continued to try to find some morally and prudentially acceptable version of perhaps the least bad of the above set of alternatives. The label I devised for such a strategy was "countercombatant," to distinguish it from counterpopulation strategies and also from counterforce strategies as commonly applied to targeting the adversary's nuclear retaliatory forces. Originally I used the term to expand my "acceptable" target-set beyond strategic retaliatory vehicles to include tactical force concentrations and supply depots, command and control centers, and militarily significant industry, transportation, internal security units and their headquarters, communications and public utility facilities. The aim would be to deny the Soviet leadership the ability to prevent hostile incursions across its borders (especially from China), to retain control over Eastern Europe or even reliably to maintain internal security and cohesion of its multinational state (Russett, 1974: chap. 14).

It later became clear that such a target-set was much too inclusive for my purposes. On the one hand, it still incorporated the destabilizing effects of including strategic retaliatory forces and command and control centers. On the other, it was so expansive as to include, at least in principle, thousands of targets located within or adjacent to civilian population concentrations and essential to the operation of any kind of minimal postwar civilian economy. Destruction on such magnitude would be hardly distinguishable from that wrought by targeting population centers per se. It would, in the expansive version, in fact be indistinguishable from current versions of the SIOP (Zuckerman, 1982).

It therefore became imperative to delimit a much more restricted target-set, one that was limited essentially to active and readily mobilizable military forces and supply depots. The number of targets should not be large, and need not be if the purpose is to degrade seriously, in the face of undamaged historic adversaries on the border, Soviet capabilities to hold territory and restive populations.

The archetypal version of such a countercombatant deterrent would be one directed against Soviet troop concentrations (nearly fifty divisions) along the Chinese border, leaving the Soviet Union vulnerable to a broad military thrust from the People's Republic. Such a deterrent would not be strategically destabilizing by requiring prompt hard-target-kill capabilities, and it would not require high accuracy either for effectiveness or, in the sparsely populated areas under attack, to spare much collateral damage to civilians. Nor would it seem to risk nuclear winter, given the relatively small number of nuclear weapons required and their targeting away from highly combustible cities, whose burning would pump great quantities of smoke and soot into the atmosphere. It is technically feasible as a limited, discriminating deterrent, directed against capabilities dear to the Soviet leadership (to contain China), and it could be deemed proportionate in the face of extreme Soviet military provocation of the West. It would seem a proportionate response to a Soviet nuclear attack on European NATO allies, or even a large conventional attack, as it would raise the risk that the Soviet Union would lose the war on a second front. It is not so extreme a threat as that of massive city destruction, but it should be severe enough to deter any kind of Soviet adventurism.

The most extreme nuclear threats are well above the threshold of threat necessary, and by the nature of their near-suicidal effects, they are simply not very credible anyway. If a countercombatant deterrent did not intrinsically raise a very great likelihood of further escalation to widespread nuclear destruction, it might actually be more credible (be perceived as having a higher probability of being carried out) than would a deterrence threat deemed likely to lead to mutual suicide. The combination of damage (disutility) and credibility (probability of execution) contained in such a threat might actually be optimal, better than that of MAD or of current policy.

I do not believe such a countercombatant deterrent is at the moment politically feasible, given the present levels and types of nuclear weapons. The current arsenal is many times bigger that it needs to be for this rather "minimal" deterrent (not a minimum deterrent in the traditional sense of the minimum necessary for countercity MAD). The bureaucratic and political pressures to enlarge the target-set beyond this minimum, and thus to blur into traditional counterforce and counterpopulation capabilities, would be very severe.[15] It will be hard to persuade decision makers to forgo prompt hard-target-kill weapons. Neither in the popular understanding nor in the U.S. security elite community is there sufficient appreciation of the possibilities and requirements of a countercombatant strategy. To be workable, such a strategy would require some indication of Soviet willingness to respond analogously, and the United States does not face a readily analogous security threat on its own (Mexican and Canadian) borders. The command and control demands on both sides are also formidable, beyond what is currently in place, and one must be fearful about breaching the firebreak to use of nuclear weapons under any circumstances. Such a strategy could not be carried out with the current or projected "tight coupling" of conventional to tactical nuclear to strategic nuclear weapons in Europe.

For deterring nonnuclear attacks, many people (I among them) may continue to prefer in principle a policy of only a nonnuclear response, even recognizing the difficulties of making such a policy fully effective in Europe and the often different preferences of Europeans themselves. The concept of a countercombatant deterrent for such purposes nevertheless should not utterly be dismissed. Moreover, for deterring *nuclear* attacks, some form of limited and countercombatant deterrent is all that, in my opinion, can be morally acceptable by the traditional just-war principles of proportionality and discrimination, and for that reason alone it demands continued attention.[16] An intriguing possibility is that of identifying targets, not before the war (as in SIOP), but after it has begun—for example, supplies and reinforcements, including those in movement, essential to carrying on tactical military operations then in process. Such intraconflict target acquisition with strategic weapons was not possible earlier, but with contemporary electronic surveillance measures it probably is now. Even so, I cannot remotely imagine such a strategy for extended war-fighting but only in conjunction with a negotiating strategy intended to bring all use of nuclear weapons to an immediate halt.

It is conceivable that a countercombatant deterrent could become feasible sometime in the future, given the will of governing authorities to make it so, and an understanding of its possibilities seems to be growing in the circles of strategic analysts (Nye, 1986: chap. 7). It combines some of the virtues of "realist" analysis, emphasizing the need for some deterrent in a world of conflicting nation-states, with some of those of "idealist" analysis, emphasizing the need for moral constraints and for a deterrent that does not exacerbate international fears and instabilities. It is, I believe, more feasible than is a bluff deterrent, in which use is threatened but not intended.

A countercombatant deterrent is compatible with a major mutual reduction in strategic arms and with a reduction in East-West tensions, especially as those tensions breed on a denial of the adversary's basic humanity. Such a denial of humanity is inherent in the kind of deterrent that envisages inflicting heavy civilian casualties. Only so long as we can be persuaded that an adversary's population is evil, hostile, and subhuman can that kind of a deterrent be made to seem morally tolerable. Movement toward a very limited countercombatant deterrent, therefore, could be fully compatible with aims, well articulated by the German bishops' statement, to move toward a wider, more comprehensive, and truer peace.

Epilogue: Deterrence After the Cold War

The present historical context is of course very different, and therefore modification of the above conclusions is required. In many analysts' judgment, the Cold War is over. With far-reaching political liberalization in the Soviet Union and Eastern Europe, progress in reducing the volume of nuclear and conventional armaments on both sides, and equally important changes in international atmospherics, the bishops' demand that nuclear deterrence serve only as "a step on the way toward progressive disarmament" needs to be recalled.

The threat of a deliberate Soviet attack on Western Europe has dropped to the vanishing point for the foreseeable future. Under the doctrines of reasonable sufficiency and defensive defense, some of the troops and equipment have been demobilized or withdrawn from the front lines; with a better conventional balance, the pressures on the West to escalate to nuclear weapons are therefore diminished. The intentions of the Soviet leadership seem concentrated on domestic economic and political reforms and far from military aggression, and the cooperation of Eastern European governments in any military move against the West is unimaginable. U.S. Defense Department analysts, previously expecting a fourteen-day strategic warning of a Soviet attack in Europe, now assume that the combination of political transparency and military unreadiness in the Soviet Union would provide a warning period of one to three months. The most common scenario for the eruption of inadvertent war in the heart of Europe—a revolt in East Germany that drew in first Soviet and then West German forces—is now irrelevant.

General theories about the obsolescence of major war between economically advanced and interdependent states for whom the cost-benefit ratio has become skewed drastically toward peace (Mueller, 1989 and Chapter 5),[17] or of the near-complete unacceptability of war between bourgeois democracies (Russett, 1990a: chap. 5), seem increasingly pertinent to emerging conditions. Should war somehow occur anyway, the military possibilities for retaining all or most of NATO Europe without the use of nuclear weapons are immensely better than previously. In other words, it is hard now to imagine what it is that nuclear weapons must deter.

Under these new circumstances, very substantial reductions in the Soviet and U.S. nuclear armories appear both needed and likely. Arms control measures can especially address the kind of first-strike-capable weapons discussed above as an integral part of planning for extended deterrence. Other arms control measures to verify the reductions, and to enhance confidence in achieving tactical and strategic warning of attack, are likely to be forthcoming. Even if, in the realist's world of interstate conflict and never-ending threat, a Soviet-U.S. crisis were to occur again, expectations that it would escalate to nuclear war would be much lower. These changes make the kind of eventuality outlined above—an eventuality requiring some credible strategy for the very limited use of or threat to use nuclear weapons—seem very distant indeed.

Yet the vision of "a world without nuclear weapons," a vision repeatedly invoked by both Mikhail Gorbachev and Ronald Reagan, also still seems far away. Even deep cuts will leave several thousand strategic nuclear weapons, and thousands more of tactical ones, in the arsenals of both superpowers. British and French nuclear modernization programs continue unabated, and each of those countries is on the path to having over 500 weapons by the early 1990s. Chinese nuclear weapons are unaffected by recent developments, as are those of near-nuclear and closet-nuclear powers (India, Israel, Pakistan, South Africa, and others). The fewer superpower nuclear weapons there are, the greater the instability that could occur should either side somehow cheat, and the greater the risk posed by nuclear weapons in the hands of smaller states. The knowledge of how to build nuclear weapons has spread across the global technological culture and cannot be eradicated. It is hard to imagine a world of zero nuclear weapons until sometime in the twenty-first century, if then.

As long as nuclear weapons do exist, some thought will be required about their function as deterrents. Even though no one in the command structure of a great power may imagine using nuclear weapons first, most of those same individuals will consider their country's weapons necessary to prevent someone else—ambitious, frightened, or deranged—from going first. Existential deterrence, the mere presence of the weapons with no plans whatever for their use, will remain unsatisfactory for the reasons outlined above regarding a bluff deterrent. However unlikely any use of nuclear weapons may be, having no prior plans would make any use all the more uncontrolled.

Many analysts would be satisfied with an arsenal and a command structure devoted to minimal deterrence; that is, with only a few weapons (hundreds?) to be used, or threatened to be used in extremis as counterpopulation instruments.[18] But that solution cannot be acceptable to anyone who accepts the reasoning of the bishops' letter: "Under no circumstances may nuclear weapons or other instruments of mass slaughter be used for the purpose of destroying population centers or other predominantly civilian targets" (National Council of Catholic Bishops, 1983: 46). This statement leaves only the very limited and controlled countercombatant use of nuclear weapons as possibly acceptable.

Some readers may reply that in a world of states governed democratically, the notion of a quarrel with the government of another state, but not with its people, would be irrelevant. Whereas the distinction might have been maintained in the days of Stalinist repression, a "quarrel" with the government of a truly democratic Soviet Union would necessarily also be with its people, which would perhaps raise the likelihood that any conflict would be intense and total. Yet blurring the sharp distinction would not legitimate the deliberate destruction of the mass of civilians who, even in a modern representative democracy, cannot be held directly guilty for their government's actions. Also, I take seriously the historical experience, alluded to earlier, that the mutual perceptions of self-governing (democratic) peoples greatly inhibit their resort to lethal violence against each other. This phenomenon is receiving increasing scholarly attention; it could be expected to attenuate the intensity of conflict.

In a world of fewer weapons, lower tensions, and diminished ideological antagonisms, nuclear weapons might indeed become "just another weapon"—not to be used like any other weapon but maintained without any intention whatever to use them on a mass scale, and with hardly any expectation of using them at all. In such a world, the idea of turning such weapons against the populace of another nation would be more repellent than ever. Insofar as inhibitions against using nuclear weapons on the government or military personnel of another nation were also strengthened, we could welcome that idea with few reservations. Nuclear weapons would not lose their horrific theoretical potential, but they might, like other weapons, someday become anachronisms—things our descendants might not quite know how to abolish but which no longer cast a fearsome shadow.

A final and more radical question also needs to be asked. The bishops' "strictly conditioned" acceptance of nuclear deterrence was based on the perception of a real threat from the Soviet Union to essential Christian and human values. Some of the sharper passages to this effect include:

> The fact of a Soviet threat, as well as the existence of a Soviet imperial drive for hegemony, . . . cannot be denied. . . . Many peoples are forcibly kept under communist domination despite their manifest wishes to be free. . . . Americans need have no illusions about the Soviet system of repression and the lack of respect in that system for human rights. [National Conference of Catholic Bishops, 1988: 249, 250]

Now, however, the Soviet threat has vastly receded, the continued existence of a Soviet imperial drive can indeed be denied, Eastern Europe is no longer kept under communist domination, and the Soviet system of repression of human rights has been greatly relaxed. True, there remains room for substantial progress, and the possibility of some reversal certainly exists. But given the progress that has been made, if the Soviet Union can no longer be characterized as an "evil empire," can the brandishing of nuclear threats and even the continued existence of nuclear weapons any longer be morally justified? Or, on the other side, has the Soviet Union's willingness to permit a de facto dissolution of the Warsaw Pact been predicated on the security that *its* nuclear weapons offer for deterring any attack on itself?

Events had not moved nearly so far at the time of the bishops' spring 1988 review of the earlier pastoral letter, and these questions were not faced. It is now time to do so, in the spirit of humility and pluralism manifested in the writing process and conclusions of the letter itself, and in Chapter 9, Cardinal Bernadin forcefully argues for greater vision on this and other dimensions of a new world order. Increasingly, the major barrier to nuclear disarmament appears to stem less from political ambitions of the superpowers than from the dangers of managing mutual nuclear disarmament. The problem of how to get rid of the weapons without risking some kind of instability from somewhere is anything but trivial. But at least it lacks the previous ideological and political overlay, and there can be no excuse for failing to address it with clarity.

Notes

Portions of this chapter appeared in an earlier version published in 1988 in the *Review of Politics*, vol. 50 (2), pp. 282–302. Published here by permission of the *Review of Politics*.

1. On the denial-punishment distinction, see Mearsheimer, 1983, and for the defense-retaliation distinction, see Snyder, 1961.

2. The Germans do not, of course, go nearly so far as do the French bishops in their letter, as the latter treat deterrence as so imperative that they endorse their government's explicitly counter-city targeting policy. The letters are appropriately titled, *The Challenge of Peace: God's Promise and Our Response* (American), *Out of Justice, Peace* (German), and *Winning the Peace* (French).

3. They seem to differ in some of their estimates of probabilities; e.g., the Germans may be somewhat more sanguine about the likelihood that deterrence (perhaps even a bluff deterrent) will work and less skeptical than the Americans (who are very skeptical) that escalation could be controlled if deterrence should fail. I believe the policy recommendations of the two groups reflect these differences.

4. Some people still do not choose to see this ambiguity, most recently Winters, 1986, and at least the first version of James Johnson's chapter in this volume (Chapter 11). I believe I conclusively refute their view in Russett, 1986. The U.S. bishops' 1988 follow-up report further clarified this matter, repeating the "absolute categorical" prohibition against deliberately targeting civilians, restating the very strong presumption against any first use, and saying that their "presumption against second-use," while "not a prohibition," was "to place the burden of proof on those who assert that 'limited use' is politically and morally possible" (National Conference of Catholic Bishops, 1988: sec. I.A.).

5. Hehir's reasons why a bluff deterrent would not be acceptable were (a) democratic governments must be candid with their citizens, (b) it would be inconsistent with the promises given in international alliance relationships, (c) expectations and predelegations in the chain of command would not permit

reliably withholding use under an intended mere bluff, (d) if the reasoning supporting "bluff only" were understood by the adversary, the threat would have no deterrence credibility. Hence "threat without use" for nuclear deterrence would imply morally questionable behavior (a and b), and in execution would either result in immoral acts (c) or simply not work (d). Hehir's comments were made at a conference in Bonn, Germany, in September 1987. Note that Hehir shifted from his earlier espousal of a bluff deterrent, as in his contribution to Gessert and Hehir, 1976.

6. For a rigorous demolition of invasion and occupation myths, see Shepherd, 1986.

7. Our data base has been sharply criticized in Lebow and Stein, 1990, but in Huth and Russett, 1990, we show our results to be extremely robust.

8. Contrary conclusions are suggested by Weede, 1983. Both the Kugler and Weede studies, however, suffer from rules for including and excluding cases that make their conclusions somewhat suspect; I referred to the problems with the Weede analysis in an "Editorial Comment" immediately following his article.

9. For instance, the Argentine government seems never to have anticipated that Britain might use its nuclear weapons in the Falkland/Malvinas War. Although common in the first two decades of the Cold War, *no* overt nuclear threats, for coercion or deterrence, have been made since 1980 (see Betts, 1987, and Halperin, 1987).

10. The recent Soviet withdrawal of significant offensive capabilities from Eastern Europe modifies this conclusion.

11. See National Conference of Catholic Bishops, 1983: paragraph 150: "We do not perceive any situation in which the deliberate initiation of nuclear warfare . . . can be morally justified."

12. More recently with the document by French Catholics, *La Paix Autrement.*

13. I am not referring here to the form of SDI that would provide only a limited point defense for hardened targets such as nuclear retaliatory forces. If cost effective, such a limited capability would be strategically stabilizing. Although technically it could "limit damage" to those retaliatory forces, it would not be damage limiting in the more common sense of being able to preserve the nation's basic social, economic, and political structures. As for protection of cities against small powers or accidental missile launches (as suggested in Chapter 11), the cost-benefit ratio again looks dubious to me. At the final meeting before releasing the third draft of the U.S. bishops' letter, the committee approved a sentence expressing great skepticism about SDI—which had just been sprung on the nation by President Reagan in a March 23, 1983, speech. Unfortunately, the sentence was omitted because of a "clerical error"; equivalent sentiments had to wait for the bishops' 1988 report.

14. For an excellent exposition on notions of targeting elites and protracted war-fighting, see Herken, 1985.

15. For a sobering though not fatalistic appreciation of these pressures, see Nolan, 1989, especially chap. 6.

16. Soviet troops on the Chinese border—in many cases not morally culpable for their position, not a direct threat to the United States, and perhaps not yet

engaged in any hostile action toward China—would probably constitute a licit target, but nonetheless a regrettable one.

17. It seems to me that Mueller's assessment in Chapter 5 gives insufficient credit to the role of religion in affecting motives. Whereas religion doubtless incited crusading wars, the Christian just-war tradition, especially in contemporary manifestations, works to raise the moral costs of war-making and so to discourage it.

18. This seems to be the view of Paul Kattenburg in Chapter 7. Although I share his preference for much smaller arsenals and second-strike-only weapons, his suggestion of counterpopulation weapons (to "perform horrendous countervalue retaliation") to deter "irrational" leaders (like Qaddafi) seems perverse, morally and practically. Overall, my position closely parallels that of Sir Hugh Beach in Chapter 2.

Part III

The Views of Moral Philosophers and Religious Leaders

In the past, it was possible to destroy a village, a town, a region, even a country. Now it is the whole planet that has come under threat.

Pope John Paul II

9

Ordering Our Destiny:
Politics, Strategy, and Ethics

Joseph Cardinal Bernardin

The political, strategic, and ethical dimensions of nuclear deterrence have particular meaning for me because of my experience in chairing the U.S. National Conference of Catholic Bishops' committee that drafted the pastoral letter, *The Challenge of Peace*, in 1983. Although I had always been interested in the significance of the nuclear age as a citizen, the task of writing the pastoral letter forced me to address the specific elements of deterrence, strategic doctrine, and arms control in a new way. I drew from this experience the conviction that the quality of the policy and the academic debate about nuclear strategy is one of the primary resources the United States possesses in exercising responsible control of nuclear weapons.

The official U.S. nuclear policy—the strategy that guides the actual development, deployment, and role of nuclear weapons—has a unique status. But official policies are formed in light of our understanding of the meaning of the nuclear age, the relationship of strategic weapons and foreign policy, and the responsibilities of being one of the two nuclear superpowers. Although the world is clearly passing through political changes that will mark a new and hopefully safer chapter in the nuclear age, the need for continuing analysis will not decline. The contributors to this book, *After the Cold War*, demonstrate a welcome willingness to exercise public responsibility by advancing proposals for enhancing our understanding of the nuclear age.

The intense involvement with the nuclear question I had from 1980 to 1988, preparing both the pastoral letter and the 1988 review of the bishops' position, left a powerful impression on me. But it did not provide me with the detailed knowledge of the nuclear question that many professional students of the subject take for granted. Hence, when I approached the challenge of writing this chapter, I thought it best to shape my remarks as one interested in public policy but not a specialist in nuclear questions and to offer a general framework of analysis rather than to focus on a particular aspect of the nuclear debate.

A general framework seems especially needed to enlighten discussion of nuclear policy in the year 1991 and beyond. Even among people who have studied this topic closely, I find a growing consensus that the next decade of analysis and action will clearly not be a continuation of the nuclear debate of the last four decades. What changes must be made, intellectually and politically, to adapt nuclear policy in the post–Cold War world is the question that now cuts across strategic doctrine, arms control, and budgetary policy.

Two books published at the end of the 1980s, McGeorge Bundy's *Danger and Survival* (1988) and Robert Jervis's *The Meaning of the Nuclear Revolution* (1989), capture the historical drama of the nuclear age and the way nuclear weapons have reshaped standard expectations about international politics. Together they reflect much of the political wisdom that living with nuclear weapons has produced in the last half-century. But these recently published books may come to be seen by historians as symbolizing the end of the *first stage* of the nuclear age. Clearly, in 1991 one has the sense of living on the other side of a fault line from what has been the experience of nuclear politics previously.

Obviously, nuclear weapons are very much with us—over 50,000 jointly held by the superpowers (Sivard, 1989)—and negotiations that promise reductions proceed. But they remain to be completed. The physical means to threaten civilization as we know it stand ready to be used, either purposefully or accidentally. But in spite of these signs of continuity with what has been, the historical fault line marked by 1989 is real, and the rationale for superpower conflict has declined dramatically. The frailty of human nature and the folly often evident in political history keep us all vigilant and cautious, but even the most careful voices today say the superpower agenda for the 1990s will demonstrate change rather than continuity.

The nuclear question has been at the center of the superpower relationship, and it will continue to be close to the center but in a new context. I wish to highlight three themes from the 1980s that will be part of this new context and then try to locate where nuclear deterrence, strategy, and arms control will fit in the new context.

The 1980s: Policy, Ethics, and Public Opinion

One characteristic that set the 1980s apart from most of the nuclear age was the degree of public engagement in the policy debate. The nuclear debate had been an elite discussion, engaging a highly sophisticated but tightly knit corps of specialists drawn from the government, a few think tanks, and some major universities. Within this circle, the nuclear discussion acquired the character that historically has been associated with the great doctrinal disputes within Christianity. There were canonical concepts, established patterns of reasoning, and views that were regarded as orthodox and heretical. A shift from massive retaliation to flexible response, or from superiority to sufficiency, was regarded as a doctrinal change—an event accorded the intellectual attention once reserved for the decisions of popes and their theologians. Books that trace these doctrinal shifts, like Fred Kaplan's *The Wizards of Armaggedon* (1983) or Gregg Herken's *Counsels of War* (1985), read like ecclesiastical history.

The general public seldom was aware of either the character of the debate or the specific conclusions that divided the experts. Even in the U.S. Congress, the intricacies of the argument were the concern not of all 535 members who voted on defense budgets annually, but of only those who sat on specialized committees like the armed services, intelligence, or appropriations committees.

The 1980s saw the nuclear debate spill over the boundaries of elite discussion and engage the electorate. In the first six years of that decade, at least, the general lines of U.S. strategic policy, if not the intricate arguments, were debated in city councils in California and town meetings in New England. The merits and risks of deterrence were explored in parish halls and meetings of the local medical societies. The nuclear-freeze movement was the most visible symbol of this broader public discussion, and in retrospect, its significance lay less with its specific proposal than with its capacity to draw ordinary citizens into an argument that had always affected them but had hardly ever included them.

In his book, *The Nuclear Debate*, Robert Tucker (1985b) contended that the upsurge in public engagement was sparked by a fear that the U.S.-Soviet relationship in the early 1980s was slipping out of control. In an attempt to reestablish confidence, the public wanted more attention paid to efforts for arms control. Although it is always difficult to establish causality in large social movements, I believe this public pressure did influence the U.S. to return to arms control negotiations, first through a series of proposals, then through the summits of 1985 to 1988.

By the end of the 1980s, however, with the INF Treaty signed and ratified, with START proposals for deep cuts on the negotiating table, and with the entire political order that generated the nuclear arms race in flux, the public in the United States was not focusing on arms control. Primary concerns in 1989 revolved around drugs and the environment, but this reorientation was not because the public was fickle. Instead, to use Tucker's argument, the general public had perceived that the nuclear threat was being addressed by responsible proposals and negotiations.

Some who are part of the elite debate would argue that the general public's reaction in the early 1980s was misplaced—the nuclear danger was not objectively greater than it had been in the immediate past— and that the present situation is more complex than the public believes. My own sense is that the public played a very useful role in pressing the policy process toward negotiations; the fact that attention has shifted to other issues like drugs does not mean that public engagement on the nuclear question is a thing of the past.

The interest generated in the 1980s produced an increased under- standing of the nuclear age: its dangers, challenges, and possibilities. In a sense, the U.S. public came out of that decade with a better grasp of their responsibility as citizens of a nuclear nation, a better understanding of how and when to engage their government, and a greater awareness that decisions taken in Moscow and Washington on the nuclear question are never purely national decisions, for they can threaten the international community. The elite debate about nuclear weapons is still the core of the policy argument (Wittkopf, 1990), but in the 1990s it will be pursued in the context of an electorate that is more capable of entering the nuclear discussion when it believes the elite is either too complacent or too adventurous.

The second major theme of the nuclear debate in the 1980s was the attention paid to ethics and nuclear strategy. From the beginning of the Christian era, war has been regarded as not only a political but also a moral problem. The nuclear age transformed the moral problem. In the prenuclear period, the ethical questions concerned the ethics of war— when force could be used, under what conditions, and by which means. In the nuclear age, these questions were joined with others concerning the ethics of nuclear peace—about whether deterrence, our way of keeping the peace, is morally acceptable. In the prenuclear age, right up through World War II, the moral arguments began with the circum- stances under which recourse to war could be justified. Under conditions of nuclear deterrence, the key moral questions about targeting, declaratory doctrine, and the relationship of strategic policy and arms control were all discussed and decided under conditions of peace.

The new moral challenge posed by both the destructive capabilities of nuclear weapons and the dynamics of nuclear deterrence was grasped early by theologians like Reinhold Niebuhr (1959) and Paul Ramsey (1961) in the Protestant community and by John Courtney Murray, S.J. (1959) in the Catholic community. But the questions about the ethics of strategy and deterrence remained at the edge of the policy arguments until the 1980s.

In that decade, however, the ethical issues moved to the center of the public discussion at both the elite and the popular levels of the nuclear debate. The religious communities continued to address the moral questions but with much greater systematic preparation (as Janice Love documents in Chapter 10). Moreover, religious voices were now joined by many who were visible participants in the strategic literature. Robert Tucker (1960), Stanley Hoffmann (1981), Herman Kahn (1960), Albert Wohlstetter (1959), Joseph Nye, Jr. (1986), Bruce Russett (1983), Lawrence Freedman (1989), George Kennan (1983), and George Quester (1970) were only some of the participants in the ethics and strategy arguments, which followed different lines of reasoning and moral traditions.

The range of participants and the centrality of the ethical concerns were new in the 1980s, but the structure of the ethical argument followed the categories sketched out in the 1960s and 1970s. One pole of the deterrence debate held that the moral limits of means and ends could be maintained with nuclear weapons; hence, a credible and morally justifiable deterrent could be sustained. Ramsey (1968) and Murray (1959) had espoused this position in the 1960s; Wohlstetter (1985), James Johnson (1984), and William O'Brien (1981) renewed the argument in the 1980s. The other pole of the deterrence debate was given renewed emphasis and systematic statement by John Finnis, Joseph Boyle, and Germain Grisez in their book, *Nuclear Deterrence, Morality and Realism* (1988). This position held that an inevitable contradiction exists between the requirements of credible deterrence and the central moral tenet that one can never intend to kill the innocent; hence, one can never target civilians in any form of a deterrent threat. Both of these polar positions offered internally coherent and very detailed policy judgments. Both positions also conveyed a sense of confidence that the move from ethical assessment to policy conclusions was both possible and self-evidently imperative.

The third general position in the debate of the 1980s was the one found in the U.S. Catholic bishops' pastoral letter, *The Challenge of Peace* (1983), and developed by other analysts. It was less confident than the attitude of Wohlstetter and others that new technologies of accuracy and miniaturization could be used to reconcile moral and strategic objectives of deterrence. But even though this position upheld strongly the principle of protecting civilians, there was a reluctance to reduce the totality of the deterrence question to the role of moral intention, as Finnis and his colleagues seem to do in their analysis.

This third position sought to place restrictions on deterrence—restrictions governing targeting, deployment, and declaratory doctrines—and then to work for a transformation of the political and strategic relationship that surrounds the deterrence relationship. This position, described as a conditional acceptance of deterrence as an interim strategy for the nuclear age, sought to forestall use of nuclear weapons, reduce the risks of deterrence, and then relativize the role of deterrence over the long term. The third position was less clear and coherent than either of the poles of the ethical argument. It was a political ethic as much as a strategic one; it conditioned ethical acceptance of deterrence by seeking to reshape the political setting in which deterrence functioned.

As someone identified with this third position, I must admit that I conceived of the time frame needed to change the political setting as something to be measured in decades. Even while advocating political changes to reduce the central role of nuclear weapons, I never expected immediate steps in this direction.

But the final major theme of the 1980s was precisely the political changes recently experienced in the superpower relationship, in the Soviet Union, and in Eastern Europe. I have already noted the fragility of this process, but its significance for the nuclear question should be recognized. For the last forty years, both the strategic literature and the ethics of strategy were built on the premise that fundamental political change in the superpower relationship was nearly impossible. The presumption of the strategic debate was that since political progress was not a realistic goal for U.S.-Soviet relations, the highest objective of policy should be to guarantee stability in the nuclear relationship. The threefold goal of crisis stability, arms race stability, and political stability was the centerpiece of the strategic and arms control literature, and ethical assessments often presumed this logic without spelling it out.

The possibilities that now exist as a result of the political changes occurring in East-West relations—from U.S.-Soviet relations, through European politics, to German unification—make it necessary to review the political presumption that was the foundation of previous strategic thinking. In the 1990s, fundamental political change is imperative, not optional. The strategic relationship, with its goal of stability, should take second place to the wider effort of shaping political relations that will reduce the danger, centrality, and salience of the regime of nuclear deterrence. If this assertion is correct, if the political dimension of superpower relationships should now have primacy, then it is possible to locate the ethics of nuclear strategy in a new setting for the 1990s.

The 1990s: Ethics, Order, and Politics

In this section, I should like to sketch a framework rather than to draw a blueprint for the primacy of the political dimension. The first imperative is to recognize that changing the content of political relationships will not do away with nuclear weapons, but it could substantially relativize their role. For 100 years, France and Germany sustained a hostile military posture, but in the post-1945 political setting, the evolution of their relationship has made war between them virtually unthinkable. This is the kind of political transformation that should be the long-term goal of the primacy of the political.

The second imperative is to address the strategic relationship, relying on the traditional objectives and methods of arms control. In the 1990s, three broad areas of arms control will need to be pursued simultaneously: the strategic relationship addressed in the START negotiations; the reduction of conventional forces in Europe as negotiated in the October 1990 CFE agreement; and the long-neglected topic of proliferation, now understood to mean preventing proliferation of nuclear weapons, chemical weapons, and ballistic missiles. The new possibilities of the political do not render these hard-core strategic objectives any less urgent.

Finally, allow me to turn to a definition of the ethical issues we face in the 1990s. Here too, we need to recast the issues, which does not mean moving away from the ethics of deterrence but addressing it in a different context. The nuclear question retains its intrinsic importance and urgency, and it must be addressed on its own terms, in continuity with the analysis of the 1980s, which will have to be extended and deepened. The moral analysis of nuclear deterrence has been an "ethic of control." Like its secular counterpart of arms control, the aim of nuclear ethics has been to contain and control the nuclear threat. Since the threat still exists—embodied in 50,000 warheads—the work of control must continue.

But I would suggest that the question for the 1990s is, not the ethics of strategic control, but, rather, an ethic of political order. The shift in perspective from control to order arises from the need to address the political changes already occurring. They have, in fact, eroded the order of international relations that has sustained the nuclear relationship since 1945. Today, the task before the international community, as it was in 1815 and 1945, is to shape a viable order of political relations that can control, contain, and direct strategic relations.

The difference of the 1990s is that the call to order today is to the first international system to encompass all the actors in the global community. In his 1987 encyclical, *On the Social Concern of the Church*, Pope John Paul II argued that the East-West issues need to be related to North-South issues. His appeal is for what he calls "a real international system." The immediate task created by changes in the Soviet Union and Eastern Europe is to reshape the order of superpower and European relations. But the world is just the superpowers or Europe. From proliferation to pollution, from deterrence to debt, the demands of world politics today, ethically and politically, require a new conception of order.

This broadly defined political challenge is both a moral and an empirical task. We need to construct an order that works, but one that works justly and can be maintained peacefully. At the heart of this order, the fact of nuclear weapons remains. The ethic of control, the ethic of reducing the nuclear danger must continue. But it is too narrow a conception of political responsibility; we should move toward more ambitious goals.

Control in international relations—whether control of weapons, the environment, or our common economic future—requires cooperation, and cooperation, in turn, must be built on a common conception of a shared destiny. It is this common destiny of the international community that the moral argument about an ethic of order seeks to grasp. Two decades ago, a prophetic Jesuit, Pierre Teilhard de Chardin (1969), said the task of this century was "to build the earth." The search for order is another way to say that we must build our common future in peace, in justice, and ultimately, in love.

10

From Pacifism to Apocalyptic Visions: Religious Perspectives on Nuclear Deterrence

Janice Love

War presents moral and ethical dilemmas that have evoked lively debate among religious authorities across the world and throughout history. Directly or indirectly, religion often plays an important role either in the causes of war, the justification of particular wars, the means of conducting a conflict, or in the conscience of those who ponder their own participation. Three moral traditions have dominated religious groups' positions: pacificism, the just-war position, and a righteous invocation of war as the means to personal or communal salvation. These traditions have endured through millennia of dramatic social and political changes, with each exhibiting substantial depth and a nuance of considered discussion regarding the particular conflicts of the time. The prospect of nuclear war in the late twentieth century, however, has stimulated religious communities to test these traditions for their adequacy as moral guidelines.

Religious authorities usually have fairly limited political and technical expertise regarding questions of national security, crisis management, strategies and tactics in the conduct of war, weapons systems, or other important aspects of potential violent conflict between and within societies. Their basis for evaluating warfare rests on a claim they make to a more fundamental expertise regarding the nature of good and evil, human potentialities and frailties, the search for truth and justice, and God's work in human history. When societies face crucial moments and imminent choices concerning issues of life and death, religious leaders often invoke this fundamental expertise to cross over into the domain of narrower political and technical expertise to give moral and ethical counsel or to make a prophetic witness. The outcomes of such religious advice on national and international conflict are quite mixed, with entire wars sometimes being either blessed or condemned, some behavior in warfare positively or negatively sanctioned, and even some weapons systems singled out for special signification. Political leaders' reception of such counsel and prophecy is also quite mixed. If religious authorities agree with the politicians' military program, they are often acclaimed for their wisdom. If not, religious leaders are, at the very least, accused of meddling in matters that are none of their business.

Although the world witnessed the impact of the atomic bombs dropped on Hiroshima and Nagasaki, as well as more than three decades of superpower rivalry and nuclear competition, religious communities remained fairly quiet on questions related to nuclear weapons and war until the massive military buildup under the Reagan administration in the 1980s. This buildup, combined with greater articulation of the nuclear war-fighting doctrine and alarming evidence about the ecological consequences of a nuclear exchange, provoked many in the religious community to believe that one of those historical moments involving pivotal choices concerning life and death had arrived. The time had come to state their positions on the moral dimensions of issues related to nuclear weapons.

These positions drew on the foundations provided by the three traditional religious perspectives on war. However, the massive destructive capability of nuclear weapons and their potential to end life as we know it raised new questions not previously considered in great depth in discussions of conventional warfare. This chapter discusses the range of opinions on nuclear war held by religious organizations in the United States. The continuum begins (as the traditional categories do) with a position rejecting all forms of violence, including nuclear weapons, continues into a large category of detailed debate on the ethics of particular nuclear strategies, and ends with the embrace of nuclear and other weapons that can be used against adversaries that are presumed to be inherently evil. The chapter also discusses some programs that have been created to provide alternative models of conflict resolution.

This examination is based on a survey of official positions taken by the national governing bodies of forty-seven Christian denominations (including Catholic, Protestant, Orthodox, Mormon) and Jewish movements. Other religious groups, such as Muslims and Buddhists, were not surveyed because they have less of an impact on public discourse in the United States. National governing bodies usually hold regular meetings (every one, two, three, etc. years) and broadly represent the organization's constituency. Twenty-seven leaders of denominations and movements responded to the survey with statements and other documentation. The groups surveyed are listed in an appendix at the end of this chapter.

Among the replies to the survey, nine indicated that their organization has no official position on this public issue, which is probably also the case for a number of others who made no response to the survey. For example, many Orthodox groups and others interpret their faith as being one that should make little or no public comment on issues of the day. In another case, an African-American religious leader suggested that although his denomination regularly passes resolutions on questions of public policy, issues other than that of nuclear war tend to dominate the agenda. The same was the case for the United Synagogue of America. Given the broad variety of organized religious expression across the country, it is not surprising that a substantial segment takes no official public stand. Nor should we interpret this outcome as complete disengagement from the issue. Organizations, leaders, and congregations may well find other means of expressing their interest within and outside the confines of their own group.

In contrast, at least four national organizations have each published one or more books to demonstrate the depth of their concern about the issue, among the more prominent being the 1983 and 1988 statements of the National Conference of Catholic Bishops. Others such as the United Methodist Council of Bishops (1986), the Christian Church (Disciples of Christ) (1985), and the Union of American Hebrew Congregations (1983) have issued lengthy, detailed discussions of the nuclear debate, which draw on substantial technical as well as theological expertise and are often accompanied by sophisticated study guides for use in congregations. Many groups that have not developed such substantial policy documents nonetheless have educational materials to promote discussion within their constituencies. The World Council of Churches published a major piece examining the question from a global ecumenical perspective (Abrecht and Koshy, 1983). Few, if any, other social issues in recent years have prompted such extensive research and publication among religious organizations to support an outpouring of clear, careful, and high-profile articulations intended to help shape public opinion and policy.

A number of the formal statements of policy positions by religious organizations are considerably shorter and go into less detail than the materials they publish to educate and stimulate discussion among their constituencies. These organizations usually do not have a particular label for the positions they take. Indeed, they might resist the category labels provided here as being too narrow to capture the nuances of their formal policy positions, which are sometimes deliberately more ambiguous than their educational materials would suggest. When a formal position lacks clarity or might fit more than one category or even fall between categories, this fact is noted.

Although the research results reported here do not include a systematic survey of informal or nondenominational religious groups or leaders, undoubtedly their public positions also affect the debate on the morality of nuclear arms. For example, televangelists and the editors of major religious magazines help shape perceptions about and opinions on this question within and outside the religious community. Some examples of these leaders' positions are included in the discussion.

Categories of Moral Positions

A basic division among religious positions on war is between those that make a presumption against war and those that make a presumption in favor of it. Most religious groups hold positions that fall in the first category, but the second is significant enough to be influential, even in the nuclear age. If most groups agree that peaceful resolution to conflict is preferable, they disagree substantially on the conditions under which violence, and especially nuclear weapons, can be used. These differences within the first category will be discussed in some depth before examining the positions related to the presumption in favor of war.

Pacifism

Pacifism is an old and honored tradition in a number of religions. It was the dominant position of the Christian church until the fourth century (Dwane, 1988), but from that point on, the people holding this perspective have been in the minority, as they have always been in the Jewish tradition. Pacifists claim that there are no circumstances under which the taking of human life is acceptable. This standard is applied to individual behavior as well as social policy and is based on the principle that all life is a sacred gift from God and not to be violated. Christian pacifists base their convictions in part on Jesus' ministry and teaching, which they argue were consistently nonviolent. Many Christians who do not subscribe to pacifism generally agree that Jesus is portrayed in the New Testament as never advocating, endorsing, or condoning violence and that a pacifist position has a solid biblical foundation.

Pacifists sometimes retreat from engagement in the world into monastic or other isolated communities and make little attempt to promote this perspective in the public realm. Others are more determined to shape public policy. The latter actively seek to create incentives and programs to encourage individuals, groups, and governments to de-escalate confrontations and resolve conflicts without resort to physical harm. Many are social activists who risk personal danger in an attempt to end particular wars, arms races, or other forms of institutional or individual violence. Advocates engage in substantial debate about whether various strategies of social change enhance or detract from life-affirming principles. Nonviolent methods of political engagement can involve significant levels of coercion, and they have been known to draw violent responses either from political authorities or others. Courage in the face of danger (but, more often, social ridicule) characterizes many who hold this position. Mahatma Gandhi, one of the most famous, creative, and provocative pacifists of this century, argued that if "cowardice is the only alternative to violence, it is better to choose violence" (Villa-Vicencio 1987: 234).

Clearly rooted as being against all forms of violence, pacifism argues against the possession or use of nuclear weapons and in favor of nonviolent resolution of any and all disputes between nations as well as immediate steps for complete nuclear disarmament. Religious groups that hold official positions in keeping with pacifism include the "historic peace churches"—the Church of the Brethren (1982), the Religious Society of Friends (Quakers) (1976), and the Moravian churches (Northern Province, 1982; and Southern Province, 1982).

Nuclear Pacifism

Like traditional just-war theory, the nuclear pacifist position departs fundamentally from complete pacifism by accepting the possibility that in rare instances violence may be used as a last resort to resolve conflicts between nations, groups, or individuals. The emphasis here, as with both pacifism and the just-war tradition, is on nonviolent resolution of all disputes. Only when all peaceful possibilities of settling the conflict are exhausted is the resort to war accepted as an extreme and a regrettable necessity.

Often relying on *jus ad bellum* criteria developed for judging when conditions allow for the resort to force and *jus in bello* criteria developed for judging how such force should be used, advocates of nuclear pacifism may come to varying conclusions when examining whether particular disputes warrant the use of violence. They are united, however, in the judgment that the use of nuclear weapons or the threat of their use is *never* justified and thus their possession serves no legitimate military or defensive purpose.

There are basically two foundations for this conclusion. One very broadly calculates the costs of nuclear deterrence; the other relies on two criteria offered under the just-war doctrine, proportionality and discrimination. This second foundation will be examined first. Proportionality requires that the damage inflicted and the costs incurred by war must be proportionate to the good achieved. The harm caused by war must not exceed the good outcome of war. Discrimination requires that noncombatants be immune from direct attack. It also rules out atrocities, reprisals, looting, and wanton violence.

Nuclear weapons are weapons of mass destruction. Because of the enormity of their blast as well as the resultant fires, fallout, and long-term ecological impact, their damage cannot be contained to small geographic areas or to combatants. Although remarkable advances in technology have produced a range of somewhat smaller, apparently more accurate weapons, especially in the U.S. nuclear arsenal, these arms are nonetheless basically indiscriminate in their immediate and long-term far-reaching effects. Noncombatants located near military sites will die in the blast, and the offspring of survivors will suffer the effects of radiation for generations to come, even though they are not the direct targets. Although nuclear weapons may be aimed at or used against military targets alone (a counterforce strategy), nuclear pacifists judge these weapons to be incapable of measuring up to the principle of discrimination.

Furthermore, advocates of this position see no reasonable hope of bringing about greater justice by engaging in a nuclear war, even if it could somehow be a "limited" war. Owing to the massive destructiveness of the weapons and the possibility of general war resulting from *any* use, even in a small exchange, nuclear war is judged to be incapable of doing more good than harm, and therefore it violates the principle of proportionality. When contemplating the worst case of the USSR or some other authoritarian government threatening to take over the United States and/or Western Europe, nuclear pacifists hold fast to the belief that the resort to nuclear weapons would not be justified. The quite dismal prospects of living under a terribly oppressive political system are judged to be better than the possibility of ending life for humanity and the rest of creation across most of the globe.

The other foundation for denying any legitimate use or possession of nuclear weapons rejects the doctrine of nuclear deterrence and a wide array of burdens associated with it. Deterrence is discussed in depth in other parts of this volume and will be examined here only as it relates specifically to moral positions. Proponents of nuclear pacifism argue that the superpowers have placed too much emphasis on nuclear deterrence as a way of preventing a war between the United States and the Soviet Union or between Western Europe and the Eastern bloc. Policymakers in both camps have presumed that the possession of these weapons of terror keep the peace among those who hold them, when in reality a number of other considerations could be deterring direct confrontation (Mueller, 1988). If nuclear arms cannot be seen as causal to stable relations or peace between the superpowers, why not fully develop other instruments of conflict resolution that are now underutilized?

Furthermore, these advocates claim that the total costs of nuclear deterrence are enormous and too high to bear. Total costs would involve calculations of the ecological, social, economic, political, and psychological burdens of nuclear weapons and war preparedness. Such costs are both direct (cost of resources) and indirect (alternative opportunities lost or delayed). For example, the environmental damage and consequent health hazards owing to the production of plutonium and tritium for weapons are already evident but have not yet been systematically surveyed.

Economic commitments to arming for deterrence divert resources, which might otherwise be used to address domestic or international social problems, and they may be implicated in the decline of U.S. goods' competitiveness in world markets. The United Methodist bishops declared:

> The human costs of this buildup in the name of "defense" are borne most directly by those who are actually most defenseless: the poor, the elderly and the very young, who are the main targets of severe cuts in social programs.
> . . .
> Furthermore . . .
> The productivity of the American economy has seriously slackened during these same years of high military spending . . . [because of] (1) the dispro-portionate allocation of scientific and technical personnel to military production; (2) the commitment of seventy percent of government research and development funds to weapons programs; and (3) the preference of basic US industries for maximum short-term profits at the expense of long-term planning and modernization. [United Methodist Council of Bishops, 1986: 57]

Lifton and Falk (1982) point to "psychic numbing" as one of the personal costs of nuclear arms races. This is a phenomenon in which individuals experience a denial that the nuclear problem exists while at the same time feeling a sense of hopelessness to cope with it. The United Methodist bishops argue that policymakers also suffer pycho-logically and spiritually when they tend "to escape into the wonderland of technology, to construct intellectual defenses behind jargon such as 'nuclear exchange' and 'strategic defense initiative,' and to ignore the uniquely human and spiritual capacities of persons" (United Methodist Council of Bishops, 1986: 60).

This kind of evaluation of the costs of nuclear deterrence and the arms race, together with a judgment that alternative routes to conflict resolution remain underutilized or unexplored, led the United Methodist bishops to label the doctrine of nuclear deterrence "idolatrous": "De-terrence has too long been reverenced as the unquestioned idol of national security. It has become an ideology of conformity too frequently invoked to disparage dissent and to dismiss any alternative foreign policy proposals. In its most idolatrous forms, it has blinded its proponents to the many-sided requirements of genuine security" (United Methodist Council of Bishops, 1986: 46). A holistic assessment of the destructive capacity of nuclear weapons production, deployment, and use led the General Assembly of the Christian Church (Disciples of Christ) (1981) to decry them as a "heinous obscenity." The World Council of Churches declared them to be a "crime against humanity" (Gill, 1983: 136).

The religious groups that take this position argue that both superpowers must rid themselves of nuclear weapons through a careful, orderly, and verifiable process, and they call on the United States to give leadership to this effort. Although one might argue that the logic of a nuclear pacifist position would point toward U.S. unilateral disarmament (Love, 1986), none of the official statements calls for such. The United Methodist bishops, for example, advocate an "ethic of reciprocity" as a means through which nuclear disarmament can take place.

As early as 1968, the National Council of Churches of Christ in the USA (NCC) passed a resolution expressing support for the concept of nuclear pacifism, complete with a critique of nuclear deterrence, without ever using this terminology. The statement was reviewed and updated in 1977 after passage of additional declarations that advocated independent U.S. initiatives, including reductions in U.S. nuclear stockpiles, to enhance the goal of worldwide nuclear disarmament (National Council of Churches of Christ in the USA, 1977). Still further, after expressing deep gratitude for the National Conference of Catholic Bishops 1983 pastoral letter on the nuclear threat, the NCC questioned the morality of one of the letter's key components, an acceptance of nuclear deterrence as an interim ethic until complete nuclear disarmament can be negotiated (National Council of Churches of Christ in the USA, 1983).

Although their statements do not specifically address the moral status of deterrence, the American Baptist Church (1985), the Christian Church (Disciples of Christ) (1981), and the United Church of Christ (1985) also all take positions in keeping with nuclear pacifism. For example, the American Baptist Church states unequivocally, "We call on all nations to abolish their nuclear weapons and to dispose of such weapons in a manner that is not harmful to either the physical or political environment." (American Baptist Church, 1985: 12). The World Council of Churches, with 25 of its 310 member churches located in the United States, also fits in this category and explicitly rejects deterrence "as morally unacceptable and as incapable of safeguarding peace and security in the long-term" (Gill, 1983: 136). The United Methodist bishops' pastoral letter (1986) basically takes a nuclear pacifist stance, but the formal position of the denomination as a whole, as articulated by its General Conference in 1988, fits in the next category.

Interim Deterrence

Positions in keeping with what might be labeled "interim deterrence" agree fundamentally with the assessment by nuclear pacifists about the dangerous and destructive nature of the production, deployment, and use of nuclear weapons. Advocates of this position would also agree about the toll that nuclear deterrence and war preparedness have taken on the environment, the society, and the psychological as well as the spiritual well-being of individuals. The difference in these two categories is in their evaluation of the short-term utility of nuclear deterrence.

Proponents of interim deterrence advocate a long-term goal of nuclear disarmament. In addition to wanting to ensure that nuclear war never occurs, however, groups like the U.S. National Conference of Catholic Bishops (building on the position taken by Pope John Paul II) also stress the need to guarantee preservation of "key values of justice, freedom, and independence which are necessary for personal dignity and national integrity" (National Conference of Catholic Bishops, 1983: 75). This proviso leads them to accept nuclear deterrence in the short term as a balance that prevents either side from gaining superiority or being tempted to try to overtake the other. The Episcopal Church contends that the only morally legitimate purpose of nuclear deterrence is to buy "a little more time to work for other, more peaceful, less apocalyptic alternatives" (Episcopal Church, 1988: 15). Aware of the dangers of deterrence, this "strictly conditioned moral acceptance of nuclear deterrence" urgently favors disarmament and vigilantly cautions that "this minimum . . . is always susceptible to the real danger of explosion" (National Conference of Catholic Bishops, 1983: 79–80).

The Catholic bishops argue that any change in the nuclear arsenal or doctrine should be judged as to whether it contributes to movement in the direction of disarmament. On the basis of this criterion, the Catholic bishops and others in this category debate in detail particular programs and proposals. Those who take the position of interim deterrence usually reject the concept of nuclear superiority, nuclear war-fighting capability or the contemplation of a "limited exchange," the development of weapons likely to enhance a first-strike capability, and proposals that have the effect of lowering the nuclear threshold (e.g., battlefield nuclear weapons). In their 1988 update of the pastoral letter, the Catholic bishops (National Conference of Catholic Bishops, 1988: 15) reiterate and further develop their categoric rejection of countervalue targeting, i.e., targeting cities and industrial centers, which the Episcopalians condemned in 1985 as "repugnant to the Christian faith and tradition" (Episcopal Church, 1988: 15). In contrast to others in this category who reject the Strategic Defense Initiative, the Catholics argue that the SDI should be maintained only as a research and development program contained within the restraints of the Anti-Ballistic Missile Treaty.

A number of positive proposals toward disarmament are often applauded by proponents of interim deterrence (as well as nuclear pacifists). These would include no-first-use policies (discussed by Paul Warnke in Chapter 4); a halt by both sides to the testing, production, and deployment of new nuclear weapons systems; deep cuts in both arsenals; a comprehensive test ban treaty; removal of short-range nuclear weapons, as well as others close to the front lines of confrontation; a strengthening of command and control systems to prevent inadvertent or unauthorized use; support for existing treaties; support for nonproliferation; and conventional arms control.

In addition to the Catholics and Episcopalians, other groups whose positions generally are in keeping with interim deterrence are the American Lutheran Chruch (1982) and the Lutheran Church in America (1984) (both being predecessor bodies of the recently formed Evangelical Lutheran Church in America), the Greek Orthodox Archdiocese of North and South America (1984), Presbyterian Church (U.S.A.) (1984), the Southern Baptist Convention (1982, 1983), the Union of American Hebrew Congregations (1989), and the United Methodist Church (1988).

The position of the Mormons, as articulated in April 1981, is ambiguous on the specific issues under consideration here. It might possibly fit in this category or one of the next two. The statement declares that "we deplore the use of nuclear weapons" but at the same time "we realize that such weaponry exists in a number of nations and we understand the responsibility of our military leaders . . . to prepare measures to repel any agression [sic]" (Church of Jesus Christ of Latter-Day Saints, 1981).

Minimum Deterrence

As with all the previous categories, this one continues to make a presumption against war, and like the two previous positions, it argues that all possibilities for resolving disputes peacefully must be exhausted before governments resort to war. The minimum deterrence position also agrees with that of interim deterrence about the short-term utility of nuclear weapons for deterrence purposes. This category, however, can be distinguished by its assessment of the long-term value of deterrence and its insistence on defending the United States' embodiment of the values of freedom and democracy at all costs. Advocates make little moral judgment regarding the ecological, economic, social, or psychological burdens of nuclear deterrence.

Although minimum deterrence proponents acknowledge that no absolute *proof* exists that the possession of nuclear weapons has caused the United States and the Soviet Union not to fight each other directly, they believe deterrence is a pivotal factor in the stabilization of superpower relations. Therefore, future policies should emphasize maintenance of such a deterrent. The current large stockpiles of nuclear weapons are probably not necessary for such a policy, however, and might be cut substantially. In addition, proponents assert that the utmost care and vigilance are necessary to prevent an accidental or unintended launch.

Another rationale for cutting the stockpiles is that these people have little enthusiasm for extending the threat of nuclear deterrence to the United States' Western allies. Most argue that the use of nuclear weapons should be reserved to protect against an attack on the United States itself, not against an attack on Western Europe. Thus, they assert that Western Europe may need to strengthen its preparedness in conventional forces. The United States and its allies should not contemplate fighting a "limited" or a "protracted" nuclear war in Europe, as advocated by people who subscribe to the next category's position, for at least two reasons: any limited nuclear war would have a high probability of escalating into a total nuclear exchange, and strategies based on the usability of nuclear weapons will make war more likely and thereby undermine their utility for homeland deterrence.

Advocates of minimum deterrence believe that the terror nuclear weapons appropriately instill in people and governments is precisely what makes them useful. Those who possess such arms must be perceived as ready and willing to use them in order for the deterrent to be credible. An adversary must be wholly convinced of the horrible and suicidal consequences of starting a nuclear exchange so as to be discouraged from it. In this regard, countervalue targeting (against cities and industrial centers) is considered to be practically and morally superior to counterforce targeting (against military installations). In addition, for minimum deterrence to have the desired effect of preventing any use of nuclear weapons, both sides must be convinced that any initial small exchange will necessarily escalate into a full exchange (Kattenburg, 1985).

The morality of minimum deterrence rests on the argument that the values which are fundamental to the life of each superpower's society (sovereignty, freedom, and democracy in the case of the United States) have priority over any others, and that to protect them, each power must scare the other away from any direct challenge. Nonetheless, the consequences of one side or the other not being scared away from an attack are clear—a full-scale nuclear war in which both sides, including the values each holds dear, are destroyed. With the possible exception of the Mormons (noted above), no reply by any religious group surveyed fits in this category. Chapter 7 by Paul Kattenburg, however, is a good illustration of the position.

Just Nuclear War

The position that can be labeled "just nuclear war" is the first among those listed so far to not have a clear position regarding a presumption against war. Based on the view that humans are by nature irredeemably evil, aggressive, and greedy, advocates of this position see little likelihood of settling fundamental differences between nations short of war. In a hostile world, governments that stand for and uphold values of freedom and democracy have an obligation to use any means at their disposal to protect their countries from would-be aggressors and to extend protection to other nations or groups that hold values similar to their own. These proponents do not actually advocate war, but they are pessimistic about the possibility of avoiding it. Furthermore, they argue that the best way to prevent war is to prepare for it.

Those who hold this position do not believe that disarmament is possible because international tension and danger will always be present. They are willing, however, to consider arms control proposals if those proposals do not impinge substantially on the growth and diversity of the arsenal. An emphasis on East-West rivalry is the context within which any assessment of issues related to domestic or international justice is made, and attempts to bring about greater international cooperation through the United Nations or international law are viewed as possibly naive and dangerous.

This category, like minimum deterrence, asserts the value of nuclear arms in safeguarding peace between the superpowers. It breaks with all the previous positions, however, in extending deterrence to the Western allies of the United States, thereby contemplating a variety of conditions under which nuclear weapons should be launched. Criteria from the just-war tradition are used to help establish these conditions. This perspective emerged in part from analyses that suggested the USSR was preparing to fight and win a nuclear war. An appropriate response by the United States, advocates claim, is to do the same.

The concept of extended deterrence rests on two basic judgments. One concerns the difference between Eastern and Western Europe in preparedness to fight a conventional war. Advocates of the just nuclear war position assert that the nations of Western Europe do not possess sufficient capability in conventional weapons to defend themselves should the Eastern bloc and/or the Soviet Union attack with conventional weapons. Using nuclear weapons to supplement Western Europe's conventional capability is the most efficient and cost-effective way of bolstering its defense. Therefore, should a war break out between Eastern and Western Europe, nuclear weapons may well be used by the West to undermine the East's conventional strength, prevent it from overtaking the West, and demonstrate resolve. This first use threat is judged to have substantial moral appeal, not only because it is deemed to provide protection for the values of freedom and democracy in Western Europe, but also because, if implemented, it would presumably end the war quickly with a potentially smaller loss of life. Both of these rationales are seen to fulfill the just-war criterion of proportionality.

The second judgment on which extended deterrence is based concerns the need for a credible homeland deterrence. Proponents suggest that as long as the use of nuclear weapons is "unthinkable" because of their massive destructive effects, leaders may be hesitant (or be seen by the adversary to be hesitant) to use them, even if the country were attacked. If, in contrast, strategies are developed to detail the circumstances under which nuclear weapons might be used for more limited purposes, the overall credibility of deterrence would be strengthened. With such strategies, no one would doubt the West's resolve to use every means necessary to prevent a conquest by the East.

Proponents of a just nuclear war position go to great lengths to apply the traditional just-war criterion of discrimination to different kinds of nuclear weapons to judge which ones have greater capacity for moral use. Advocates acknowledge that such arms are, by definition, weapons of mass destruction, but they make substantial distinctions within the arsenal as to just how massive the destruction would be. They often argue for continued technological improvements and the development of small weapons to enhance a discriminating capability. Furthermore, proponents also assert the moral merits of counterforce targeting (against military installations) because, depending on the number of weapons used, fewer noncombatants would die in the immediate blasts and fires.

Although no religious group responding to the survey took this position (again with the possible exception of the Mormons), many of the groups included in the nuclear pacifist and interim deterrence categories carefully scrutinized the arguments of this position and explicitly rejected them. Some denounced them. Many who take a position of interim deterrence prefer counterforce targeting, as does the just nuclear war category, but for the purposes of achieving long-term disarmament, not long-term war-fighting capability.

Articulations of the morality of the just nuclear war position can be found within circles of military analysts and strategists (Wohlstetter, 1985) as well as among televangelists who campaigned for the military buildup based on the war-fighting position proposed by President Reagan.

For example, in advertisements printed in a number of major newspapers, Jerry Falwell said:

> War in any form is abominable. We all know that. But there is something at least as abominable, and that is life without liberty—life without the freedom to write and speak and pray. . . . We cannot afford to be number two in defense! But, sadly enough, that's where we are today. Number two. And fading! . . . But right now—at this very moment—it is not too late to rebuild our defenses. . . . We have a President who wants to build up our military strength. . . . He and the loyal members of Congress need to know that you are with them. [Falwell, 1983: B18]

If the position of nuclear pacifism could be characterized as "better red than dead," just nuclear war prefers "better dead than red."

Apocalyptic Militarism

Premillennial eschatology foretells the end of the world. It posits that biblical scriptures can be appropriately interpreted to predict the conflictual sequence of events, beginning with war in the Middle East, that will lead up to a physical return of Christ to earth. Then, this perspective announces, Christ will establish a 1,000-year reign on earth before transforming this kingdom into an indestructible eternal form.

From this point of view, the Antichrist is communism, embodied especially in the USSR and the People's Republic of China. As war in the Middle East escalates to include the superpowers, the Antichrist will necessarily have to be militarily defeated by the "Christian" nations of the West through the use of nuclear weapons. Much of civilization as we know it now will be destroyed in the process. Just prior to total obliteration, however, Jesus will return to bring lasting peace for the whole world. Individuals can experience personal peace and salvation at any point in history by becoming disciples of Christ, but the world can be relieved of war only after Armageddon. Thus, in contrast to all the positions listed previously, this one makes an unequivocal moral presumption in favor of war.

The category labeled here as "apocalyptic militarism" argues in favor of war preparedness. Little debate is generated over issues that preoccupy some of the other moral positions, like the types of weapons built or their targeting. Since the governments of the West are assumed to be morally superior, they require military superiority as well. How this is achieved is left to the policymakers and technicians. One of the most highly developed articulations of this position is that by Hal Lindsey in *The Late Great Planet Earth* (1977) when he prophesies:

The conflicts will not be limited to the Middle East. The apostle John warns that when these two great forces meet in battle the greatest shock wave ever to hit the earth will occur. Whether by natural force or an earthquake or by some super weapon isn't clear. John says that all the cities of the nations will be destroyed (Revelation 16:19). . . . He also predicts that entire islands and mountains would be blown off the map. It seems to indicate an all-out attack of ballistic missiles upon the great metropolitan areas of the world. [Lindsey, 1977: 155]

As was the case with the previous category, several groups included under nuclear pacifism or interim deterrence specifically mentioned this position and explicitly rejected it. The Lutheran Church in America (one of the predecessor bodies of the Evangelical Lutheran Church in America), for example, stated: "We reject the notion that the conflict between the nuclear superpowers is an apocalyptic struggle between absolute Good and absolute Evil. While there are profound differences between the political values of the Western and Eastern systems of government . . . to absolutize these historical differences is theologically heretical and politically irresponsible. Such prideful absolutizing invites policies of total war unrestrained by morality or prudence" (Lutheran Church of America, 1984: 6).

Programs for Peacemaking

In addition to passing official policy positions on the question of nuclear war, religious organizations promote a wide range of programmatic emphases on peace. Foremost among these is educational activity. As stated earlier, many survey respondents indicated that they publish and promote substantial study guides and other curricular material for their constituents to use in local congregations and elsewhere, and during the 1980s, educational activities to deepen believers' understanding of the issues involved in nuclear war were pervasive.

One of the denominations that apparently takes no official policy position but organizes a significant educational emphasis on peacemaking is the Reformed Church in America (RCA). Much of the material it distributes for education is in keeping with the nuclear pacifism position. In addition, however, the group addresses the economic aspects of nuclear weapons production (RCA, 1985) and has an official policy of minimal investment in companies developing and producing nuclear systems to protest those activities. Other organizations also employ this method of trying to persuade the corporate world to end its participation in nuclear war preparedness; some simply divest themselves of any holdings in companies involved in development or production; and some take positions in favor of "peace conversion" in an attempt to reorient the U.S. economy away from weapons production toward production to meet human needs.

Another popular program for religious groups is engaging in people-to-people exchanges with religious organizations in the Eastern bloc. The National Council of Churches of Christ in the USA has organized such exchanges for many years, for example. Travel in both directions to see how the "adversary" lives is viewed as an important way to promote goodwill, greater understanding, clarity about genuine differences, and a human face for the "enemy." Many hope that across time, the fruits of such contact can spill over into dampening the hostilities between East and West.

Emphases on peacemaking and training for conflict resolution are promoted in some seminaries, like those of the Christian Church (Disciples of Christ). This denomination, and others like the Religious Society of Friends (Quakers), also endorse tax resistance. Their efforts to achieve a "peace tax" would allow citizens legally to designate that personal tax payments not be used for military expenditures.

The United States Institute of Peace (USIP) came into being in part because of the lobbying efforts on the part of many religious and other groups to have a national, government-sponsored, peace academy to research and promote, among other things, nonviolent methods of conflict resolution. Other examples of work by religious organizations to achieve peaceful settlement of conflict could be cited, demonstrating that the issue is an important one for many of the faithful and their leaders.

Conclusion: Nuclear Morality After the Cold War

Religious people throughout time have worried over and made pronouncements about issues of war and peace, and deep concern over the prospects of nuclear annihilation in the late twentieth century has given rise to a great deal of research and articulation of moral positions by religious authorities. As demonstrated above, eight U.S. groups with official positions fall into a category of interim deterrence. The remainder, with one exception, fall into the categories of pacifism (four groups) or nuclear pacifism (five groups), positions even more restrictive regarding the use or possession of nuclear weapons. Nine respondents did not take official policy positions on the question of nuclear war, and the same is likely for most of the groups that made no response to the survey. Nonetheless, with the possible exception of abortion, this issue has apparently generated more debate within the religious community than most other public policy questions in recent years. Furthermore, the groups that do formulate official resolutions make pronouncements that contrast sharply with the moral judgments articulated in U.S. government policies during the 1980s, most of which could be represented in the category of just nuclear war.

Such opposition to the government raises several important questions. For example, does it mean that these churches have little or no influence on government? Or perhaps the reverse, does it mean that the government has little influence on churches? This is a complex problem that warrants investigation beyond the scope of this chapter, but raising it generates curiosity regarding the overall efficacy and impact of public policy pronouncements by religious authorities.

Unlike experiences with previous administrations, "mainstream" religious leaders had little access to the White House during the Reagan presidency, as Ronald Reagan took most of his religious counsel from televangelists. Thus, even if their institutions' opinions had been more in keeping with those of the president, it is doubtful whether the leaders of the organizations represented in this survey would have been able to affect public policy initiatives of the executive branch. Nonetheless, other arenas of influence were available. Perhaps one impact of the various denominations' positions on issues related to nuclear war was to help legitimize and buttress people outside of government who strove to lobby and mobilize public opinion against the massive military buildup of the Reagan administration. By making declarations compatible with those of activists in the peace movement, religious groups may well have (intentionally or unintentionally) served to increase the credibility of this social movement during its controversial confrontations with, what was at the time, a popular administration. Such a hypothesis also deserves further investigation.

If most of the religious institutions surveyed here basically opposed official policy on nuclear issues, does that mean that their constituents did, too? Again, this is a question that requires more research, but a safe assumption is that there was less consensus on these issues among the constituencies than there apparently was among their leaders. In this regard, religious authorities are not elected or appointed to echo the opinions of the faithful but, rather, to give insight, wisdom, counsel, and challenge regarding appropriate interpretations of the faith for the circumstances in which peoples and societies find themselves.

Another interesting question raised by the survey has to do with why some religious institutions with a reputation for theological and social conservatism did not take public positions that were in line with the more-conservative moral categories listed in this chapter or more supportive of the Reagan administration. With the exception of the statement made by leaders of the Church of Jesus Christ of Latter-Day Saints (Mormons), no group adopted a stance in the categories of minimum deterrence, just nuclear war, or apocalyptic militarism. The likely explanation is that conservative groups are somewhat reticent to issue such declarations on any issue. For example, officials from one well-known conservative institution, the Assemblies of God, responded to the survey by indicating that the denomination had no public position on the question of nuclear war or deterrence. If one were to investigate the content of sermons, educational material, and other sources from such groups, however, the data might offer a better understanding of the scope of their positions articulated in a less formal, but perhaps nonetheless powerful, fashion. One of the surprises of the survey, however, is that the Southern Baptist Convention, a denomination historically known for its conservatism, declared a position in the more liberal category of interim deterrence.

Whether or not religious groups will continue to place a high priority on programs and policies regarding nuclear war is unclear. The extraordinary changes taking place in Eastern Europe and the Soviet Union offer new opportunities to those who want to press further for nuclear restraint and disarmament, at the same time that the urgency for such pressure is apparently diminishing. Should the superpowers and other states possessing nuclear weapons succeed in moving toward substantial or complete reductions in their nuclear arsenals, those who make a moral presumption in favor of war will need to find new justifications for that stand. The apocalyptic militarists may even be forced to revise their predictions about how the world will come to an end.

With a lessening of East-West tensions and perhaps a greater preoccupation in the United States with domestic problems, the future would also seem to point to increasing adherence to moral positions that advocate a holistic accounting of the impact of nuclear war preparedness rather than those that focus more narrowly on the ethics of how and when to use various forms of these weapons. The categories of interim deterrence, nuclear pacifism, and pacifism—which examine a wide spectrum of ecological, social, economic, and psychological costs for individuals, groups, society, and the world—may become more popularly acceptable than the categories of minimum deterrence and just nuclear war, which attempt to tell us how to wage nuclear war responsibly. Apocalyptic militarism has never been a widely held point of view in the religious community, and it is not likely to gain many more converts.

Appendix: Groups Surveyed

African Methodist Episcopal
African Methodist Episcopal Zion
American Baptist Churches*

Antiochian Orthodox Christian Archdiocese of North America*
Apostolic Catholic Assyrian Church of the East*
Armenian Apostolic Church*
Armenian Church of America
Assemblies of God*
Christian Church (Disciples of Christ)*
Christian Methodist Episcopal Church
The Church of God in Christ
The Church of Jesus Christ of Latter-Day Saints*
Church of the Brethren*
Coptic Orthodox Church in North America
Episcopal Church*
Evangelical Lutheran Church in America*
Federation of Reconstructionist Congregations
Friends General Conference
Friends United Meeting
Greek Orthodox Archdiocese of North and South America*
Hungarian Reformed Church in America*
International Council of Community Churches*
International Evangelical Church
Moravian Church in America (Northern Province)*
Moravian Church in America (Southern Province)*
National Association of Evangelicals
National Baptist Convention of America
National Baptist Convention, USA, Inc.
National Council of Churches of Christ in the USA*
Orthodox Church in America
Philadelphia Yearly Meeting of the Religious Society of Friends*
Polish National Catholic
Presbyterian Church (USA)*
Progressive National Baptist Convention, Inc.*
Reformed Church in America*
Roman Catholic Church (National Conference of Catholic Bishops)*
Serbian Eastern Orthodox Church
Southern Baptist Convention*
Synagogue Council of America
Syrian Orthodox Church of Antioch
Ukranian Orthodox Church in America
Union of American Hebrew Congregations*
Union of Orthodox Jewish Congregations
United Church of Christ*
United Methodist Church*
United Synagogue of America*
World Council of Churches (Geneva, Switzerland)*

*Responded to the survey

11

Can Contemporary War Be Just? Elements in the Moral Debate

James Turner Johnson

The Shape of Recent Debate over Moral Issues in Defense Policy

Discussions of ethics and military issues have followed a cyclical pattern in the United States since World War II, with three major phases in the debate. The first, which began in the late 1950s and peaked in the early 1970s, was focused on strategic nuclear deterrence. Such books as Herman Kahn's *On Thermonuclear War* (1960) and Paul Ramsey's *War and the Christian Conscience* (1961) were epicenters of this phase of the debate, and the parameters laid down in this period have continued to provide much of the framework for subsequent discussion of the nature of nuclear deterrence and its morality or immorality. A quite different sort of debate raged throughout the period of the U.S. involvement in Vietnam, with issues related to nuclear weapons and strategic deterrence taking second place to discussions about the justness of U.S. participation in that war and the moral issues raised by insurgency-counterinsurgency conflicts. After the U.S. withdrawal from Vietnam, the center of gravity in the moral debate over defense policy shifted back to nuclear weapons and strategic deterrence. The cycle of analysis and argument that began about 1978 and continued through the mid-1980s had mostly to do with the morality of nuclear weapons, their potential uses, and most of all the possession of large numbers and certain kinds of nuclear forces for the purpose of deterrence.

The peak of this phase in the debate occurred between 1982 and 1984, and its benchmark was the appearance in 1983 of the U.S. Catholic bishops' much-discussed pastoral letter, *The Challenge of Peace* (National Conference of Catholic Bishops [hereafter NCCB], 1983). This work was without doubt the most widely noticed contribution to the discussion of moral issues in defense policy in the 1980s. By the time it appeared, the ongoing debate of the immediately previous years had already been significantly influenced by the shape of what the bishops were thinking, as the pastoral letter went through first one draft, then another radically different one, then a further version. The process was consciously designed to engage response from a wide variety of perspectives—not only Catholics but people from other religions and of no religion; not only moral theologians and philosophers but persons from the policy community, the military, and scientific fields; not only scholarly but political and popular discussions of the issues raised.

The intention to stimulate debate succeeded brilliantly; the second draft of the letter—still far from being the final version—was front-page news in both the *Washington Post* and the *New York Times*. (When else has the second draft of any religious document had such attention?) The academic world responded with numerous conferences and symposia, some purely scholarly, others designed to engage broader segments of public expertise and concern. Simultaneously, whether spurred on by the Catholic bishops or proceeding independently, a number of Protestant denominations held conferences and prepared position papers on issues related to defense policy and deterrence. The discussion that centered on *The Challenge of Peace* continued vigorously for a year after it appeared, and this document continues to be a focus for further reflection and argument.

There were, of course, other factors that also contributed to there being an especially active debate about ethics and defense policy in the early 1980s. These included the still recent experience of the Vietnam War; the perception of the Soviet threat to U.S. interests both locally (in Central America) and globally; the policies of the Reagan administration, which included a less conciliatory attitude in international relations and giving new life and strength to U.S. military forces; and the perceived need in the policy community and the military to find an efficacious yet justifiable way to respond to terrorism directed against U.S. citizens and interests.

Alongside the preoccupation with nuclear weapons and strategic deterrence that characterized most of the ethical debate in the religious and academic spheres, a more broadly construed interest in ethics developed within the professional military community during this period. Although this interest included concern for moral issues raised by nuclear weapons and their potential uses, that concern was never the sole focus of the military's sharpened interest in ethics.

Within the U.S. Army, lingering problems of professional identity planted by the Vietnam experience and a new emphasis on readiness for low-intensity conflict joined the exploration of moral and policy dimensions of the nuclear debate to become major factors in the introduction of courses on ethics at the Army War College, the inclusion of ethics in the program of the Army Command and General Staff College, and the program of the U.S. Military Academy's Senior Conference XXI (held in 1983). Similarly, the use of naval forces to project U.S. military power into areas of armed conflict stimulated reflection on ethics in such contexts. The involvement of naval and marine forces in the conflict in Lebanon led to conferences at the Naval War College on the ethical parameters of responses to terrorist activity, and "Ethics in Naval Service" provided the theme for the Navy Chaplain Corps' Professional Development and Training Course (attended annually by all chaplains on active duty) in 1985 and 1986. But though factors other than concern about the nuclear weapons policy helped to create the new debate over ethics and defense policy within the U.S. military and to give it a particular color or texture as compared to the civilian debate, outside the military sphere issues raised by nuclear weapons and deterrence remained at center focus.

Just-War Tradition and Recent Moral Debate over Strategic Deterrence

Just-War Tradition in Outline

The use of categories and tools of reasoning drawn from the just-war tradition of Western culture has been a major feature of the moral debate over defense policy since World War II, particularly that part of the debate that focuses on nuclear weapons and strategic deterrence. Although the tradition has developed out of both secular and religious sources and is carried in the contemporary world by such institutions as the international law of armed conflicts and military codes of conduct, it is the revival of this tradition as a source for religious moral analysis that is new and notable in the moral debate over defense policy.

In its fullest and classic form, the just-war tradition has two aspects, one having to do with the justness of resort to war (*jus ad bellum*) and one on the limits to be observed in the justified use of force (*jus in bello*). These aspects are defined, in turn, by a series of concepts usually called criteria for judgment, and a full list of these criteria is provided in Table 11.1 (see also Johnson, 1984: 1–29). Some of these ideas have a logical, and perhaps a normative, priority over others; for example, it is necessary to have a competent political authority in order to assess the other requirements, and a just cause is needed before any of the other requirements come into play.

The relative importance given to *jus ad bellum* or *jus in bello* reasoning has been different in various time periods and among the sources and

Table 11.1.   Just-War Criteria

Jus ad bellum (When is it right to make war?)

Just Cause: The protection and preservation of value

Right Authority: The person or body authorizing the war must be a responsible representative of a sovereign political body

Right Intention: The intent must be in accord with the cause and not with territorial aggrandizement, bullying, etc.

Proportionality of Ends: The overall good achieved by the war must not be outweighed by the harm it produces

Last Resort: No other means of settling the matter in question will work

Reasonable Hope of Success: No imprudent gambling with military force

The Aim of Peace: Among the ends for which a war is fought should be the establishment of international stability and peace

Jus in bello (Limits to be observed)

Proportionality of Means: Means causing gratuitous or otherwise unnecessary harm should be avoided

Discrimination/Noncombatant Immunity: Protection of noncombatants from direct and international harm

carriers of the tradition. For example, in the Middle Ages the religious analysts were more concerned about the decision to go to war than about what might morally be done in war; in the current debate, as we shall see in more detail, *jus in bello* issues have dominated religiously based use of the tradition.

Historically, the deep roots of many of the just-war ideas can be found in classical Greece and Rome and in the Hebraic religion, though the earliest comprehensive and continuing expressions of the tradition are from the Middle Ages. It is a mistake to conceive of it as a purely religious tradition, as it has been shaped as much by nonreligious as by religious forces over its development. Indeed, throughout most of the twentieth century, the major institutional carrier of this tradition has been a secular one: international law. That law has changed markedly with the revival of the just-war tradition as a source of religious ethical norms in the U.S. debate over morality and defense policy during the last thirty years. (On the historical development of the just-war tradition, see also Johnson, 1975 and 1981.)

Just-War Reasoning in the Work of Paul Ramsey

The revival of just-war reasoning began with Paul Ramsey's *War and the Christian Conscience* (1961) and the essays he wrote during the 1960s collected in *The Just War* (1968). His work has had a pervasive and continuing influence in the debate since that time. Ramsey focused almost entirely on questions related to the moral use of force (*jus in bello*) and, within this framework, made an explicit connection between the idea of noncombatant immunity and the requirements of Christian love for neighbor. This proved to be a powerful argument in the context of religious ethical reflection during the late 1950s and 1960s, which was dominated by the concept of love as the principal uniquely Christian ethical norm. Concentration on love also allowed Ramsey to engage directly, and refute, Christian pacifists who argued from the example of Jesus' nonviolence to a rejection of all things military in American life.

Briefly stated, Ramsey (1961, chaps. 1 and 2) argued that the Christian idea of love gives birth to a "twin-born" just-war theory, including both justification and limitation of the use of force. Love for neighbor requires that he or she be protected from unjust assaults, even (if necessary and as a last resort) at the price of using violent force against the assailant. The just-war *jus ad bellum* is this normative insight extrapolated to the level of the political community. At the same time that force is justified, however, Ramsey continued, it is also limited—and by the same consideration, love of neighbor. Since the unjust assailant is also a neighbor who must be loved, one may not do to him or her more than is necessary to protect the victim. Nor is the protector justified in harming others than the guilty in order to achieve that protection. The *jus in bello* principles of proportion and discrimination express this normative limitation on force that derives from the idea of love for neighbor.

For Ramsey, the principle of discrimination means, in Christian terms, that it is never moral to directly, intentionally attack noncombatants— people whose personal circumstances or social function set them apart from direct involvement in the war effort of their society. By contrast with proportionality, which proceeds by a utilitarian calculus of goods versus evils, discrimination expresses a moral absolute: it is never justified to directly, intentionally attack the innocent. Thus for Ramsey, within *jus in bello* the principle of discrimination has normative priority. If it cannot be satisfied, no amount of reasoning from proportionality can supplant it.

Ramsey's analysis accordingly concentrates on discrimination and its implications. In his first book, in which he developed this idea theoretically, he applied discrimination directly to nuclear deterrence and the possibility of use of nuclear weapons. Arguing against the regnant doctrine of counter-city targeting of nuclear weapons, Ramsey rejoined that nuclear deterrence is immoral for Christians if it rests on such counterpopulation targeting; this targeting doctrine violates the principle of discrimination by making the intended targets of a potential nuclear attack precisely the people who should be shielded from direct, intentional harm. On the other hand, he continued, deterrence based on counterforce targeting puts the intent to harm where it justly belongs: on the enemy's combatant forces. Although it is clear that except for attacks on forces located in remote areas, counterforce strikes will inevitably also kill and otherwise harm noncombatants, this formally unintended and indirect harm is not forbidden by the principle of discrimination. In counterforce strikes, the principle of proportionality provides the only moral limitation. This constraint may still be sufficient to rule out such strikes on certain targets as too costly in collateral lives lost and damage done; this determination will have to be made for each case. Yet such strikes are not ruled out in principle, as are counterpopulation attacks.

Through the diffusion of his ideas in the subsequent debate, Ramsey may be judged to have established his point, at least in theory and partly in practice. The theoretical point was brought out in the debate that preceded the U.S. Catholic bishops' pastoral letter. Responding to a query from the bishops, the Reagan administration formally replied that the United States does not directly, intentionally target noncombatant populations as such. This principle had been part of official deterrence policy prior to the debate over the bishops' letter, and it remains so today.

Practically, of course, it is difficult to distinguish the intention of killing noncombatants from that of attacking military forces in the case of legitimate targets located in or near enemy cities. Here, moreover, the principle of proportionality calls for efforts to lower total collateral destruction from counterforce attacks, and this aim, in turn, implies avoidance of high-yield weapons with a high circular error probability (CEP) in counterforce attacks. Yet there are technological limits to the reduction of yield of nuclear warheads and to increased accuracy of delivery systems. Moreover, powerful voices in the debate over strategic deterrence oppose low-yield, low-CEP weapons as being destabilizing because of their prospective utility as first-strike weapons. Nonetheless, in the process of upgrading the nuclear strategic forces, there has been movement toward increasing accuracy and reducing yield, so that the present force is more capable of proportionate counterforce strikes than was the U.S. strategic deterrent force when Ramsey was writing in the late 1950s.

The use of just-war theory in theological and philosophical ethical writings on nuclear deterrence since Ramsey's time has, in great part, been a development of his fundamental argument from the absoluteness of the principle of discrimination (see, for example, Finnis, Boyle, and Grisez, 1988; O'Brien, 1981; O'Brien and Langan, 1986; O'Donovan, 1989). Conversely, opponents of even a qualified acceptance of deterrence like Ramsey's have mostly based their arguments on the inability of existing forms of nuclear weapons to satisfy the principle of proportionality, and they have gone on to call in question the very possibility that war can be just in the nuclear age. Such "nuclear pacifism" thus invokes just-war reasoning, though its proponents are generally unwilling to admit the contemporary relevance of anything else from this tradition (see Douglass, 1968; United Methodist Council of Bishops, 1986; Yoder, 1984).

Just-War Theory in the Thought of the U.S. Catholic Bishops

The Challenge of Peace (1983), while making reference to the work of Ramsey (a Protestant) as well as to that of other theorists, explicitly grounded its description of the just-war tradition, as well as its overall moral analysis and argument, in the broad Catholic tradition, including the Scriptures. Its description of the just-war criteria was much fuller than Ramsey's and more sensitive to the historical development of the concepts defining it (though a bit more truncated than the classic doctrine I have just summarized), and it included a lengthy discussion of *jus ad bellum*. Nonetheless, the concrete judgments made by the bishops about nuclear weapons and strategic deterrence (NCCB, 1983: sections 146–161, 178–198) focused on the difficulty of satisfying the moral requirements of the just-war *jus in bello*.

An important part of the argument of the document was the way it attempted to resolve the dilemma of deterrence: that nuclear deterrence seems to help to prevent war but to use a deterrent force in war would be gravely immoral (i.e., indiscriminate and disproportionate). A major section of *The Challenge of Peace* (Part 3, "The Promotion of Peace") sought ways out of the dilemma; yet within the framework of the dilemma, the Catholic bishops addressed it in two chief ways. First, they called for the development of nonnuclear defensive strategies and avoidance of the use of nuclear weapons of all sorts. This aspect was connected to their general policy judgment that nuclear strategic deterrence is able to be morally tolerated only so long as there is no viable option. Second, they distinguished between the possession of nuclear weapons for deterrent purposes and planning for the actual use of those weapons, including the development and possession of nuclear weapons for war-fighting. According to this conception, nuclear deterrence exists "only to prevent the use of nuclear weapons by others" (NCCB, 1983: section 188), not to retaliate against a nuclear attack already launched by another nation.

Exactly what this latter point means in practical terms, and specifically whether it amounts to bluff deterrence, has been much debated. In the context of the pastoral letter, the ruling out of use of nuclear weapons is a "prudential" judgment about nuclear war, not a judgment based on the universally binding moral principles of noncombatant immunity and proportionality. The debate centers on whether, either logically or in practical terms, this is not a distinction without a difference. On the one side (arguing against the interpretation that the pastoral letter endorsed bluff deterrence), there are such commentators as J. Bryan Hehir and Bruce Russett, both of whom worked closely with the bishops' committee that drafted the letter; taking the opposing view are people such as Francis X. Winters (1986), who was also close to the bishops' committee, and Paul Ramsey (1988), who testified before the committee and later published a closely argued analysis of elements of the pastoral letter. (For a general analysis of the morality of a bluff deterrent and of the pastoral letter, see Finnis, Boyle, and Grisez, 1988; the positions of Hehir, Russett, Winters, and others are treated at some length in the notes of that work.)

Some Critical Reflections

Ramsey and the U.S. Catholic bishops, then, present two widely respected and influential moral arguments based on a Christian reading of the just-war tradition that differ substantially in their conclusions about the morality of nuclear deterrence and the relation of strategic nuclear deterrence policy to the possibility of involvement in war. Each argument reflects the political and technological conditions of the historical period in which it was prepared as well as the shape of the moral debate in each of those periods. Both are products of the Cold War and do not extend their discussion of nuclear deterrence strategy to embrace issues raised by conflicts outside the superpower relationship or moral issues raised by contemporary forms of nonnuclear war (though Ramsey in the late 1960s extended his use of just-war theory to a discussion of the Vietnam War).

This deficiency is still significant in the moral argumentation over nuclear weapons and deterrence policy. Neither Ramsey nor the Catholic bishops took seriously the secular dimensions of the just-war tradition or sought to integrate these into their arguments (though the bishops more directly sought to address the policy community). In providing parameters for a moral discussion of defense policy, both have had great influence, but both are limited.

An Assessment of the Moral Debate

Can Modern War Be Just?

Responding to the issues as they were defined in the early 1980s and building on my ongoing historical study of just-war tradition (see Johnson, 1975 and 1981), in 1984 I published a book with the title, *Can Modern War Be Just?* (Johnson, 1984). Much of that book has to do with nuclear weapons and with deterrence; yet I believed then (as now) that it is a mistake to focus the lens of moral judgment so exclusively on these subjects as to lose sight of the need to apply ethical analysis to other forms of contemporary war that have proved themselves more likely to occur and thus are more characteristic expressions of war in the present age. I also believed it is a dangerous mistake, one made in a great deal of the argumentation focused on the uniqueness of the moral problems of the nuclear age, to forgo the possibility of employing traditional ethical insights and reasoning to contemporary forms of armed conflict, and accordingly, my book consciously applies moral standards rooted in the historical development of the just-war tradition to the types of conflict identified.

One of my targets was admittedly the widely spread argument of nuclear pacifists who, having established to their satisfaction the immorality of all nuclear weapons, conclude that in the nuclear age no forms of military action to resolve international disputes or respond to threats to national interests can be justified. This sort of reasoning illustrates the problem of tunnel vision that is induced by reducing the moral issues of modern war to the specific moral dilemmas associated with nuclear deterrence.

The Challenge of Peace appeared while *Can Modern War Be Just?* was in press, so I did not have the opportunity there specifically to address the Catholic bishops' understanding or application of the just-war tradition or their conclusions about nuclear weapons, strategic deterrence, and war-fighting. Although I have reservations about their comments in all these areas, my book was not intended as a criticism of the views of the U.S. Catholic bishops or any other theorists as such. Rather, my intention was to broaden the question about the justice of contemporary war and to apply just-war reasoning across the whole range of such conflict. In the wake of the Vietnam War, with the introduction into Europe of tactical and theater nuclear weapons of high accuracy and relatively low yield (compared with earlier generations of such weapons and the majority of the strategic deterrence force), and with the U.S. involvement in the tensions of the Middle East, I thought it critical to attempt this broadening of the moral debate. In light of the events that began in fall 1989, such a broadening seems even more necessary, and a single-minded focus on deterrence in the fashion of earlier years of the moral debate has become all the more inappropriate.

What Is Contemporary War?

What is the shape of war in the nuclear age, anyway? In *Can Modern War Be Just?* I posed this question, arguing in response that at least five types of armed conflicts need to be included in a moral analysis of war in the present age (Johnson, 1984: chap. 2).

Two of the types I identified were nuclear: war between the United States and the Soviet Union involving strategic nuclear weapons and a war, most likely between NATO and Warsaw Pact forces in Western Europe, involving tactical/theater nuclear weapons. In contradistinction to those moralists, policy analysts, and others who believe that a limited use of nuclear weapons should be judged by the same standard as an all-out strategic exchange, I sought to show that so long as the firebreak holds between the two sorts of nuclear war, there are substantial and morally significant differences between them. In particular, the arguments against strategic nuclear weapons and deterrence policy that are based on the principles of discrimination and proportion do not lead to the same results when applied to nuclear weapons of lower yield, higher accuracy, and specifically counterforce function.

The differences are even greater, I argued, between strategic nuclear exchange and three other types of contemporary armed conflict: those between established powers using conventional weapons, such as the Falkland/Malvinas War of 1982; insurgency-counterinsurgency conflicts in which only conventional weapons are used but the means of war are unconventional; and terrorism as a means of war. Unlike the possible forms nuclear war might take, all of these types of nonnuclear conflict have actually occurred in the post–World War II era, and there is good reason to argue that this fact makes such conflicts the reality of what "modern war" is. Reducing the moral debate to a focus on issues concerning strategic nuclear weapons distorts the moral issues raised by these other forms of contemporary warfare and deflects moral reasoning and judgment away from what is to what might be. At the same time, casting the moral debate so as to include the whole range of types of armed conflict is also good for analysis of the moral issues raised by deterrence, since it locates discussion of deterrence within the larger framework of the justified use of force to protect values and the limits to be observed in such justified use of force.

Moral Issues in Planning Defense Policy for the Future

The same sort of concern noted above needs to be advanced in the context of this section, especially since, if anything, the relative importance of the two types of nuclear warfare most prominent in earlier discussions—a superpower strategic exchange and a NATO–Warsaw Pact conflict using tactical/theater nuclear weapons—today seems radically diminished beside other forms of armed conflict. The Iran-Iraq war showed how costly in lives and resources a nonnuclear war with contemporary weapons can be, and that war also returned to center stage a problem many believed had been relegated permanently to the wings: the use of poison gas and other poison chemical agents against troops in the field and against civilian populations. The cheapness and ubiquitousness of highly toxic chemicals—in particular, those that form the basis of some fairly common pesticides—together with the lack of consensus on their control has led to the characterization of chemical warfare as the poor nations' equivalent of the nuclear warhead.

Although there has been a diminution of insurgency warfare and terrorist activity since 1984, both forms of contemporary armed conflict still persist in the world, and, to a greater or lesser degree in each instance, they may threaten to involve the major powers. At the same time, other examples of bloody conflict have erupted in which combatant-noncombatant distinctions and other limits have been ignored: the Chinese repression of dissidents in June 1989; the Rumanian revolution; the emergence of ethnic and religious strife at the edges of the Soviet empire added to that in the Middle East, Northern Ireland, Sri Lanka, and elsewhere.

In short, today, as much or more than in the early 1980s, there is reason to believe that debate over moral factors related to national defense should include serious consideration of how to impose restraints on nonnuclear forms of contemporary war as well as of how morally to conceive possible U.S. responses to such conflicts. Discussions of the future role of nuclear weapons and of strategic deterrence should proceed with this broader defense agenda in mind. It is notoriously difficult to peer into the future, yet it is equally necessary to plan for the future in the light of present conditions and perceived movements toward change. The following comments are offered with this point in mind.

The diminished threat of superpower nuclear war. The justifying rationale behind U.S. strategic deterrence has always been, not the simple possession of nuclear weapons by the Soviet Union, but the climate of enmity between the United States and the USSR that made the Soviet nuclear capability a threat. The size of the Soviet nuclear strategic force in turn rationalized the size of the U.S. force. In this context, arms control has been pursued as a means of managing the competition between the superpowers, not (as antinuclear activists would have preferred) abolishing nuclear weapons entirely. The moral dilemma posed by strategic nuclear deterrence was sharpened by the impossibility of finding an alternative to deterrence that could be reasonably perceived as equally stabilizing of the East-West rivalry.

With the transformation of that role of enmity into one of greater openness and cooperation between the Soviet Union and the Western world, the edge has been taken off the moral debate over deterrence. The same problems still remain in the formal sense—broadly, how to conceive and construct deterrence in a form that will satisfy the requirements of discrimination and proportionality—yet with the diminution of the threat of possible attack, the possibility of use of strategic force has also been diminished, and the rationale for the existence of such a force in its present form has been similarly weakened. The United States does not possess strategic nuclear weapons to deter the United Kingdom or France from attack; those countries are friends and allies. The United States has not built up such a large strategic force to deter China from a nuclear attack; though U.S.-China relations are often difficult, there is no credible nuclear threat from China that would require such a massive retaliatory capacity. The deterrence policy of the United States has been aimed at the Soviet Union; its existence has been justified by the threat of Soviet expansionism, and its nature has been driven by the development of Soviet military power.

Although it is still too early to declare that all threats from the nuclear capability of the Soviet Union have dissolved in the warm milk of superpower amity, it is hardly credible that if Soviet-U.S. relations and the perception of relative national power (not simply nuclear forces) had been the same from 1945 to 1989 as they are today, we would have developed deterrence policy or the strategic nuclear forces as we have. The same may be said of the Soviet Union, which after all has suffered proportionately larger economic and environmental burdens in the development and maintenance of its own strategic deterrent. The question is whether this same level of deterrence preparedness can be justified today, in the light of altered East-West relationships, changed patterns of Soviet behavior, and modified perceptions of Soviet intentions and capabilities.

I think not, and accordingly I think one of the priorities in the moral debate as well as in the broader policy debate over defense capabilities is to consider how mutually the two superpowers might reduce their deterrent forces and scale back their readiness for strategic retaliation. Obviously the call to take these steps has been issued previously by nuclear pacifists and other opponents of strategic deterrence; what is different now is the diminution of the threat that in the past has justified deterrence. I previously believed that such pacifist arguments should not be taken seriously, given the shape of international affairs. Today, those affairs have a different shape, and the arguments now make sense.

Also making new sense are arguments to increase protection against the accidental use of nuclear weapons. Steps have been taken toward this end in the past, with concentration on control of access to such weapons, the installation of "hot lines" for rapid intercommunication, and so on. An area of protection that has been highly controversial, however, is the development of defenses that can destroy nuclear weapons in flight. There is need in the ongoing debate over SDI to consider whether a strategic defense system developed and shared among the nuclear powers might not provide worthwhile protection against accidentally launched strategic weapons, as well as providing security against attacks on other nations by smaller powers who have purchased missile technology and decide to use it malevolently.

The diminished likelihood of a NATO–Warsaw Pact war. With the breakup of the Soviet empire in Eastern Europe and the move of the Eastern European states toward democratic politics and closer ties with the West, it is generally accepted that the likelihood of a war between the Warsaw Pact nations and NATO nations has become small. Even granting, in the worst case, that there remains a remote possibility of an attack on the West from some combination of Warsaw Pact forces, the timetable for the preparation of such an attack has been lengthened so much as to diminish the threat to NATO still further. In this context, there have already been significant nuclear force reductions, and agreements to conventional force reductions were reached in October 1990. As in the case of the superpower relationship, a diminished threat can justify only a diminished military capability.

The new watchword in both U.S.-Soviet relations and in relations among the European states is "mutual security." One may ask, security against what? And what kind of military forces are needed to provide such security? So far as U.S.-Soviet relations are considered in the world as a whole, mutual security implies a condominium to police rogue powers and prevent them from threatening world order. In Europe, the term implies both security against threats from outside and security against threats from within.

As to the former, a case can be made for the maintenance of military forces to participate in a condominium to police world order. Such a conception has regularly figured in plans for European and world unity, all the way back to the "perpetual peace" plans of the seventeenth and eighteenth centuries. As to the latter, I will here only comment that there remains great potential for internal strife in the nations of Eastern

Europe, as is evinced by the bloodiness of the Rumanian revolution and the ethnic strife in Bulgaria as well as the ongoing tension between Greeks and Turks and similar ethnic and religious tensions within the Soviet Union and in the Middle East. Moral discussion of the future shape of European military forces needs to take account of the role they might play in preserving peace and justice in the presence of such strife and the potential for it.

Rethinking the nature and role of deterrence. For nearly half a century, the word "deterrence" has been linked, on the one hand, to the concept of strategic bombing as it developed in the period between the two world wars and particularly during World War II and, on the other hand, to the existence of the nuclear weapons that form the strategic deterrent force. Deterrence in its present form would not exist if either of these conditions were absent.

Deterrence depends on the development, during the 1930s and World War II, of a conviction that it is justifiable in war to attack enemy population centers as a way of weakening "home front" morale and undercutting support for the military forces. This idea, which was tied directly to the growth of air power capable of delivering bombs on enemy cities well behind the fighting lines, was justified by a utilitarian argument that such bombing would shorten the war and save lives— the argument that was eventually made to justify the atomic strikes against Japan. In the context of World War II, strategic bombing as practiced by the Allies was also clearly a response of retaliation against Hitler's Germany and Tojo's Japan for beginning the war and for their own modes of prosecuting it. The fact that strategic bombing could be accepted is a sign of the degree to which the earlier consensus on noncombatant immunity had disappeared by this period.

Although the tactic was hotly debated within the military, there was no substantial civilian moral outrage against this expanded form of warfare. Pacifist voices raised against the war as such did not distinguish among the means of war. For the pacifist opposition, war as such was evil, and all its means were evil. The combatant-noncombatant distinction was entirely foreign to this perspective. Ironically, this stance put pacifist opponents to the war in somewhat the same camp as the advocates of strategic bombing, who also thought the distinction was nonsense.

By the end of the war, strategic bombing was a well-established practice, and the postwar development of deterrence doctrine took it for granted that enemy cities could be targeted. Despite formal changes in targeting doctrine since that time, strategic deterrence is still heavily dependent on the mutual foreknowledge that a nuclear strike would demolish cities and kill overwhelming numbers of noncombatants.

The characteristics of nuclear weapons and the available delivery systems also have decisively shaped the nature of strategic deterrence. The great destructive power of these weapons, coupled with the inaccuracy of the delivery vehicles, has meant that, in practice, counterforce targeting is a distinction without a difference from countervalue/counterpopulation targeting. Given the indiscriminateness and disproportionate destructiveness of these weapons systems, strategic deterrence could be developed only in a context of acceptance of strategic bombing. Conversely, the only way strategic bombing could be credible as a deterrent and not as a war-fighting method was to couple it to nuclear weapons.

Deterrence is commonly described as a means of defense, but in fact a strategic deterrent force does not properly defend anything. Rather, it provides a means of punitive retaliation against an enemy who has already launched a nuclear strike. The punitive nature is assumed in the term "mutual assured destruction"—the destruction the enemy wreaks will surely be answered in kind.

All of these factors—the link between deterrence and noncombatant targeting, the link to nuclear weapons, and the nondefensive, punitive nature of strategic retaliation—suggest that something else should be found to provide for national defense than the strategic nuclear deterrent force. But what? I conclude this chapter with several observations.

1. The best security is found in a stable international system in which disputes are avoided and modes of dispute resolution short of armed conflict are generally employed. It is in our national interest to promote such a system.

2. The present historical context offers a previously unavailable opportunity to scale down strategic deterrence forces and to remove the most disproportionate and indiscriminate weapons from them. It is in our national interest to pursue this opportunity.

3. The lessening of East-West tensions and the scaling back of offensive power create an opportunity for the development of genuinely defensive forces to provide national security. Although these may not, realistically speaking, replace strategic deterrent forces, they have the potential to provide greater security than the existing nuclear deterrent provides. It has been forgotten in the age of strategic deterrence that a good defense is itself a strong deterrent against attack. It is in our national interest to pursue such a deterrent.

Those three observations respond to the most serious moral faults with deterrence. To rethink deterrence along such lines would enhance its ability to discharge what the just-war tradition regards as the only justification for military force—to protect and preserve value. One of the ironies about strategic nuclear deterrence is that it attempts to protect values while at the same time it sharply contradicts other values, notably, the value of not putting innocent life at risk. A moral defense policy should seek the end to that irony.

Part IV

New Thinking About Old Questions

Only when East and West can work out ways of not dying together may humanity at large work out ways of living together. . . . Talk of the end of the Cold War, of [the consequences of] a reunited Germany and of the dissolution of the military blocs has suddenly become common and further immense changes are certainly now on their way. Yet terrible shocks and reverses are also still possible so, although there can be larger hopes for a secure peace, there must be anxiety about a phase of inevitable instability.

Ronald Higgins

12

On the Scholarly Study of Nuclear Deterrence: Historical Roots of the New Discourse

Steven W. Hook
William A. Clark

Today's revived dialogue regarding the morality of nuclear deterrence can be more easily understood if viewed in its historic context. This chapter attempts to trace the rich legacy underlying the contemporary debate by reviewing the work of major theorists and the issues they have advanced. The survey should reveal how the dialogue has consistently reflected the changing international climate confronting national leaders and analysts and how today's discourse is being shaped by changes in the world *After the Cold War*.

After largely sidestepping the moral dimensions of nuclear deterrence during much of the Cold War, strategic analysts, theologians, and mass publics became absorbed by these questions in the 1980s. Whether reflecting the tense revival of superpower tensions, an escalating arms race alongside parity in their nuclear arsenals, or widespread fear of publicized strategies to "prevail" in a nuclear war, the 1980s "witnessed a resurgence of ethical concern about the implications of nuclear weapons" (M. J. Smith, 1987: 2).

Yet this modern form of our timeless fixation with issues of war and peace is daunting and disconcerting. One initially wonders whether the juxtaposition of morality and nuclear weapons is the ultimate oxymoron, the two unworthy of being mentioned in the same breath. But, as a review of the literature on nuclear deterrence illustrates, the conjunction has an intrinsic moral dimension that encompasses both the traditional issues of just-war doctrine and the analyses relating to such nonmilitary issues as economic instruments of statecraft, technology, and global interdependence.

In this sense, nuclear weapons policy is only the most recent dimension of global politics to be placed in a moral context. The roles of personal and social morality have been central to political theory since Aristotle, and realpolitik observers from Thucydides to Machiavelli and Hobbes have framed the debate among theorists of international relations, regarding such ties as inherently amoral and imploring national leaders to treat them as such. Reinhold Niebuhr's distinction between *Moral Man and Immoral Society* (1932) has been extended further by such theorists as Hans J. Morgenthau. He noted that selfish interests, which dominate both interpersonal relations and those within polities, are even more prevalent in relations among states, where "the civilizing influences of law, morality, and mores are less effective . . . than they are on the domestic political scene" (cited in Lefever, 1957: xvi).

The Moral Assessment of Nuclear Weapons

Viewed in this context, the introduction of nuclear weaponry has certainly not changed classical views about the problematic place of morality in international affairs. Although the relationships between morals and politics have remained as uncertain as ever, nuclear weapons have rendered neglect or misunderstanding of morality far more dangerous.

As a result, nuclear deterrence—the management of nuclear arsenals in a manner that precludes their use—has spawned a vast and distinct literature of its own, and in the late twentieth century, nuclear doctrines have received nearly as much scrutiny from moral theologians as they have from strategic analysts and policymakers. Many observers have echoed Albert Einstein's well-known remark that nuclear weapons have "changed everything save our modes of thinking" and have questioned whether the superpowers' awesome strategic arsenals—and those of the other nuclear powers—have left the world's 5 billion inhabitants exposed permanently to the threat of sudden annihilation.

The intense dialogue regarding the morality of nuclear weapons, then, is a recent and unique phenomenon. During the first two decades of the Cold War, as nuclear technologies were refined and the bipolar world became entrenched, public discourse was starkly ideological and polemical. Although U.S. defense experts tended to argue about the capabilities and limitations of nuclear weapons in the *Bulletin of the Atomic Scientists*, political leaders and theologians focused much of their attention on the relative virtues of the competing political systems—communist and capitalist—that dominated the postwar environment. The latter group generally paid little attention to the inherently *moral* implications of the doctrines and force postures the superpower rivals devised to carry out their ideological contest.

The nature of the dialogue in the United States shifted after the first phase of the Cold War, but it still was not greatly concerned with the central issues of nuclear morality. From the late 1960s and for much of the 1970s, the debate about the ethics of war "focused on intervention, just-cause, proper authority, and conscientious objection as the [United States] struggled, not with the rarified rationality of nuclear strategy, but with the intractable contradictions and passions of the Vietnam experience" (Hehir, 1989: 279). Yet nuclear doctrines underwent modifications, and nuclear stockpiles expanded exponentially.

The moral debate intensified during the early 1980s as U.S.-Soviet relations deteriorated. Unlike the "first" Cold War, the superpowers' nuclear arsenals had by then reached rough equivalence, and mutual "overkill" became a central feature of the strategic relationship. The heightened tensions and renewed arms race prompted not only literature that focused on the technical aspects of nuclear weapons[1] but also works that examined their moral dimensions and implications. Suddenly, the relationship between *Morality and the Bomb* (Fisher, 1985) began to receive widespread attention.

Contributing to this effort were studies by the Ambio Study Group (see Peterson and Hinrechson, 1982), Carl Sagan (1983–1984), and others who advanced evidence that a nuclear war would destroy life in areas far beyond the warring states, possibly across the entire planet. Some analysts (Sederberg, 1986) concluded that the nuclear-winter scenario had fundamentally altered the assumptions under which nuclear war strategy was based.

Although some assessments of nuclear strategy are couched in the boldest realpolitik language, every nuclear argument is implicitly representative of a "moral" position. Militaristic "hawks" and pacific "doves" alike insist their views have superior moral validity. But, as we shall see, that is about all they have in common. The debate has been, and to some extent remains, widely diffused among those who demand immediate disarmament, those who promote strategic dominance through nuclear superiority, and those who espouse innumerable stages between those two extremes. Even people who assert the most self-interested, Machiavellian ethics argue their case in moral terms. Whether nuclear deterrence is regarded primarily as a theory, a method, a strategy, or an academic discipline, students of the phenomenon frequently incorporate a "consequentialist" morality into the content of their argument.

Nuclear deterrence, as old as the weapons themselves, has been the subject of impassioned debate at many levels of analysis. The collective dialogue, within the United States as well as other nuclear states, has "gradually transformed nuclear deterrence from a theory and policy into a dogma and doctrine" (Vasquez, ed., 1990: 266). Yet this deterrence remains among the most salient and controversial aspects of international relations; huge nuclear arsenals seem stubbornly to resist any reduction of their meaning to a simple, compelling interpretation. No single school of thought has commanded sufficient respect to dominate the others as a Kuhnian paradigm (Kuhn, 1970).

Moreover, the attention paid to moral precepts by the contending schools of thought have been reduced by the seemingly amoral nature of nuclear weapons. Karl W. Deutsch (1988), while conceding that nuclear weapons have forced national leaders to be much more deliberate in their strategies, captured a common concern about nuclear deterrence when he noted that the debate over nuclear weapons has slipped beyond the rational and moral boundaries of strategic analysis:

> Among various people it has encouraged some callousness, some hardening of sensibilities, some belief that the end justifies all means, and some willingness to lower emotional barriers against considering the admitted equivalents of mass slaughter and torture as potential means of public policy. [Deutsch, 1988: 164]

Students of international relations customarily base their evaluations on a recognition of the fact that deterrence relationships are ubiquitous between states of asymmetrical power (see Naroll, Bullough, and Naroll, 1974; Quester, 1966). Yet the relationships in the nuclear era, while retaining some timeless dimensions of deterrence strategy as they apply to conventional weapons (Mearsheimer, 1983), have fundamentally altered the debate and inferences about how *all* wars can best be deterred. Thomas C. Schelling was among the first to draw attention to the peculiar ways in which nuclear weapons have shaped the relationship between *Arms and Influence* (Schelling, 1966), and he creatively explored the consequences stemming from the "new reality" of the nuclear age, in which "the atomic bomb seems so far to overshadow any military invention of the past as to render comparisons ridiculous" (Brodie, 1946: 34).

In the ominous new thermonuclear world, a few strategic analysts began trying to conform nuclear weapons to existing deterrence models. As noted, Schelling (1960, 1966) was among the first scholars to probe theoretically the novel dynamics of international relations in the nuclear age. The sophistication of the new technology notwithstanding, Schelling found that the most primitive aspects of interpersonal conflicts were present in nuclear politics: as in the game of "chicken," a credible threat was all-important, and advantages were to be gained by willfully appearing irrational or reckless. Yet Schelling concluded that common interests—namely, peaceful coexistence—prevailed between even the most bellicose states and that such survival instincts could be expected to subdue "nuclear temptations" (Draper, 1983).

Another pioneer of nuclear deterrence strategy, Herman Kahn (1960, 1966, 1968), submitted deterrence to computer simulation and "systems analysis." His research broke new ground by attempting to lend "scientific" rigor to such analysis. This effort stimulated great controversy, with critics such as Philip Green contending that it was absurd to "fit essentially political questions into the strait jacket of so-called scientific analysis" (Green, 1966: 259). To Green, the *Deadly Logic* sometimes derived from scientific methods needed to be tempered by consideration of the moral implications of the analysis. To his mind, dangerous conclusions and policy prescriptions often flowed from the assumptions on which purely deductive scientific models relied. Many of these models abused scientific principles of discovery to rationalize ideological beliefs about the most efficient methods of waging and deterring war in the nuclear age. Green thus agreed with the view that "deterrence theory [had] long parted company with science and has become the ideological lubricant of the arms race" (E. P. Thompson, 1982: 13).

Yet the effort to find ways to assist defense planners without considering their ethical implicatons continued in the area of defense and deterrence policy. Soon after Schelling's and Kahn's analyses appeared, Bruce Russett (1963) published the first of his many empirically grounded research findings in modern deterrence theory. Breaking new ground by approaching the problem inductively, Russett noted the continuity between nuclear and prenuclear deterrence relationships. He found that traditional rational-choice modeling retained its explanatory power, and he accurately predicted that nuclear tensions would be tempered by growing economic and ecological interdependence among states.[2]

Other analysts, such as Anatol Rapoport (1964) and Alexander George and Richard Smoke (1974), were more alarmed by the empirically weak foundations on which nuclear deterrence rested. Rapoport noted the salience of psychological factors but argued that too little was known about them to draw credible inferences: "The truth of the matter is that we do not know how and why nations become or cease to be 'aggressive' " (Rapoport, 1964: 169).

After a relatively slow start, this type of scholarly research expanded in several directions, enhanced to some degree by the amount of time modern states had managed to survive without bloodshed in the shadow of nuclear weapons. Analysts in the 1980s focused on such aspects as *Psychology and Deterrence* (Jervis et al., 1985), "The Long-Term Stability of Deterrence" (Kugler and Zagare, 1990), and *Extended Deterrence and Arms Control* (Gantz, 1988). With new evidence at hand, and a broadening empirical base on which to draw, one of the central questions of the

1990s is largely epistemological: Has nuclear deterrence "worked" and if so, how do we know?

Today's Moral Discourse: Intellectual Origins

The rest of this chapter explores major thinking regarding nuclear deterrence as it has evolved in the United States (a more elaborate global review is beyond the scope of this inquiry). As can be ascertained by this introduction, analyses sprang from many sectors of society as researchers probed the functions, limitations, strategic attributes, and moral implications of nuclear deterrence. As inquiry has progressed, it has moved from broad conjecture toward balance and rigor, even if consensus has not been achieved (Schell, 1984), and the effort continues to make nuclear deterrence theory credible (Powell, 1990).

The preceding chapters in this volume reflect the progress that has been made toward a fuller understanding of the moral status of nuclear deterrence. In this chapter, we illustrate the intellectual origins of today's dialogue and trace the divergent approaches and positions from which assessments of the morality of deterrence *After the Cold War* originate. Just as this book brings together disparate voices speaking about the nuclear debate, this chapter illustrates the analytical disparity that has persisted throughout modern history.

The following account of the literature cannot be exhaustive. Instead, a representative sample of the most prominent works published on the morality of deterrence, largely from U.S. experts, is surveyed. Many of the authors cited made contributions that advanced the overall inquiry and generated subsequent research. Others less analytically voiced the critical normative concerns that captured widespread sentiment at the time. Brought together, their collective efforts sensitized policymakers who controlled the potent arsenals and helped the American public come to grips with the nuclear era. The authors' contributions formed the intellectual backdrop and leading ideas from which strategists, academic specialists, and moralists now frame their views about the moral status of nuclear deterrence on the eve of the next century, at a time when the Cold War has thawed and a new global environment is forming.

Following the subject division of the first three parts of this book, in the rest of this chapter we first explore such thought as it is found within the centuries-old just-war doctrine. Then we review literature that traces the origin and evolution of the nuclear age, along with the varying arguments about the deployment and possible uses of U.S. nuclear weapons. Finally, we highlight the changed moral debate of the

1980s and place the overall dialogue in the context of the extraordinary global changes that have recently swept the world.

Just-War Doctrine and Nuclear Deterrence

The doctrine of just war has a long and distinguished pedigree, dating to the writings of St. Augustine, St. Thomas, Hugo Grotius, and Francisco Suarez (see Johnson, 1981, for a comprehensive history). Emerging from both religious and secular origins, evolving ecclesiastical, legal, diplomatic, and military practices have combined over the centuries to produce what is now referred to generically as the just-war doctrine. This doctrine, in its various and developing forms, has been a core concept in the Western intellectual tradition and in the attempt to justify and limit war. Despite the seemingly disparate interests and motives of those that have sought to develop a tradition of just war, the overall consistency and results of their individual contributions have been noteworthy.

Generally speaking, the just-war doctrine is often seen in the context of two central elements. First, the doctrine seeks to establish the conditions under which war may morally be waged. This *jus ad bellum* component focuses on the circumstances that would provide just cause for a state to go to war (see O'Brien, 1981). Although the specific justifications cited by religious, military, legal, and diplomatic figures have varied widely over time, the nature of their justifications falls into this broad category.

St. Augustine was among the first of the Christian thinkers to consider the issues of just war systematically (Holmes, 1989). Defining the *jus ad bellum* component of the just-war doctrine, Augustine established three general criteria for the permissible recourse of Christians to war. First, he stipulated that just war required "competent authority": the power and decision to declare war should lie with recognized state governors; private individuals were unauthorized to declare or wage war. Second, there must be a "just cause" for declaring war. Here, Augustine referred mainly to the avenging of wrongs done by another state, to the restoring of the state of affairs that obtained prior to the wrong being performed (status quo ante), and to the use of force to promote international law and maintain international stability. Finally, Augustine pointed to the requisite of "right intention": entering into war must be only for the goal of achieving some higher good or to avoid some evil.

The second major component of the just-war doctrine deals primarily with the rules for war-fighting. Unlike the *jus ad bellum* criteria, which were developed mainly by religious thinkers, the *jus in bello* standards have been the primary concern of military, legal, and diplomatic figures.

This aspect of the doctrine of just war has traditionally focused on the two major principles of "discrimination" and "proportionality."

Discrimination evaluates a state's conduct in war by the degree to which combatants and noncombatants are distinguished; the unwarranted targeting of noncombatants violates this aspect of the just-war doctrine. The concept of proportionality deals with the types and extent of weaponry employed in war-fighting and the amount of permissible destruction. At various points in history, certain types of weapons (e.g., chemical and biological weapons) have been deemed inappropriate for use in "civilized" warfare. Moreover, at times more extreme uses of force have been rationalized by the purely "consequentialist" claim that mass destruction could end a war quickly and thereby terminate the further loss of life that would occur in a protracted conflict. Sherman's march in the American Civil War, the saturation bombing of cities during World War II, U.S. tactics in Vietnam and Cambodia—even the use of nuclear weapons against Japan—were all "justified" by this standard (Alperovitz, 1965; Reston, 1984).

As we discuss later in this chapter, this consequentialist perspective has been extended to military strategies in peacetime and has come to dominate modern analysis of nuclear deterrence. Among the earliest proponents was Paul Nitze, who argued that deterrence "makes possible the preservation of the values of freedom, diversity, and cultural growth" (Nitze, 1960: 29) and thus makes possible *The Recovery of Ethics* in a nuclear world.

George I. Mavrodes (1985) and others have taken issue with the just-war principle of discrimination, or what has been called the "immunity thesis." Although those proposing a just-war standard of evaluation assume the innocence of noncombatants, Mavrodes argues that if the concepts of "guilt" and "innocence" are to have moral content, then noncombatants can be guilty and combatants can be innocent. "Noncombatants are citizens of warring nations," he states, "in exactly the same sense as are soldiers" (Mavrodes, 1985: 55). In other words, he and others represent the unorthodox view that the distinction maintained by just-war theorists between innocents and combatants does not withstand logical examination.

In addition to these central components of the just-war doctrine, other factors have been applied by theorists and theologians. For example, some have suggested that the probability of success should guide national leaders in their deliberations; engaging in a war with little chance of victory is immoral. Others have demanded that the resort to war be demonstrably a last resort. Both of these *jus ad bellum* components have been adopted, whether explicitly or implicitly, by most contemporary just-war theorists. Taken as a whole, the standards have served as guiding ethical norms by which strategic planning and policies have been judged.

During the nuclear era, contemporary theorists and moral philosophers have attempted to subject the realities of the nuclear age to a rigorous analysis based on just-war principles and have thus structured much of the debate on the morality of nuclear deterrence. But some early writers, such as Robert Tucker, believed modern technology meant that many accepted moral components of *The Just War* (Tucker, 1960) had to be forsaken. Given these deep-seated cleavages, it is not surprising that moral theorists still disagree about the proper formulation of the just-war doctrine and its implications for strategic policy.

William V. O'Brien (1983: 195) articulated a new position on which many strategists and military planners agree and rely to support the war-waging policies they have formed. Emphasizing the legal principle of military necessity as a circumstance that authorizes the use of force for defense and, sometimes, preemptive assault, O'Brien maintains that the serious application of just-war doctrine would go far to satisfy Vatican II's call for an entirely "new attitude" to the problem of nuclear deterrence and war. In his view, while just-war doctrine has a centuries-old history, concerted efforts to apply it and abide by its conditions and prescriptions have been very rare.

For O'Brien, just-war doctrine applies more directly to war-fighting than to the deterrence of war. Therefore, he tends to emphasize the doctrine's *jus in bello* prescriptions of proportionality (the benefits that accrue from fighting for even a just cause must not be out of proportion to the harm that results) and discrimination (direct intentional attacks on noncombatants are impermissible) over *jus ad bellum* considerations. O'Brien holds fast to the principle of proportionality even though he acknowledges the difficulty of maintaining the integrity of the principle of discrimination when there is a serious overlap of counterforce and countervalue targeting strategies (the targeting of military installations and weapons versus the targeting of population centers).

Consistent with this just-war position, O'Brien advocated the adoption of a flexible-response, counterforce strategy as the moral alternative to the mutual assured destruction (MAD) strategy, which, in his view, violates both major principles of the just-war doctrine's *jus in bello* prescriptions. "The important point to be made about strategic nuclear counterforce deterrence," he wrote, "is that, as a war-fighting posture for the contingencies where deterrence has failed, it could offer the greatest hope for conformity to just-war conditions and principles" (O'Brien, 1983: 217).

With Robert Tucker, Paul Ramsey (1961, 1968) was among the first to apply traditional components of just-war analysis to nuclear strategy, setting the stage for much of the contemporary discourse. More specifically, he emerged as the foremost Protestant proponent of the strict principle of discrimination as the foundation of *jus in bello* limitations on war.

Following St. Augustine and Thomas Aquinas, who articulated a full range of moral and "just" reasons for going to war, Ramsey sought to elaborate those *jus in bello* requisites that would maximize "noncombatant immunity." Since the resort to war is at times a moral necessity and since, in his view, proportionality is a lesser priority than discrimination, Ramsey made the latter the cornerstone of his just-war prescriptions. In his view, acts of warfare that directly and intentionally bring about the death of noncombatants, or threaten to do so, are akin to murder and must be condemned. However, Ramsey was fully aware that in modern warfare it is impossible at times to attack combatants without endangering the lives of innocents, and he felt that so long as the death of noncombatants was the "indirect" effect of an attack, it could be said to adhere to the principle of discrimination. If the principle of proportionality is honored (Ramsey, 1968: 149), apparently even large-scale unintentional or "collateral" civilian deaths can be accepted.

This troublesome question of *intentionality* has been a pervasive issue in the just-war dialogue. The apparent willingness of some just-war theorists to jettison the principle of noncombatant immunity through the analysis of strategic intent has contributed to the division of theorists into "absolutist" and "consequentialist" camps (see M. J. Smith, 1987); the perceived virtues of one's cause leads some to condone a variety of dubious war-fighting measures. The debate still persists and is reflected in the ongoing confusion and controversy surrounding NATO's strategic doctrine.

According to J. Bryan Hehir (1989), a key participant in the formulation of the Catholic bishops' 1983 pastoral letter (*The Challenge of Peace*), the just-war principle of noncombatant discrimination emerged as the key point of debate between the bishops and the Reagan administration. Sensitive to the perception that U.S. policy failed to satisfy the preconditions of the Catholic bishops' view, the administration went to some lengths to justify its strategic targeting policy. William Clark, then President Reagan's national security adviser, insisted that Soviet civilian population centers were not targeted "as such" and that U.S. policy did "not threaten the existence of Soviet civilization by threatening Soviet cities" (Hehir, 1989: 284). This statement was followed by Defense Secretary Caspar Weinberger's declaration that the policy of the Reagan administration was that such weapons must not be used for the purpose of destroying populations.

The bishops, however, took the view that as long as counterforce targeting could possibly violate the just-war criterion of proportionality, any moral justification of strategic doctrine based solely on the principle of noncombatant discrimination would represent "an inadequate moral posture" (Hehir, 1989: 285). Since nuclear weapons are so massively destructive of both military targets and the people who reside in their vicinity, the distinction between counterforce and countervalue targeting is meaningless; both "targets" would be destroyed in an attack. As a result of this dilemma, many modern theorists of just war advocate the adoption of counterforce targeting strategies.

However, this position carries its own internal contradictions and has been rejected by some on at least two grounds. First, as many strategic thinkers have argued, a counterforce strategy is *escalatory;* once nuclear weapons are introduced, there is a high likelihood that the level of use will be elevated by one or both parties. Second, a war-fighting strategy may be destabilizing in that such a nuclear strategy introduces the fear of a first-strike, "disarming" attack on the nation being so targeted. This fear presumably generates a case for preemption and thus drastically destabilizes the nuclear balance (see Bundy et al., 1982, and Chapter 4).

Thus, some would argue that there seems to be an internal logical flaw in just-war theory as it applies to the nuclear age. A counterforce strategy is regarded by some as preferable to countervalue targeting, since the latter grossly violates the principle of discrimination between combatants and noncombatants. To these people, low-yield weapons are preferable because they can marginally conform to both the proportionality and the discrimination precepts. Thus, if developing technology brings weapons to the point where they are more accurate (more discriminate) and less powerful (more proportionate), closer adherence to the two major standards of the *jus in bello* tradition may be possible. However, as we have seen, developing weapons that can produce more discrimination and increased proportionality may destabilize the nuclear balance and make the probability of the use of the weapons greater.

Many of the arguments proffered by the just-war theorists have been challenged on other grounds, and two basic challenges to the Augustinian *jus ad bellum* exist within the Christian tradition. Representing one position are the pacifists, who can point to numerous instances in the New Testament where violence of all types is categorically rejected. The biblical prescription "Whosoever shall smite thee on thy right cheek, turn to him the other also" (Matthew 5:39) is only one of a large number of similar admonitions against retaliation and violence (see Sibley, 1963). Many just-war critics refer to Jesus Christ's outright rejection of violence, regardless of its purpose or tactics, and regard subsequent "amendments" as immoral. Indeed, this pacifist tradition in Christianity predates St. Augustine's development of the just-war doctrine (Bok, 1990: 147).

On the other end of the spectrum lies the strong historical tradition of Christians crusading against the infidels. As Mueller observes in Chapter 5, even a cursory look at the history of Europe in earlier centuries shows a decidedly bellicose element in the Christian tradition, which, rather than restricting the use of force, served to rationalize its initiation and to justify unlimited damage. Autocratic internal rule, frequent attacks against neighboring states, and subjugation of native populations were often justified in the name of the Catholic church and its Christian mission.

As one can see, the moral assessment of nuclear strategy is far more varied and complex than blanket condemnations or endorsements would suggest, and in the next section, we explore how these persistent questions have been addressed by U.S. policymakers. Although they have approached the issues from a different position, their deliberations have confronted the same issues of principle and expedience that have dominated moral analysis since the dawn of the nuclear age.

Nuclear Politics: The Evolving Doctrinal Debate in the United States

The emergence of the atomic age prompted substantial debate regarding the inclusion of nuclear weapons in existing U.S. military doctrine. Although experts disagreed as to how the United States should respond to the new technology, most agreed with Bernard Brodie (1946) that averting rather than winning wars should be the primary goal of nuclear strategy. The doctrine of nuclear deterrence was born with the nuclear age itself (see Freedman, 1989).

The United States, with its atomic monopoly and its predominant military and economic power in the wake of World War II, was temporarily placed in a position to set the postwar security agenda. For a brief time, the idea of turning nuclear facilities over to international agencies was given serious consideration by the U.S. leaders, but that idea was quickly eclipsed by national anixiety over the challenge of communism and mounting concern that Stalin's Soviet Union and the People's Republic of China in 1949 were expansionist powers with global ambitions. The challenge of "containing" communism, seemingly exacerbated by the Czechoslovakia coup in 1948, the Berlin blockade in 1948–1949, and other ominous developments, was perceived to be the central task of U.S. foreign policy makers.

The United States, which had fairly consistently pursued an isolationist foreign policy during its first 150 years (T. Bailey, 1980), was irreversibly thrust into a role of world leadership in the wake of World War II (Ambrose, 1988). In marked contrast to its tradition of avoiding foreign entanglements, the new U.S. containment doctrine embraced a willingness to establish regional security blocs and international organizations (Acheson, 1969). Through the Marshall Plan, selective foreign-aid packages, and other economic development efforts, U.S. leaders sought to promote the nation's interests worldwide.

It can be said that the nuclear debate began when the U.S. nuclear monopoly was erased by the Soviet detonation of an atomic bomb in August 1949. U.S. military leaders, led by Paul Nitze, responded by composing NSC-68, a sweeping proclamation vowing to resist the worldwide "assault on free institutions" (see Quester, 1973). President Harry Truman's containment approach, viewed by prominent critics such as John Foster Dulles (1950) as too passive, gradually gave way in the 1950s to a more aggressive "rollback" strategy aimed at reversing communist gains through "compellence."

Guiding these changes was the moral outlook of U.S. leaders concerning the perceived evils of communism and the virtues of democracy. The increasingly messianic nature of U.S. foreign policy rhetoric was best articulated by Dwight Eisenhower during his 1952 presidential campaign: "We can never rest until the enslaved nations of the world have in the fullness of freedom the right to choose their own path" (cited in Ambrose, 1988: 132). The United States, the "city on the hill" offering itself as the world's role model, would no longer lead merely by example but actively and ubiquitously.

The central components of the current debate—minimum versus maximum nuclear deterrence, counterforce versus countervalue targeting—were largely absent at this stage of the Cold War. Instead, given the continuing U.S. superiority in nuclear armaments, a consensus emerged early in the Eisenhower administration around the prospect of "massive retaliation" against any Soviet advances. Secretary of State Dulles, to whom the doctrine is widely attributed, felt it would most clearly deter Soviet aggression "through the threat of immediate, large-scale, nuclear attacks against military, leadership, and urban industrial targets in the Soviet Union" (Carlucci, 1989: 35). This simplistic military doctrine provided Eisenhower with "stunning inflexibility . . . [the only military response involved] launching *all* available forces against *every nation* in the Sino-Soviet bloc" (S. Sagan, 1989: 25; emphasis in original).

Yet, while publicly espousing this strategic doctrine, Eisenhower also worked to integrate nuclear weapons into the defense structure so they could also be used in less-than-apocalyptic circumstances. "Administration officials . . . made a concerted public effort to blur the distinction between nuclear and non-nuclear weapons" (Gaddis, 1982: 149). Quite possibly, Eisenhower was responding to the views expressed by "realists" such as Hans J. Morgenthau and Henry Kissinger. The former urged strategists to move beyond cataclysmic assumptions about nuclear war, arguing that "to the extent that we assume the impossibility of all-out atomic war and act on those assumptions, we increase the very possibility of such a war" (Morgenthau, 1956: 9). Kissinger's influential works, *Nuclear Weapons and Foreign Policy* (1957) and *The Necessity for Choice* (1961), called on military leaders to consider waging "limited" nuclear war as a means of retaining the weapons' credibility.

Similarly, Herman Kahn concluded that a nuclear war would not necessarily end in total destruction, so Americans "might want an ability actually to fight and survive a war" (Kahn, 1960: 96). His position was refuted by Tom Stonier (1964) and others, but the view that a nuclear war is survivable was widely accepted during this period. Advocates generally dismissed deontological condemnations of nuclear weapons; their vision of possible conflict scenarios claimed to be a more responsible approach to deterring or minimizing nuclear violence. Their arguments, advanced in later years by Fred Charles Iklé (1971) and Colin Gray (1977), among others, extended this line of reasoning to a degree that justified the Carter administration's adoption of a "countervailing" strategy and the Reagan administration's endorsement of a "prevailing" nuclear strategy (see Scheer, 1982, for a critique of these strategies, especially the revival of civil defense in the early 1980s).

Eisenhower often suggested that nuclear weapons could be used in an armed conflict "as you would use a bullet or anything else" (cited in Gaddis, 1982: 149). He and Dulles viewed nuclear weapons as a comparatively low-cost addition to the U.S. defense forces, providing "more bang for the buck" and a more cost-effective military establishment.[3]

This consensus on nuclear doctrine developed within the pervasive anticommunist atmosphere in the United States in the 1950s, most publicly symbolized by Sen. Joseph McCarthy's search for closet communists in the U.S. government and society. The moral debate regarding nuclear deterrence remained largely dormant as U.S. leaders maintained agreement on the nature of "the threat" (Iklé, 1990) and the methods necessary to combat it. The perceived moral comparability of nuclear and conventional weapons went largely unchallenged; consequentialist rationales—that peaceful and democratic ends justify morally ambiguous means—prevailed in both scholarly and public-policy literature.

When John F. Kennedy took office early in 1961, a new consensus began to emerge around the view that the massive-retaliation doctrine was too narrow, that it could lead a U.S. president into an all-or-nothing decision. McGeorge Bundy, Kennedy's national security adviser, argued that "the current war plan is dangerously rigid. . . . In essence [it] calls for shooting off everything we have in one shot, and so is constructed to make any more flexible course very difficult" (cited in S. Sagan, 1987: 23). Thus was born the doctrine of "flexible response," which "increased the number of options available to the president, and provided the capability either to respond to Soviet aggression at the level which it was initiated, or to escalate the conflict to a higher level" (Carlucci, 1989: 35). As President Kennedy told the nation in July 1961, "We intend to have a wider choice than humiliation or all-out nuclear war" (cited in Gaddis, 1982: 203). The doctrine became official NATO policy in 1967 and survives even in 1990, despite the fact, as Bruce Russett points out in Chapter 8, that the threat of a Soviet attack on Western Europe has virtually vanished.

But let us also recall that not only was Kennedy reacting to the policy innovations of his defense advisers, he was also coming to terms with the emergence of the Soviet Union as a formidable nuclear power and adversary.[4] "Compelling" agreeable behavior would not be so simple with the military stakes so much higher; U.S. nuclear weapons would now be used to "deter" the Soviets from invading states of vital interest to the United States. Nuclear deterrence, a product of nuclear rivalry, would henceforth be the strategic—and moral—objective of nuclear weapons policy.

Although Kennedy embraced the new doctrine of flexible response, its conception is frequently attributed to his secretary of defense, Robert S. McNamara. He was the one who refined the counterforce approach of targeting military sites of enemies rather than population centers, so as to give "a possible opponent the strongest possible incentive to refrain from striking our own cities" (McNamara, 1962: 628).

The new doctrine, integrated into U.S. defense strategy, was adopted by the NATO alliance in 1967 (although with the loss of France as a part of NATO's military organization). But a key element of the strategy, as in the policy of massive retaliation, prompted growing dismay among many European citizens and theorists of nuclear morality: the first use of nuclear weapons. As McNamara noted, "despite my confidence in the feasibility and desirability of a major nonnuclear option, we cannot exclude the possibility that, under heavy pressure, NATO's nonnuclear defenses might begin to crumble" (cited in S. Sagan, 1989: 39). Thus, NATO strategy continued to include a first-use contingency.

Although military leaders are not prone to framing their doctrinal arguments in moral terms, there is an implicit moral component to any prescribed strategy that seeks the best protection for a state's population. On this level, the counterforce strategy has often been justified in ethical terms. As Theodore Draper observed, "No one can contemplate with equanimity a devastating attack on the social fabric of any country

. . . but an attack on its nuclear weapons or even military establishment does not arouse quite the same repulsion" (Draper, 1989: 34).

Not all analysts of this period were fixated on relative force structures and nuclear doctrines. Some, such as Klaus Knorr, saw opportunities in growing commercial and diplomatic ties among states and suggested that "their rise has tended to curtail the utility of military power for a range of foreign-policy purposes, and may well have made the appeal to force entirely irrelevant in some cases" (Knorr, 1966: 16; this "interdependence" school would gain momentum through the 1970s and 1980s; see Keohane and Nye, 1989). Knorr and other analysts focused less on the immorality of nuclear deterrence than on its obsolescence in the modern world (see Mueller, 1991, for an update of this view).

Although Kennedy, his successor Lyndon Johnson, and McNamara refined the flexible-response strategy in the context of various small- and medium-scale conflict scenarios, they embraced the notion of "assured (Soviet) destruction" in response to a direct attack on the United States. As the Soviets continued to approach nuclear parity with the United States, mutual assured destruction (MAD) became the central dynamic of the spiraling arms race. President Nixon, in supporting the U.S.-Soviet antiballistic-missile (ABM) accord, argues that it "would make permanent the concept of deterrence through 'mutual terror.' . . . Each side therefore had an ultimate interest in preventing a war that could only be mutually destructive" (cited in Ambrose, 1988: 244–245).

The ABM agreement was a central component of the SALT I Treaty concluded by the two superpowers in 1972. That treaty, and its follow-up in 1979, were designed to set limits on each side's strategic arsenals and set the stage for actual reductions through subsequent pacts. Nixon, with Kissinger as his powerful national security adviser, continued to develop broader parameters for deployment and possible use of nuclear weapons—all in the name of deterring the Soviet Union from directly challenging U.S. interests. Gerald Ford followed the same approach, and Jimmy Carter extended it further in 1980 when he issued Presidential Directive 59. Its countervailing strategy involved meeting Soviet threats "at any level of aggression" and maximizing U.S. options in any confrontation.

The arguments in favor of wide-ranging nuclear capabilities were assessed throughout the 1970s and 1980s. Using the familiar psychological arguments cited above, such evaluations stressed that if "retaliatory threats are not credible, then potential attackers may gamble that retaliation might not be carried out and they may not be deterred successfully" (U.S. Office of Technology Assessment, 1989: 108). This reasoning reflects the entrenched interest in strategic *stability* that has prevailed throughout the age of nuclear deterrence; ideological appeals have often been obscured by this overarching goal of superpower peace (see Gaddis, 1982, and Chapter 5 for detailed discussions of this aspect).

In the early 1980s, Ronald Reagan advocated, and achieved, sweeping increases in funding for U.S. nuclear forces. He claimed that the Soviet Union had moved beyond parity to nuclear supremacy over the United States and that the United States could soon be vulnerable to Soviet "compellence" if the gap widened further (see Figure 1.2). Reagan also revived the notion of missile defenses and launched the controversial Strategic Defense Initiative (Star Wars) program. By this stage in the nuclear arms race, the spectrum of issues being debated had widened considerably (see Keeny and Panofsky, 1981–1982). And, as will be surveyed in more detail in the next section, the debate was joined by a widening array of observers—church leaders, peace researchers, and members of public-interest groups. Their contributions helped move the debate beyond the highly technical issues that had dominated earlier, in which the morality of nuclear deterrence was implicitly assumed; the outpouring of literature in the 1980s, in addition to examining the strengths of the competing strategic doctrines, squarely questioned the intrinsic morality of nuclear deterrence and its propriety under then-prevailing conditions.

Not only did public debate move beyond the technical aspects of strategic competition, but the convulsive changes of the late 1980s and early 1990s have prompted political leaders to question their established and most basic assumptions regarding their countries' national security policies. As James N. Miller perceptively observed with respect to the prospect of U.S.-Soviet arms control, "Political rather than technological factors will probably determine the prospects for vast reductions in nuclear weapons" (Miller, 1988: 31). The same could be said for the broader issues of Eastern European sovereignty, European integration, and internal reforms in the Soviet Union and other communist states.

As the Soviet Union's abrupt demise began, Secretary of Defense Caspar Weinberger (1988) urged continued vigilance and nuclear deterrence in the name of stability. But when policymakers such as Zbigniew Brzezinski (1988) called for U.S. leaders to formulate a "new geostrategy" in response to the global changes, moral theorists questioned whether the demise of the Cold War had undermined the rationales many people had used in defending nuclear deterrence.

The Rise of Nuclear Moralism

As noted, the geopolitical climate in the early 1980s was dominated by renewed tension between the Soviet Union and the United States. The election of Ronald Reagan as the U.S. president and his heated references to a Soviet "evil empire" increased global anxiety. Unlike the "first" Cold War, when U.S. military and economic power far exceeded that of the USSR, U.S. officials alleged that the Soviets by 1981 had achieved parity with the U.S. nuclear arsenal and had deployed far larger conventional forces in Europe than the NATO alliance. The "nuclear clock," many feared, was ticking toward midnight.

Jonathan Schell's *Fate of the Earth* (1982) was among the first of many books to capture the public's growing anxiety, which was exacerbated by the escalating arms race and talk of the "winnability" of a nuclear war. In that work, he reflected on the sense of moral estrangement that prevailed among many at the time when he noted that "it is not obedience to our moral feelings but resistance to those feelings that is presented as our obligation" (Schell, 1982: 200). In the years to follow, hundreds of books and articles explored the causes of and possible escapes from the nuclear stalemate. This energized dialogue included academics from several disciplines as well as theologians and policymakers. U.S. television viewers watched a disturbingly realistic depiction of nuclear Armageddon in "The Day After," and on the streets of many major European cities, large antinuclear protests reflected the aroused passions of certain segments of the general public. Similar concerns grew regarding peaceful nuclear power in the aftermath of the accidents at Three Mile Island (1979) and Chernobyl (1986), and the uncertain management of nuclear waste also prompted public protest.

Beyond raising tactical or ideological questions, Schell questioned the *moral* right of nuclear powers tempted by the use of their strategic arsenals to endanger the global population. These fundamental moral questions far outweigh issues of throw-weights or second-strike capabilities, Schell argued, issues that had deadened the debate throughout the nuclear era. He urged citizens to avoid being overcome by the "numbness and inertia" that he felt resulted from the spiraling superpower tensions, and he asked his readers to contemplate, in the spirit of Einstein, the practicality of abolishing nuclear weapons while replacing the competitive nation-state system with a world government (Schell, 1984).

The growing dialogue regarding the morality of nuclear deterrence was punctuated in 1983 by the U.S. National Conference of Catholic Bishops. Their pastoral letter, *The Challenge of Peace: God's Promise and Our Response*, provoked criticism from both the right and left; it enraged as many militarists as it did pacifists. Critics on the right objected to the letter's restricted posture regarding nuclear deterrence, arguing that the menacing nature of the Soviet system justified making the threat of use credible on moral grounds (*jus ad bellum*). Those on the left, conversely, criticized the bishops for their acceptance of nuclear deterrence, however anguished and qualified. Given the pastoral letter's important role in generating dialogue in the 1980s, we will discuss it at some length.

The passionate reaction to the U.S. Catholic bishops' pastoral letter was partly owing to the lengthy and highly visible deliberations that preceded its publication in May 1983. Preliminary drafts were released in the spring and autumn of 1982, and the drafting committees met frequently with lay members of the Catholic church as well as with outspoken members of public interest groups. In addition, the authors conferred with top-level members of the Reagan administration to clarify their assumptions regarding the technical and strategic bases of U.S. nuclear policies (see G. Cheney, 1991, for a review of the drafting process). As Jim Castelli, who observed and documented the bishops' labored deliberations, noted: "The public nature of the process surrounding the pastoral will not be repeated on every issue the bishops address, but it will remain the standard by which everything else will be compared. The bishops involved far more Catholics and, for that matter, non-Catholics at the grass-roots level than ever before" (Castelli, 1983: 181).

True to its purpose, The Challenge of Peace raised public consciousness regarding the moral ends and means of nuclear deterrence.[5] (Not to be outdone, other religious denominations, as Janice Love surveys in Chapter 10, were provoked into forming their own positions.) The central finding of the bishops' letter, and the point that drew the most wrath from the left, was that nuclear deterrence, despite its volatile and precarious nature, was a morally *acceptable* policy for nuclear powers if accompanied by steps toward arms control and disarmament. Actual use of such weapons, the bishops emphasized, would be morally reprehensible in almost any context.

Although the bishops offered this strictly conditioned moral acceptance of nuclear deterrence, they rejected the practice as a long-term basis for peace. Their conditions included the rejection of nuclear war-fighting strategies, deployment of tactical nuclear weapons, efforts to achieve nuclear superiority, first-use doctrines, and targeting strategies that included population centers. The bishops implored leaders to achieve deep cuts in nuclear arsenals, sign a nuclear test ban treaty, and strengthen command-and-control facilities to reduce the chance of accidental nuclear war. Among their other controversial findings was that the extended deterrence of NATO-based nuclear weapons was morally acceptable. "Especially in the European theater," the bishops noted, "the deterrence of a nuclear attack may require nuclear weapons for a time, even though their possession and deployment must be subject to rigid restrictions" (National Conference of Catholic Bishops, 1983: 66).

Catholic bishops from France and West Germany (see Schall, 1984) released their own surveys of nuclear morality in the wake of The

Challenge of Peace. More than their U.S. counterparts, the European bishops focused on the aggressive designs of the Soviet Union; conversely, they were more positively disposed toward nuclear deterrence as a means of self-defense. While the Germans deplored the "Russian tradition of a fearful distrust," the French bishops derided the "aggressive and dominating character of Marxist-Leninist ideology. . . . In this ideology, everything, even the aspirations of nations for peace, must be utilized for the conquest of the world" (Schall, 1984: 104).

The U.S. bishops renewed their conditional acceptance of nuclear deterrence in a revised 1988 report entitled *Building Peace,* suggesting that nuclear deterrence had been a significant factor in the continuing restraint of nuclear powers. They repeated that nuclear deterrence must never be adopted as a permanent feature of superpower doctrine, and they called for global efforts at arms control and nonproliferation. In addition, the bishops supported early U.S. research efforts in developing a missile-defense system.

The bishops' acceptance of nuclear deterrence, however qualified, was questioned by the United Methodist Council of Bishops, who proclaimed that deterrence "has become a dogmatic license for perpetual hostility between the superpowers" (United Methodist Council of Bishops, 1986: 47). Although they went further in condemning nuclear deterrence than the Catholic bishops, the Methodists also fell short of advocating immediate unilateral disarmament. Instead, they called on nuclear states to adopt an "ethic of reciprocity" and begin phased, parallel reductions in nuclear arsenals.

The Catholic bishops' obvious moral anguishing, as reflected in the letter's qualified wording, raises the point of the deceptive complexity of moral reasoning with regard to nuclear weapons. To the bishops (and many other observers), the issue of nuclear morality is not as absolute as many intuitively believe. All such moral judgments are intractably shrouded in more immediate questions of unilaterally disposing of existing nuclear stockpiles, achieving reciprocity, and maintaining the perceived nuclear "balance" that has presumably restrained the superpowers. Absolutist reasoning yielded to innumerable compromises as growing numbers of analysts weighed in.

As many analysts came to share the bishops' short-term acceptance of nuclear deterrence, the arguments returned to the more technological areas, which had dominated in earlier decades. Nuclear "absolutists," who demanded immediate unilateral disarmament, were few in number; most analysts debated whether "minimum" or "maximum" stockpiles are more inclined to keep the peace (see Table 12.1 for a sampling of the leading analysts in the three areas).

Table 12.1.   A Typology of Moral Positions on Nuclear Deterrence

Absolutists	Minimalists	Maximalists
Boyle (1988)	Bundy (1989)	Gray (1984)
Dyson (1984)	Draper (1983)	Iklé (1973)
Finnis (1988)	Fischer (1984)	Kahn (1960)
Grisez (1988)	Jervis (1979)	Kissinger (1957)
Kenny (1985)	Nye (1986)	Nitze (1960)
Schell (1982)	O'Brien (1981)	Wohlstetter (1959)

Students of the evolving Catholic role in peace issues cannot ignore the weighty critique of George Weigel (1987), who published one of the most authoritative analyses of the nuclear debate. He reviewed the church's tradition of "moderate realism" with regard to military issues and concluded that the bishops' effort amounted to "a tragically lost opportunity." To Weigel, the U.S. bishops were overwhelmed by the technical aspects of nuclear weapons and lost sight of the moral precepts that had guided Catholic judgment for centuries. In addition, nuclear revulsion dominated the bishops' thinking to the exclusion of other dimensions of the global dilemma. "The notion that sheer physical survival . . . is the highest good to which all other goods must be subordinated is not a theme compatible with Catholic ethics" (Weigel, 1987: 281).

William Au (1985) also focused on the church's historical role and the context in which the bishops composed the pastoral letter. The bishops were ultimately constrained by trying to appease the many diverse interests involved, Au concluded, and "both pacifists and realists were right in criticizing the lack of clarity in the bishops' thinking" (Au, 1985: 234). Similarly, Douglas Lackey criticized "a certain inconsistency between the bishops' ringing denunciation of most uses of nuclear weapons and their endorsement of nuclear deterrence" (Lackey, 1984: 210).

One can readily appreciate the Hobson's choice facing any analyst who attempts to reconcile nuclear deterrence with strict moral principles: the perceptible short-term "alternatives" to nuclear deterrence appear more destabilizing—hence, more dangerous—than the practice itself. These *Moral Paradoxes of Nuclear Deterrence* (Kavka, 1987) largely explain the broad utilitarian consensus that formed around the bishops' core findings. As Gregory S. Kavka observed, a "balancing of risks and benefits, rather than a rigid application of absolutist principles, should be the starting point of a moral evaluation of nuclear deterrence" (Kavka, 1987: 97).

Although consequentialism has been pervasive in the contemporary nuclear debate, and the presence of moral absolutists has thus been comparatively modest, one should not minimize the central role of strict pacifists throughout the evolution of just-war doctrine. Contemporary nuclear absolutists echo many of the same general themes enunciated by Jesus Christ, whose dictates to "turn the other cheek" were unconditional. Subsequent theologians have diverged from this position, and the same compromises are present in the writings on nuclear morality.

Not all participants in this debate have resigned themselves to consequentialist conclusions. The same factors that vexed the Catholic bishops in the 1980s—largely concerning the realistic options facing the nuclear powers under present circumstances—preoccupied most other analysts and commentators. But some felt the dangers and moral depravity inherent in nuclear deterrence are so great that an abolutist position—demanding immediate, unilateral disarmament—is the only possible one to take.

Among the contemporary absolutists, Jonathan Schell (1982) argued that the imperatives of nuclear disarmament were paramount; conventional concerns of "national security" were secondary. Taking a slightly different approach, Freeman Dyson believed a U.S. effort of "nonnuclear resistance" would compel the Soviets to abandon their own nuclear strategies: "Unilateral action may arrive at the goal more quickly and easily" than protracted arms negotiations (Dyson, 1984: 267).

Their companions in this lonely sector included the European moral theologians John Finnis, Joseph Boyle, and Germain Grisez (1988). Their collaboration rebutted consequentialist logic in deference to an unqualified condemnation of nuclear weapons and a demand for their immediate abolition by all nuclear powers. Unlike Schell, they suggested that the United States, having taken this step, may indeed fall under Soviet control, a fate they did not envision fondly. However, recalling the radical theses forwarded in the 1950s and 1960s by British Catholics such as Walter Stein and G.E.M. Anscombe, they insisted that consequentialist compromises are logically flawed and morally repugnant. "Here is a true challenge," the authors concluded, "to show, in some other way, why it makes sense to adhere, whatever the consequences, to the stringent precept against killing the innocent." Such "moral absolutes," they added, are "integral to authentic realism and self-respect" (Finnis, Boyle, and Grisez, 1988: 370).

Anthony Kenny (1985) was among many critics of nuclear deterrence who condemned the weapons as both immoral and lacking any practical utility. He echoed the absolutist rationales employed by like-minded analysts, and suggested that U.S. leaders begin disarming unilaterally. Unlike the most radical absolutists, however, Kenny added that a "minimum transitional existential deterrent" may be necessary while other nuclear powers are persuaded to follow suit.

One of the most prominent conservative responses to the bishops' efforts was composed by a Catholic lay member Michael Novak (1983), whose critique framed an entire issue of William Buckley, Jr.'s, *National Review*. Novak's view, endorsed by more than a hundred influential Catholic lay members, exposed the internal ecclesiastical debate within the church that had preceded the bishops' pastoral letter. Novak and his supporters focused on what they perceived to be the bishops' misapprehension of the Soviet threat. In the parlance of just-war doctrine, Novak stressed *jus ad bellum* rationales for condoning one's efforts—the ends being pursued rather than the means being applied. To Novak and his supporters, the Catholic bishops had improperly deemphasized the moral distinction between the nuclear superpowers, a distinction that justified U.S. deterrence policies in the name of a superior cause. No analysis of the strategic relationship is appropriate, they felt, if the natures of the competing systems were equated.

This approach led Novak and his supporters to a more "hawkish" position than that adopted by the bishops. In his response, Novak defended NATO military doctrines that did not preclude nuclear first use, supported a mixed array of counterforce and countervalue nuclear targets, and warned the Reagan administration against taking premature steps toward a nuclear freeze.

Rather than confronting the bishops directly, theologian David Hollenbach (1983) also chose to draft his own moral analysis of nuclear deterrence. Like Novak, he argued that "right intentions" carry their own moral weight and are "inseparable from an evaluation of the reasonably predictable outcomes of diverse policy choices" (Hollenbach, 1983: 74). The bishops, he argued, had paid too little attention to the "right intentions" of U.S. policymakers.

Albert Wohlstetter (1983) presented still another critique from the right immediately after the publication of the pastoral letter. Wohlstetter assailed the bishops' advocacy of nuclear deterrence as being so tightly restricted that it constituted a "self-confessed suicidal bluff. . . . Declaring—or telling oneself—that one does not really mean to use nuclear weapons if deterrence fails is one way of stilling uneasiness about threatening to kill innocents in order to deter" (Wohlstetter, 1983: 31). This view was shared by Charles Krauthammer, who called the pastoral letter "a sorry compromise, neither coherent nor convincing" (Krauthammer, 1985: 149).

Wohlstetter, like Richard Pipes, Colin Gray, and other nuclear "maximalists," relied on the same psychological assumptions most often employed by advocates of minimum or "existential" deterrence. To

Wohlstetter, small numbers of nuclear weapons would, in order to achieve a deterrent effect, have to be targeted on civilian areas. Instead, Wohlstetter suggested that the West continue deploying the increasingly accurate nuclear weapons at its disposal, which were capable of exercising a "selective but militarily useful [mission] suited to the circumstances" (Wohlstetter, 1983: 33). Such a strategy, he felt, would be more credible, and hence more likely to restrain the behavior of adversaries.

In contrast to this line of reasoning, nuclear "minimalists" (see Halperin, 1987) argued that war-fighting strategies, with their applications of low-yield, tactical weapons, had dangerously eroded the distinction between conventional and nuclear conflict and had made crossing the "firebreak" to nuclear war much easier. Beyond the range of a small "existential deterrent" (Bundy, 1988), larger stockpiles were seen as both dangerous and economically wasteful. These minimalists argued that both nuclear superpowers could cut their stockpiles by more than half and still retain the functional attributes of nuclear deterrence.

Many observers shared the bishops' concern about the moral ambiguities of nuclear deterrence but concluded that its likely endurance required that a stable modus vivendi with nuclear weapons be maintained. In 1986, Joseph Nye, Jr., explicitly promoted this consequentialist view. He advocated minimum nuclear deterrence designed to avoid the "spurious appeasement" of unilateral disarmament and the "provocation" of pursuing nuclear superiority. "Given the enormity of the potential effects, moral reasoning about nuclear weapons must pay primary attention to consequences," Nye observed. "Effective moralists will have to dirty their hands with some knowledge of nuclear strategy" (Nye, 1986: 91–92).

Along the same lines, Robert Tucker updated his grudging endorsement of nuclear deterrence by concluding that, though a "fall from grace," it may be a "manageable arrangement for an indefinite period of time" (Tucker, 1985a: 59). Such consequentialists echoed St. Augustine's view that national leaders have a greater responsibility than merely acting out their personal moral preconceptions: refusing self-defense may be moral individually but is immoral in the name of others. This viewpoint would be one of many adaptations of centuries-old just-war precepts to the modern nuclear debate.

Just before his death in 1986, strategic analyst Robert E. Osgood thoughtfully assessed this *Nuclear Dilemma in American Strategic Thought* (1988) and found the views of both nuclear abolitionists and arms control "rejectionists" fundamentally flawed. The former ignored the fact that "the political and material means of achieving abolition do not exist in the real world," Osgood observed, while the advocates of limited nuclear war displayed "an intolerable indifference not only to human suffering, death, and physical and ecological destruction, but also . . . to the requirements of effectively achieving political objectives." He concluded that "mitigation" of nuclear risks is the "only realistic and ethical approach," and suggested that policymakers focus on defensive systems, improved command and control, and enhanced conventional forces (Osgood, 1988: 95, 97).

The year after Osgood's book was published, Oliver O'Donovan crafted a similar critique of modern nuclear deterrence, advocating that the West accompany disarmament by "a slow, well-prepared build-up of usable battle-fighting forces, either at conventional or at the lowest nuclear level" (O'Donovan, 1989: 112). His labored position reflected the persistence of moral, logical, and tactical ambiguities that continued to plague analysis into the 1990s. The moral issues surrounding nuclear deterrence simply didn't lend themselves to sweeping Kantian proclamations or demands.

As mentioned previously, this revival of the debate over nuclear morality largely preceded the major changes that swept through the Soviet bloc at the end of the 1980s. In fact, it was the perceived threat of Soviet power as depicted by President Reagan that prompted much of the concern. In this sense, aspects of the debate have an anachronistic flavor (see Fischer, Nolte, and Oberg, 1989, for a more contemporary perspective that may be a harbinger of the next phase of literature on nuclear morality).

As the chapters in *After the Cold War* may suggest, however, the dialogue about continued nuclear deterrence should not end with the Cold War. In fact, the receding salience of the superpower rivalry has undermined a central rationale driving the nuclear arms race, a crucial fact that has further invigorated the moral debate. The dialogue is thus likely to continue as national leaders reconsider their long-lived assumptions around which their nuclear deterrence policies have been based.

Conclusion

As the preceding pages show, the explicitly moral aspects of the nuclear debate have, at various points in time in the public life of the United States, been held in abeyance. Despite a pedigree of just-war considerations dating back centuries, relatively little attention was paid during the 1950s and 1960s to the central questions of proportionality and discrimination. Or, to put the point alternatively, the superpower nuclear doctrines were based precisely on the violation of both of the tenets.

During most phases of the Cold War years, the nuclear debate revolved around technical issues such as the relative strengths and weaknesses of different targeting strategies, missile throw-weights, circular error probabilities (CEPs) and MIRVed missiles. Indeed, to the degree that the nuclear debate touched on ethical or moral considerations, it centered on the West's moral responsibility to halt the spread of "atheistic communist totalitarianism." This imperative prompted the consequentialist ethic, in which, morally, the ends were perceived to justify the means.

The collapse of the ideological and economic vitality of communism in the late 1980s has widened the parameters of these long-standing moral issues. Throughout the 1980s, the moral flavor of the nuclear debate became pronounced, although to be sure, the decade did not produce a "new morality" by which to judge the strategies of the various members of the nuclear club. Rather, after several decades of relative neglect or, perhaps more accurately, relative dissonance, the moral debate assumed a sharper focus. Strikingly, the wave of moralistic reasoning that swept the discourse of the 1980s left the debate much where it had been two decades earlier—in the hands of nuclear tacticians who emphasized "stability" and "credibility" over moralistic purity.

The task of those responsible for the strategic doctrine of the United States today is in many ways more challenging than at the height of the Cold War. What was for four decades a "clear and present danger" to the vital interests of the United States seems suddenly neither very clear nor very present. While the probability of superpower confrontation has become remote, the prospects of a nuclear exchange have become utterly negligible.

However, in this period of reduced tensions, when an increasing number of people are able to propose what would have not very long ago seemed to be extreme and unacceptable alternatives to the official U.S. strategic policy, the range of legitimate demands on government action has widened significantly. For example, whereas only ten years ago a proposal for drastic unilateral cuts in the U.S. nuclear arsenal would not have (and perhaps should not have) been given serious consideration by many individuals in positions of public power, in the first years of the decade of the 1990s, such a proposal is suddenly worth contemplating, and it has gained adherents on both sides of the Atlantic. The decline of the principal threat to U.S. interests—via the demise of its principal nuclear adversary—has made the range of the "thinkable" wider. In an odd twist on Herman Kahn's (1966) admonition that Americans should "think about the unthinkable," the new challenge facing U.S. policymakers today may be to consider the *peaceful* possibilities that only yesterday were scarcely imaginable.

Notes

1. For an illustrative example of this literature from the early 1980s, see Fred Kaplan's *The Wizards of Armageddon* (1983). More recent works, which adequately review the entire nuclear era, include Philip Bobbitt's *Democracy and Deterrence* (1987) and Kurt Gottfried and Bruce Blair's *Crisis Stability and Nuclear War* (1988). See also *Nuclear Strategizing: Deterrence and Reality* (1988) by Stephen Cimbala for an exhaustive analysis of the technical dimensions of nuclear-based defense strategies.

2. Russett, 1967, expanded on these findings with a provocative case study. Graham Allison, 1971, also applied a rational-choice model to empirical deterrence calculations. For a comprehensive analysis of the role of perceptions in nuclear deterrence, see Robert Jervis, 1976.

3. Defense spending, as a percentage of the U.S. gross national product, declined throughout the Eisenhower administration (Gaddis, 1982: 359) while the number of U.S. nuclear weapons grew from about 1,000 to 18,000 (Gottfried and Blair, 1988: 48).

4. As of 1961, the U.S. nuclear arsenal dominated that of the Soviet Union by a margin of 3,267 to 500 warheads (S. Sagan, 1987). Even so, Kennedy's assertion that a "missile gap" threatened the United States had been a central theme of his successful presidential campaign the year before.

5. For the most informative set of responses to the pastoral letter published immediately after its release, see Murnion, 1983, which includes essays by J. Bryan Hehir, Bruce Russett, and George Kennan. Other useful anthologies are Bridger, 1983; Blake and Pole, 1984; Dworkin and Goodin, 1985; and Sterba, 1985.

13

The Post–Cold War Context:
The Contributors' Dialogue
in Perspective

Jonathan Davidson

The chapters in *After the Cold War* capture the contributors' latest thinking about the moral status of nuclear deterrence in the newly evolving international system of the 1990s. As is clear from a reading of the preceding chapters, the contributors approached the problems surrounding nuclear deterrence from differing perspectives and arrived at different conclusions.

To better understand this diversity of perspectives, it is useful to document the exchange of ideas that occurred when the contributors convened at the University of South Carolina on February 8–9, 1990. The dialogue sparked some stimulating ideas and provocative proposals, and the purpose of this concluding chapter is to review that discourse and allow for comparisons with the chapters in this volume.

As a preface, it is necessary to offer a confession about the assignment that confronted the contributors—or rather, the obstacles they faced in evaluating the morality of nuclear deterrence at a time of extraordinary change. Cardinal Bernardin said in his opening address to the University of South Carolina conference that when he worked on the pastoral letter, *A Challenge to Peace*, with its celebrated "conditioned acceptance" of nuclear weapons (one of the conditions being a determined effort by the superpowers to reduce tensions and move toward a political accommodation), he did not realize that the political framework would change so quickly. Six years after publication of the pastoral letter, the relationship between the United States and the Soviet Union was indeed transformed.

A similar confession by the conference organizers is in order. When planning for the international conference began in the summer of 1988, there existed no basis for anticipating that such a profound shift in the international order would occur between the time the contributors first drafted their analyses and the moment they arrived to engage in debate about the positions they had taken. Nonetheless, on the basis of the ideas they exchanged and in response to the momentous changes that unfolded thereafter, the contributors rose to the challenge of revising their essays and directly confronting the new post–Cold War system that rapidly unfolded.

Crossing a Fault Line

Especially shaken to their foundations were those aspects of the world order that had fit tidily for forty years under the rubric of "East-West relations" and had conditioned most analyses of Western security and nuclear deterrence. In most minds, the essential components of the postwar paradigm were unlikely to shift for years or even decades. The convulsions of late 1989 changed everything—including the moral status of nuclear deterrence.

Amazingly, within the space of a few months, at the end of 1989:

• The communist dictatorships of six Eastern European nations fell, new political parties emerged, and democratic elections were scheduled.
• Baltic states and other Soviet republics began to seek independence or secession from Moscow, threatening to extend the anticommunist revolution to the heart of the Soviet Union.
• Presidents Bush and Gorbachev discussed withdrawing troops from Central Europe and negotiated wide-ranging cuts in short- and medium-range nuclear armaments.
• The Berlin Wall opened, and German unification, for forty years a nominal goal of the Western allies and assumed by most to be a chimera, became a virtual fait accompli.
• Soviet constitutional reforms formally terminated the permanent primacy of the Communist party and established a Western-style executive presidency.

"State-centered, command-and-control systems seem to be decomposing," one senior official (Darman, 1990: 8) observed as the events unfolded. If at the outset such a "wargame" scenario had been prepared for the conference, few would have regarded it as credible.

The conference from which *After the Cold War* was derived was thus conceived in a bygone era. In 1990, as Cardinal Bernardin said, the world finds itself on the other side of a historic fault line. The international context underwent a fundamental transformation during this book's gestation period, and with the rubble of the Berlin Wall went many of the assumptions on which defense policy and the international security order had been built. As "history accelerated around us," to borrow Czechoslovakian President Vaclav Havel's (1990) graphic phrase, it proved necessary to rethink our most basic assumptions.

When the goals for this project were originally sketched, President Reagan was still in office. A convert to arms control—and like many late converts, a passionately zealous believer—Reagan left office with the basic architecture of Western security strategy essentially intact. His successor addressed East-West relations and strategic policy cautiously and, initially at least, with even more reserve than Reagan (see Kegley, 1989), regardless of the far-reaching changes that were by then under way in and around the Soviet empire.

In May 1989 President Bush dipped a rhetorical toe in the water with hints of a possible new era in which it was conceivable to move U.S. foreign policy "beyond the containment of communism" (Bush, 1989: 700). By the time of his December 1989 summit with Gorbachev, Bush was actively looking for ways, mainly in the economic sphere, to buttress Gorbachev's efforts to breathe life into perestroika (White House, 1989).

But there was no suggestion emanating from the White House that the fundamental assumptions on which strategic doctrine had been built for many decades were necessarily about to change. On the contrary, there was some evidence that Bush was more comfortable with the doctrine of mutual assured destruction than Reagan or his predecessor, Jimmy Carter, had been and that he had rehabilitated nuclear deterrence (Hoagland, 1989). "What we have seen thus far in the new administration looks like a return to old views on nuclear deterrence, which would not be a good thing," said Georgi Arbatov, a Soviet official, in June 1989 (cited in Hoagland, 1989). In addition, the United States explicitly reaffirmed the doctrine of mutual assured destruction as the cornerstone of Western defense strategy at the July 1989 Seven-Power Summit.

Throughout the 1980s, the framework in which issues of nuclear deterrence, along with most areas of international security policy, were couched consisted of a relatively fixed set of assumptions. The threat emanated from a potentially aggressive Soviet Union; strategic doctrine was formulated to survive a first or second nuclear strike on U.S. territory and inflict devastating retaliation; and extended deterrence provided a U.S. nuclear umbrella, including a first nuclear strike option, to secure Western Europe against the threat of a Soviet or Warsaw Pact nuclear or conventional attack or invasion, most probably in West Germany.

To underscore the unshakable commitment of the United States to the defense of Western Europe and the credibility of NATO's deterrent capabilities, elaborate political and military strategies were instituted to avoid the risk or even the appearance of any "decoupling" of European-theater forward forces from their umbilical cord to the strategic nuclear triad (the land-, sea-, and air-based strategic nuclear forces of the United States). Hopes were often expressed that East-West relations would thaw to the point where serious efforts might be made to reduce the balance of nuclear terror, or that serious arms reduction negotiations might perhaps place a brake on the alarming spiral of the arms race. But for the most part, these were pious aspirations with little expectation that they would be substantially fulfilled in the near term, as Cardinal Bernardin observed (see also Kruzel, 1991).

As Professor Russett illustrates, the geopolitical architecture had a flavor of permanence about it, as if the premises on which strategic doctrine were built were all but cast in stone. Few, if any, imagined the paradigm shift in attitudes and assumptions that was to occur with such breathtaking speed and magnitude at the very end of the decade or the new opportunities these changes would create for fresh analysis of the role and morality of nuclear weapons in global security and the new international order that was being ushered in.

The intent of this project was to promote a dialogue among experts who had thought and published on nuclear deterrence in the 1980s but had rarely discussed their differences face to face. Although they approached the issues from a variety of political, ideological, and intellectual perspectives, their views were commonly advanced against the background of a stable, unchanging international order, characterized by an essentially bipolar world.

Prior to the momentous developments in late 1989, advocates of a nuclear freeze and its variants were often dismissed by those in the policy community as being out of touch with reality. The efforts of the U.S. Catholic bishops and other religious groups to devise an acceptable moral framework for deterrence elicited a muted response from Reagan administration policymakers. Exponents of nuclear strategic planning, meanwhile, conducted their business in the rarified atmosphere of secret government councils, with an occasional sally into the academic world or elite think tanks. They rarely convened with religious leaders or other concerned groups beyond the technical arena to consider the moral and ethical dimensions of the nuclear age. This project was designed to widen the circle of those in the academic community and the general public who were exposed to such crucial discussions on nuclear deterrence. Other purposes were to enlarge public understanding of the complex issues involved in nuclear strategy and its moral dimensions and to consider some fresh insights on moral and ethical dilemmas inherent in the question of nuclear deterrence. Concern for these issues had risen steadily after the release of the bishops' pastoral letter, and it was stimulated in part by the fears raised about nuclear war in the 1980s, when talk switched from why *The Absolute Weapon* (Brodie, 1946) could not be used to ways in which nuclear arsenals could be made into *The Winning Weapon* (Herken, 1980).

After a period of lively debate stimulated by the pastoral letter, however, public discussion had become somewhat sterile. Protagonists, whether scholars or moral theologians, religious leaders or policymakers, strategic thinkers or public commentators, too often talked past each other. Some practitioners of nuclear "theology," as Cardinal Bernardin pointed out in his address, were retreating to their shelters of virtually monastic seclusion and were pursuing their analyses within a tightly closed circle. Our aim, then, was to breathe new life into the moral debate.

Much of the discussion at the conference focused on whether the new political climate and the new world order that was evolving would fundamentally change the character of nuclear deterrence policy and the moral debates surrounding it. Contributors indulged in visions of the new order that would have seemed utopian just months earlier. The changes, and the debate they provoked, made it possible to bring fresh analysis to the perennial questions of international security in the nuclear age.

The upheaval in the global landscape provided an opportunity to recast the moral debate in terms of a new world order in which East-West rivalry and confrontation would be replaced by accommodation and peaceful cooperation. It was realistic to envision for the first time in four decades an increasing convergence of interests between the superpowers leading to agreements on drastically smaller nuclear stockpiles and practical cooperation in maintaining peace and global security. This new vision allowed the focus of the moral debate to shift to issues that had been neglected in the past.

As would be expected from leading authorities, the conference participants responded to the new opportunities and intellectual challenges with keen insight. Their exchanges represented truly "new thinking," and that is captured in the previous chapters, which were revised in light of the discussions that took place at the conference.

Proceedings

The conference opened with a speech by Cardinal Bernardin, a substantially edited version of which is reprinted in this volume. Subsequently, there were two sessions. The first consisted of a five-member panel discussion including Sir Hugh Beach, Father Bryan Hehir, Richard Perle, Bruce Russett, and Paul Warnke. The discussion was moderated by Paul Duke and taped for broadcast on public television. The panel members were later joined by the remaining contributors to this volume for a second session, a roundtable discussion moderated by Professor Russett. To promote a maximum exchange of views, the sessions were designed to provide for open-ended discussion. All the major issues were tackled in each session, rather than sequentially. The account of the discussions that follows therefore ranges over the conference as a whole and is not broken down according to particular sessions.

A New International Order?

Cardinal Bernardin struck a chord that resonated throughout the conference in his call for more attention to a new political relationship among the major powers rather than undue emphasis on the need for "stability." Drawing the analogy of the definitive end in 1945 of a hundred years of militant hostility between France and Germany, he suggested that such a political transformation should now be the long-term goal of "the primacy of the political"—to make war generally as unthinkable as it has become in the case of France and Germany. His assertion that in the 1990s the rationale for superpower conflict has dramatically declined met no substantial dissent, though his caveat—that vigilance is required in a still dangerous world—was underscored emphatically by Richard Perle.

Cardinal Bernardin's call for a new world order encompassing "all the actors in the global community" emerged as another resonant theme. Picking up that theme, Professor Hehir argued that the political-economic agenda raises "moral questions about ranges of distribution, about human needs, human health, and human care . . . and that we now have a chance to discuss [this agenda] under the new conditions."

Articulating the views of several participants about the new opportunities for peace and stability presented by the prospect of a newly evolving world order, Sir Hugh Beach called for a system of "common security," in which the Soviets would join with Europe and North America in guaranteeing European security and global peace and stability. Richard Perle emphatically disagreed, however, arguing that the changes under way in Eastern Europe resulted from Western strength. He rejected what he termed the "vacuous, wholly useless" concept of "common security" as a component of the future order.

Although conceding that the Warsaw Pact had collapsed and that it would be hard to imagine the Soviets reasserting the control they once exerted over their former Eastern European satellites, Perle dissociated himself from some other prescriptions for global security in the evolving order. Paul Kattenburg, for example, suggested that the time had come to explore prospects for an international authority—based on the UN Security Council—to underwrite global peace and security. Minimal nuclear forces might eventually be placed under the command of such a multilateral authority. Janice Love and Bruce Russett both urged that more attention should be given, in the new climate of East-West rapprochement, to the creative use of other forms of influence, such as economic and social sanctions, to deter conflict. Perle doubted the merit of multilateral security arrangements.

Several participants drew attention to the shifting axis of conflict at the end of the Cold War. Sir Hugh Beach voiced his "dismal vision" of a ninety-degree shift in the axis of world conflict, from East-West rivalry to "Christian North versus Muslim South." Concurring, James Turner Johnson drew the conclusion that in the new era now emerging, it would be morally acceptable and appropriate for the major powers to exert collective military force in pursuit of "just causes" such as human rights.

Bryan Hehir drew a less military conclusion. Although nuclear weaponry was perceived to be an inheritance that the world could not shed, Professor Hehir argued that it should be placed in a special category with exceptional restraints on its use. Elaborating, he maintained that we could now look forward to a period of stable East-West relations, though provision must be made to deter against nuclear mistakes and accidents. Meanwhile, he contended, it was possible and necessary to focus on the neglected agendas of domestic and Third World social and economic needs. In constructing a new international order, we should recognize the moral and political imperatives that were neglected in the past owing to intense preoccupation with East-West military and political confrontation. What was now required was a reordering of budgetary priorities to address unmet social, economic, and developmental needs at home and abroad. The ethics of strategy, nuclear stability, and nuclear control should no longer form the "leading edge" of the moral debate in the 1990s.

Strategic Nuclear-Force Cuts

There was little or no dissent concerning the proposition that the time has come to drastically reduce the nuclear arsenals of both superpowers. The new relationship of the West with the Soviet Union and the new situation in Eastern Europe make it "a lot safer to have very drastic cuts [in nuclear weapons]," Paul Warnke argued: "The argument against drastic cuts is disappearing every day." In the United Kingdom, "the Trident missile system is a gross misuse of resources," said Sir Hugh Beach. Similarly, Richard Perle recommended abandoning further modernization of U.S. offensive land-based forces, citing the proposed expenditure of $50 billion–$60 billion on Midgetman as "foolish in the extreme."

As a measure of the degree to which opinion had changed on this issue, in 1990 the sober London *Economist* called for a reduction of these ceilings to 2,000 on each side, down from the present totals of around 10,000 each and one-third the current START target of 6,000 each—a view that, in the days of the 1980s nuclear-freeze movement, would have been widely regarded as unattainable (*Economist*, 1990).

Strategic Defense

Likewise, the issue of strategic defense raised little heat, perhaps reflecting the lower temperature of U.S.-Soviet relations. Richard Perle argued that resources should be diverted from offensive missile systems to strategic defense. He suggested that it should now be possible to persuade the Soviets that a limited form of strategic defense represented no threat to their security. Strategic defense, in his view, would constitute prudent insurance against errant nuclear missiles from outlaw states or, conceivably, a disintegrating Soviet Union.

Paul Warnke responded that it would first be necessary to work out the offensive half of the equation with the Soviets, to assure both sides that there was no possibility of the other side's gaining a preemptive first-strike capability. If that could be done, he would not dismiss the prospect of an eventual strategic defense capability, though he doubted its relevance as a protection against a nuclear threat from the Third World, which more likely would materialize in the form of a gravity bomb or a cruise missile.

Has Nuclear Deterrence Worked?

In contrast, substantial disagreement surfaced about the extent to which the absence of military conflict between the Soviet Union and the West since the end of World War II could be attributed to nuclear deterrence and, by extension, about how ethical it was to maintain the nuclear deterrent and threaten its use during that period. Kenneth Boulding noted the propensity of the human race to use whatever implements are at its disposal ("if a man has a tennis racquet, he has a strong tendency to play tennis").

John Mueller implied, moreover, that there was little, if any, moral justification for the nuclear deterrent. Nuclear weapons were irrelevant as a deterrent. The Soviet Union and the United States had no interest in going to war: They were, in fact, "deterred" by a variety of factors wholly unrelated to the existence of nuclear weapons, notably their common interest, as victors in World War II, in maintaining peace. Now that we have moved another significant step toward recognition of the "obsolescence" of war, the Soviets, Mueller suggested, should be invited to join a superpower condominium—invited, in effect, to join NATO. Arms reduction talks should be abandoned on the grounds that they obstruct the reductions of arsenals that would otherwise be proceeding apace.

To the criticism that abandoning the pursuit of negotiated reductions would be destabilizing, Mueller responded that calls for nuclear stability were the product of old thinking. There is no "stability" in the military balance between the United States and Canada, but war is nevertheless unthinkable between them. Likewise, Mueller stressed, we should recognize that war between the United States and the Soviet Union could become equally unthinkable, rendering the concept of stability increasingly outmoded and irrelevant.

Bruce Russett argued that the nature of deterrence had fundamentally changed during the course of the postwar period. At the outset, unquestioned U.S. nuclear superiority may have deterred Soviet aggression against Western Europe; but this "extended deterrence" has been increasingly less credible since nuclear parity, so the factors deterring Soviet aggression, whatever they may have been, could well have changed over time. Richard Perle asserted, by contrast, that the case for nuclear deterrence had been made: if the Soviets alone had possessed nuclear weapons in that period, NATO and conventional U.S. forces would not have sufficed to deter a Soviet attack on Western Europe.

Extended Deterrence

Russett agreed with Warnke that the first use doctrine is an increasingly embarrassing anomaly of Western strategy and should be dropped. Note, here, Warnke's position, surfacing more often among today's policymakers (U.S. Congress, 1990): the collapse of the Warsaw Pact renders the doctrine of first use even more outmoded and inappropriate.

"There is an antique quality about the military budget," said Warnke. "It contains provision for the deployment in Germany of a new nuclear weapon that can hit Czechoslovakia, Poland, Hungary, and East Germany." To dramatize how outmoded this weapon has become since the collapse of the Warsaw Pact, Warnke quoted Hans-Dietrich Genscher, the foreign minister of the Federal Republic of Germany, who has asked rhetorically, Whom do I aim it at, Lech Walesa? (The U.S. administration subsequently decided to drop development of the new weapon.)

Nuclear Proliferation

Optimism about the future of superpower relations was offset by general concern about the proliferation of weapons of mass destruction to more unstable areas of the world. There were some sharp differences of view, however, on how to address the problem.

Empirically, even though the risk of nuclear war has diminished, said Bryan Hehir, there is a rising danger of nuclear proliferation. The moral agenda has not changed, he asserted, but issues are now surfacing that previously had little airing because of the intensity of the Soviet-U.S. confrontation. It is essential after the Cold War to address the underlying causes of weapons proliferation.

The single most effective step in preventing proliferation, according to Paul Warnke, would be for the major powers to enact a comprehensive test ban treaty—to implement the pledge, as he put it, voiced at the time of the 1963 partial test ban treaty and again in the 1968 nuclear nonproliferation treaty, to "stop all testing of all nuclear weapons for all times." Sir Hugh Beach argued in favor of implementing Article 6 of the Nuclear Non-Proliferation Treaty, which calls for rapid reduction of nuclear arsenals by the major powers and, more particularly, for a multilateral mechanism under the auspices of the United Nations to resolve regional disputes that are the root cause of nuclear proliferation.

Richard Perle, on the other hand, endorsed a permissive posture toward the use of preemptive strikes for particular purposes and cited the elimination by Israel in 1981 of Iraq's nuclear reactor before the latter country could achieve a weapons capability as an example of the kind of circumstances in which the use of force is justifiable. This topic led to the sharpest exchange of the conference. Perle asserted that if Israel had not taken out Iraq's reactor, the Iran-Iraq war would have become a nuclear war. Others retorted that there was adequate deterrence against such use (Warnke), that preemptive strikes are a recipe for counterstrikes (Hehir), and that, whatever its past failings, the United Nations will prove to be indispensable in maintaining world peace in the coming decade (Russett).

There was less disagreement on another aspect of nuclear proliferation: What is entailed by the risk of nuclear weapons falling into the hands of an outlaw regime? Here, the participants agreed that the major powers are obligated to retain a residual nuclear deterrent capability in the post–Cold War era. However stable U.S.-Soviet relations, consensus supported the view that after the Cold War, it would still be necessary to guard against the risk of nuclear blackmail by Qaddafi or someone like him.

No one at the conference expressed any doubt that the threat of nuclear proliferation poses severe risks in the decade ahead. Underscoring this widely felt concern, William Webster, director of the Central Intelligence Agency, warned that "nations around the world are building up their own arsenals. The proliferation of nuclear, chemical and biological weapons poses serious dangers to regional stability and to the interests of the United States" (*Washington Post*, April 13, 1990: A22).

Outlook

"The changes in Eastern Europe are of the most far-reaching magnitude and completely irreversible," said Sir Hugh Beach, "and the point of no return has probably also been reached in the Soviet Union. . . . This calls for completely recasting our thinking." Paul Kattenburg advanced a similar view, arguing that "we stand on the threshold of extremely important developments if we have enough vision and imagination to seize the opportunity."

Consensus developed, therefore, about the nature of the political earthquake that has shaken the European order as we have known it throughout the postwar and Cold War periods. Consensus was also reached on the probability that the new situation offers much promise for greatly reduced nuclear arsenals and the long-term relaxation of East-West tensions. Some participants went so far as to suggest (allowing for obvious caveats that we cannot foretell what the future holds) that a new era of meaningful cooperation between the superpowers is on the horizon, with improved prospects for long-term European peace and stability, and even world government.

There was also a feeling that the essential character of the moral issues surrounding nuclear deterrence would not change significantly. With the exception of Kenneth Boulding and John Mueller, the contributors felt that nuclear weapons are here to stay and require complex and skillful management to assure nuclear stability. But in the new post–Cold War era, the questions of nuclear strategy, control, and stability will no longer be at the top of the moral and ethical agenda. Moral energies should be redirected to global problems such as famine, AIDS, ethnic recidivism, ecological crises, and, not least, nuclear proliferation.

Notwithstanding the collective sense of sharing a new dawn that permeated the conference, the moderator of the final session, Bruce Russett, may have been nearer the mark when, in winding up, he said, "We are still stumbling into a post–Cold War world." This grim reality makes the quest for international security by effective *and* moral means as imperative as ever.

References

Abrecht, Paul, and Ninan Koshy. 1983. *Before It's Too Late: The Challenge of Nuclear Disarmament*. Geneva: World Council of Churches.

Abshire, David M. 1988. *Preventing World War III: A Realistic Grand Strategy*. New York: Harper and Row.

Accident Facts, 1985. 1985. Chicago: National Safety Council.

Acheson, Dean. 1969. *Present at the Creation*. New York: Norton.

Allison, Graham T. 1971. *Essence of Decision: Explaining the Cuban Missile Crisis*. Boston: Little, Brown.

Almquist, Peter. 1990. "The Vienna Military Doctrine Seminar: Flexible Response Vs. Defense Sufficiency." *Arms Control Today* 20 (April):21–25.

Alperovitz, Gar. 1989. "Do Nuclear Weapons Matter? An Exchange." *New York Review of Books* 36 (April 27):57–58.

———. 1965. *Atomic Diplomacy*. New York: Simon and Schuster.

Ambrose, Stephen E. 1988. *Rise to Globalism*. 5th ed. New York: Penguin.

American Baptist Church, General Board. 1985. "American Baptist Policy Statement on Peace." Resolution adopted in December.

American Lutheran Church. 1982. "Mandate for Peacemaking." Resolution adopted by the Eleventh General Convention, September 10.

Aquinas, Thomas. 1990. "Of War." In John A. Vasquez, ed., *Classics of International Relations*, pp. 8–11. Englewood Cliffs, NJ: Prentice-Hall.

Arms Control Association. 1989. *Arms Control and National Security*. Washington, DC: Arms Control Association.

Art, Robert J., and Kenneth N. Waltz. 1983. "Technology, Strategy, and the Uses of Force." In Robert J. Art and Kenneth N. Waltz, eds., *The Use of Force*, pp. 1–32. Lanham, MD: University Press of America.

Ashton, Basil, Kenneth Hill, Alan Piazza, and Robert Zeitz. 1984. "Famine in China." *Population and Development Review* 10 (December):613–645.

Aspen Strategy Group. 1989. *Deep Cuts and the Future of Nuclear Deterrence*. Lanham, MD: University Press of America.

Au, William A. 1985. *The Cross, the Flag, and the Bomb*. Westport, CT: Greenwood Press.

Auden, W. H., ed. 1956. *Selected Writings of Sydney Smith*. New York: Farrar, Straus.

Avenhaus, Rudolf, Steven J. Brams, John Fichtner, and D. Marc Kilgour. 1989. "The Probability of Nuclear War." *Journal of Peace Research* 26 (February):91–99.

Axelrod, Robert. 1984. *The Evolution of Cooperation*. New York: Basic Books.

Bailey, Alison. 1989. *Posterity and Strategic Policy: A Moral Assessment of Nuclear Policy Options*. Lanham, MD: University Press of America.

Bailey, Thomas. 1980. *A Diplomatic History of the American People*. 10th ed. Englewood Cliffs, NJ: Prentice-Hall.

Baldwin, David A. 1971. "The Power of Positive Sanctions." *World Politics* 24 (October):19–38.

Ball, Desmond, and Robert C. Toth. 1990. "Revising the SIOP: Taking War-Fighting to Dangerous Extremes." *International Security* 14 (Spring):65–92.

Barnet, Richard J. 1990. "Reflections: Defining the Moment." *New Yorker* (July 16):46–60.

Beres, Louis René. 1990. "Responding to the Threat of Nuclear Terrorism." In Charles W. Kegley, Jr., ed., *International Terrorism: Characteristics, Causes, Controls*, pp. 228–240. New York: St. Martin's Press.

Bernhardi, Friedrich von. 1914. *Germany and the Next War*. New York: Longmans, Green.

Betts, Richard K. 1987. *Nuclear Blackmail and Nuclear Balance*. Washington, DC: Brookings Institution.

Blainey, Geoffrey. 1973. *The Causes of Wars*. New York: Free Press.

Blake, Nigel, and Kay Pole, eds. 1984. *Objections to Nuclear Defense: Philosophers on Deterrence*. London: Routledge and Kegan Paul.

Blechman, Barry M., and Stephen S. Kaplan. 1978. *Force Without War: U.S. Armed Forces as a Political Instrument*. Washington, DC: Brookings Institution.

Bobbitt, Philip. 1987. *Democracy and Deterrence: The History and Future of Nuclear Strategy*. New York: St. Martin's Press.

Bok, Sissela. 1990. "Early Advocates of Lasting Peace: Utopians or Realists?" *Ethics and International Affairs* 4:145–162.

Botterweck, G. Johannes, and Helmer Ringgren. 1986. *Theological Dictionary of the Old Testament*. Grand Rapids, MI: Eerdmans.

Boulding, Kenneth E. 1978. *Stable Peace*. Austin, TX: University of Texas Press.

———. 1964. *The Meaning of the Twentieth Century: The Great Transition*. New York: Harper and Row.

———. 1962. *Conflict and Defense*. New York: Harper and Row.

Bracken, Paul. 1983. *The Command and Control of Nuclear Forces*. New Haven, CT: Yale University Press.

Bridger, Francis, ed. 1983. *The Cross and the Bomb*. London: Mowbray.

Brodie, Bernard. 1959. *Strategy in the Missile Age*. Princeton, NJ: Princeton University Press.

———. 1946. *The Absolute Weapon: Atomic Power and World Order*. New York: Harcourt, Brace.

Brown, Seyom. 1987. *The Causes and Prevention of War*. New York: St. Martin's Press.

Brzezinski, Zbigniew. 1988. "America's New Geostrategy." *Foreign Affairs* 66 (Spring):680–699.

Buchan, Alastair. 1974. *Change Without War*. London: Chatto Windus.

Bueno de Mesquita, Bruce. 1981. *The War Trap.* New Haven, CT: Yale University Press.

Bundy, McGeorge. 1990. "From Cold War to Trusting Peace." *Foreign Affairs* 69 (Summer):197–212.

——. 1988. *Danger and Survival: Choices About the Bomb in the First Fifty Years.* New York: Random House.

——. 1984. "The Unimpressive Record of Atomic Diplomacy." In Gwyn Prins, ed., *The Nuclear Crisis Reader*, pp. 42–54. New York: Vintage.

Bundy, McGeorge, George F. Kennan, Robert S. McNamara, and Gerald Smith. 1982. "Nuclear Weapons and the Atlantic Alliance." *Foreign Affairs* 60 (Spring):753–768.

Burin, Frederic S. 1963. "The Communist Doctrine of the Inevitability of War." *American Political Science Review* 57 (June):334–354.

Bush, George. 1989. "Remarks at the Texas A&M University Commencement Ceremony in College Station, Texas." *Weekly Compilation of Presidential Documents* 25, no. 20:699–702.

Butterfield, Herbert. 1949. *Christianity and History.* London: Fontana Books.

Carlucci, Frank C. 1989. *Annual Report to the Congress, Fiscal Year 1990.* Washington, DC: Government Printing Office.

Carnesale, Albert, Paul Doty, Stanley Hoffmann, Samuel P. Huntington, Joseph S. Nye, Jr., and Scott D. Sagan. 1989. "How Might Nuclear War Begin?" In Charles W. Kegley, Jr., and Eugene R. Wittkopf, eds., *The Nuclear Reader*, 2d ed., pp. 242–257. New York: St. Martin's Press.

Castelli, Jim. 1983. *The Bishops and the Bomb: Waging Peace in a Nuclear Age.* New York: Doubleday.

Chace, James, and Caleb Carr. 1988. *America Invulnerable: The Quest for Absolute Security From 1812 to Star Wars.* New York: Simon and Schuster.

Charles, Daniel. 1987. *Nuclear Planning in NATO.* Cambridge, MA: Ballinger.

Chayes, Antonia Handler, and Paul Doty, eds. 1989. *Defending Deterrence.* Washington, DC: Pergamon-Brassey's.

Cheney, Dick. 1990. *Annual Report to the President and the Congress.* Washington, DC: Government Printing Office.

Cheney, George. 1991. *Organization Rhetoric in the Management of Multiple Identities: The U.S. Catholic Bishops' Pastoral Letter.* Columbia, SC: University of South Carolina Press. Forthcoming.

Chernus, Ira. 1987. *Dr. Strangegod: On the Symbolic Meaning of Nuclear Weapons.* Columbia, SC: University of South Carolina Press.

Cheshire, Leonard. 1985. *The Light of Many Suns.* London: Methuen.

Christian Church (Disciples of Christ). 1985. *Seeking God's Peace in a Nuclear Age.* St. Louis, MO: CBP Press.

Christian Church (Disciples of Christ), General Assembly. 1981. "Resolution Concerning Nuclear Arms." Resolution adopted July 31–August 5.

Chubaryan, A., and B. Marushkin. 1987. "The Inadmissability of War in the Nuclear Age." In Raimo Vayrnen, ed., *The Quest for Peace*, pp. 97–107. Beverly Hills, CA: Sage.

Church of Jesus Christ of Latter-Day Saints. 1981. "Easter Message—A Plea for Peace." *Church News*, April 18.

Church of the Brethren Annual Conference. 1982. "Reaffirmation of Opposition to War and Conscription for Military Training." Resolution adopted July 20–25.

Cimbala, Stephen J. 1988. *Nuclear Strategizing: Deterrence and Reality*. New York: Praeger.

Clausewitz, Carl von. 1976. *On War*. Edited and translated by Michael Howard. Princeton, NJ: Princeton University Press.

Cohen, Sheldon M. 1989. *Arms and Judgment: Law, Morality, and the Conduct of War in the Twentieth Century*. Boulder, CO: Westview Press.

Commission on Integrated Long-Term Strategy. 1988. *Discriminate Deterrence*. Washington, DC: Government Printing Office.

Contamine, Philippe. 1984. *War in the Middle Ages*. Oxford: Basil Blackwell.

Crowe, William. 1990. Interview with R. Jeffrey Smith, *Washington Post* (January 8):1.

Darman, Richard G. 1990. "Director's Introduction to the New Budget." In *Budget of the United States Government, Fiscal Year 1991*. Washington, DC: Government Printing Office.

Deutsch, Karl W. 1988. *The Analysis of International Relations*. 3d ed. Englewood Cliffs, NJ: Prentice-Hall.

Doty, Paul, and Antonia Handler Chayes. 1989. "Introduction and Scope of Study." In Antonia Handler Chayes and Paul Doty, eds., *Defending Deterrence*, pp. 1–16. Washington, DC: Pergamon-Brassey's.

Douglass, James. 1968. *The Non-Violent Cross*. New York: Macmillan.

Doyle, Michael. 1986. "Liberalism and World Politics." *American Political Science Review* 80 (December):1151–1169.

———. 1983. "Kant, Liberal Legacies, and Foreign Affairs." *Philosophy and Public Affairs* 12 (Summer and Fall):205–235, 323–353.

Draper, Theodore. 1989. "Nuclear Temptations." In Charles W. Kegley, Jr., and Eugene R. Wittkopf, eds., *The Nuclear Reader*, 2d ed., pp. 25–39. New York: St. Martin's Press.

———. 1983. "Nuclear Temptations." *New York Review of Books* 29 (January 20):42–50.

Dulles, John Foster. 1950. *War or Peace*. New York: Macmillan.

Dwane, Seqibo. 1988. "Early Christians and the Problem of War." In Charles Villa-Vicencio, ed., *Theology and Violence: The South African Debate*, pp. 133–146. Grand Rapids, MI: Eerdmans.

Dworkin, Gerald, and Robert E. Goodin, eds., 1985. *Nuclear Deterrence: Ethics and Strategy*. Chicago: University of Chicago Press.

Dyson, Freeman. 1984. *Weapons and Hope*. New York: Harper and Row.

Economist (London). 1990. "The New Nuclear Age" (unsigned editorial). March 10.

Eden, Lynn, and Steven Miller, eds., 1989. *Nuclear Arguments*. New York: St. Martin's Press.

Episcopal Church, General Convention. 1988. *To Make Peace: The Reports of the Joint Commissions on Peace*. Cincinnati, OH: Forward Movement Publications.

Evangelista, Matthew. 1988. *Innovation and the Arms Race: How the United States and Soviet Union Develop New Military Technologies.* Ithaca, NY: Cornell University Press.

Falwell, Jerry. 1983. "An Open Letter from Jerry Falwell on the Nuclear Freeze." *Washington Post* (March 8):B18.

Finnis, John, Joseph Boyle, and Germain Grisez. 1988. *Nuclear Deterrence, Morality, and Realism.* Oxford: Oxford University Press.

Fischer, Dietrich. 1984. *Preventing War in the Nuclear Age.* Totowa, NJ: Rowman and Allanheld.

Fischer, Dietrich, Wilhelm Nolte, and Jan Oberg. 1989. *Winning Peace.* New York: Crane, Russak.

Fischoff, Baruch, Sarah Lichtenstein, Paul Slovic, Stephen L. Derby, and Ralph L. Keeney. 1981. *Acceptable Risk.* Cambridge: Cambridge University Press.

Fisher, David. 1985. *Morality and the Bomb.* London: Croom Helm.

Freedman, Lawrence. 1989. *The Evolution of Nuclear Strategy,* 2d ed. New York: St. Martin's Press.

Frost, Gerald. 1990. "Demilitarization Is a One-Way Street." *Wall Street Journal* (July 31):A12.

Gaddis, John Lewis. 1990. "Coping with Victory." *Atlantic Monthly* 265 (May):49–54.

——— . 1987–1988. "Containment and the Logic of Strategy." *National Interest* 10 (Winter):27–38.

——— . 1987a. "How the Cold War Might End." *Atlantic Monthly* 260 (November):88–100.

——— . 1987b. *The Long Peace: Inquiries Into the History of the Cold War.* New York: Oxford University Press.

——— . 1982. *Strategies of Containment.* New York: Oxford University Press.

Gallois, Pierre. 1961. *The Balance of Terror: Strategy for the Nuclear Age.* Translated by Richard Howard. Boston: Houghton Mifflin.

Galvin, James R. 1989. "The NATO Alliance: A Framework for Security." *Washington Quarterly* 12 (Winter):85–94.

Gantz, Nanette C., ed. 1988. *Extended Deterrence and Arms Control.* Santa Monica, CA: Rand.

Garthoff, Raymond L. 1990. *Deterrence and the Revolution in Soviet Doctrine.* Washington, DC: Brookings Institution.

——— . 1985. *Détente and Confrontation: American-Soviet Relations from Nixon to Reagan.* Washington, DC: Brookings Institution.

George, Alexander, and Richard Smoke. 1974. *Deterrence in American Foreign Policy.* New York: Columbia University Press.

Gessert, Robert A., and J. Bryan Hehir. 1976. *The New Nuclear Debate.* New York: Council on Religion and International Affairs.

Gill, David, ed. 1983. *Gathered for Life: Official Report.* Seventh Assembly. Geneva: World Council of Churches.

Goldberg, Andrew C. 1989. "Offense and Defense in the Postnuclear System." In Charles W. Kegley, Jr., and Eugene R. Wittkopf, eds., *The Nuclear Reader,* 2d ed., pp. 121–128. New York: St. Martin's Press.

Goldblat, Jozef. 1982. *Agreements for Arms Control: A Critical Survey.* London: Taylor and Francis.

Goldstein, Joshua. 1988. *Long Cycles.* New Haven, CT: Yale University Press.

Gottfried, Kurt, and Bruce Blair. 1988. *Crisis Stability and Nuclear War.* New York: Oxford University Press.

Gralnick, Alexander. 1988. "Trust, Deterrence, Realism, and Nuclear Omnicide." *Political Psychology* 9 (March):175–188.

Gray, Colin S. 1984. *Nuclear Strategy and Nuclear Planning.* Philadelphia: Foreign Policy Research Institute.

————. 1977. *The Geopolitics of the Nuclear Era.* New York: Crane, Russak.

Gray, Colin S., and Keith Payne. 1980. "Victory Is Possible." *Foreign Policy* 39 (Summer):14–27.

Gray, John. 1989. "Harsh Birth Pangs in the New Order." *Times of London* (December 28):10.

Greek Orthodox Archdiocese of North and South America. 1984. "Preventing Nuclear War." In *Statements on Moral and Social Concerns,* pp. 18–19. New York: Greek Orthodox Archdiocese of North and South America, Department of Church and Society.

Green, Philip. 1966. *Deadly Logic.* Columbus, OH: Ohio State University Press.

Greenhouse, Steven. 1988. "Zaire, the Manager's Nightmare: So Much Potential, So Poorly Harnessed." *New York Times* (May 23):48.

Hackett, Sir John. 1978. *The Third World War: August 1985.* London: Sidgwick and Jackson.

Halperin, Morton. 1987. *Nuclear Fallacy: Dispelling the Myth of Nuclear Strategy.* Cambridge, MA: Ballinger.

Harvard Nuclear Study Group. 1983. *Living with Nuclear Weapons.* Cambridge, MA: Harvard University Press.

Havel, Vaclav. 1990. "Address of the President of the Czechoslovak Republic to a Joint Session of the United States Congress." (February 21) Washington, DC: Government Printing Office.

Head, Ivan L. 1989. "South-North Dangers." *Foreign Affairs* 68 (Summer):71–86.

Hehir, J. Bryan. 1989. "There's No Deterring the Catholic Bishops." *Ethics and International Affairs* 3:277–296.

Helprin, Mark. 1988. "War in Europe: Thinking the Unthinkable." *Wall Street Journal* (November 1):A28.

Herken, Gregg. 1985. *Counsels of War.* New York: Knopf.

————. 1980. *The Winning Weapon: The Atomic Bomb in the Cold War, 1945–1950.* New York: Knopf.

Hermann, Charles F. 1988. "Crisis Stability in Soviet-American Strategic Relations." In Joseph Kruzel, ed., *American Defense Annual 1988–1989,* pp. 211–228. Lexington, MA: D. C. Heath.

Herz, John. 1951. *Political Realism and Political Idealism.* Chicago: University of Chicago Press.

Higgins, Ronald. 1990. *Plotting Peace: The Owl's Reply to the Hawks and Doves.* London: Brassey's.

Hoagland, Jim. 1990. "Bush Urges NATO to Change Strategy on Atomic Response." *International Herald Tribune* (July 3):1, 8.

———. 1989. "The Return of Nuclear Deterrence." *Washington Post* (June 27):A23.

Hoffmann, Stanley. 1989a. "Do Nuclear Weapons Matter?" *New York Review of Books* 36 (February 2):28–31.

———. 1989b. "What Should We Do in the World?" *Atlantic* 264 (October):84–96.

———. 1981. *Duties Beyond Borders.* Syracuse, NY: Syracuse University Press.

———. 1971. "International Law and the Control of Force." In Karl W. Deutsch and Stanley Hoffmann, eds., *The Relevance of International Law*, pp. 34–66. Garden City, NY: Doubleday-Anchor.

Hollenbach, David. 1983. *Nuclear Ethics: A Christian Moral Argument.* New York: Paulist Press.

Hollins, Harry B., Averill L. Powers, and Mark Sommer. 1989. *The Conquest of War.* Boulder, CO: Westview Press.

Holmes, Robert L. 1989. *On War and Morality.* Princeton, NJ: Princeton University Press.

Holsti, Ole R. 1989. "Models of International Relations and Foreign Policy." *Diplomatic History* 13 (Winter):15–43.

House, Karen Elliott. 1989. "As Power Is Dispersed Among Nations, Need for Leadership Grows." *Wall Street Journal* (February 21):A1, A10.

Howard, Michael. 1987. *War and the Liberal Conscience.* New Brunswick, NJ: Rutgers University Press.

———. 1984. *The Causes of War.* 2d ed. Cambridge, MA: Harvard University Press.

Huth, Paul. 1990. "The Extended Deterrent Value of Nuclear Weapons." *Journal of Conflict Resolution* 34 (June):270–290.

———. 1988. *Extended Deterrence and the Prevention of War.* New Haven, CT: Yale University Press.

Huth, Paul, and Bruce Russett. 1990. "Testing Deterrence Theory: Rigor Makes a Difference." *World Politics* 42 (July):466–501.

———. 1988. "Deterrence Failure and Crisis Escalation." *International Studies Quarterly* 32 (March):29–45.

Hyland, William G. 1990. "America's New Course." *Foreign Affairs* 69 (Spring):1–12.

Iklé, Fred Charles. 1990. "The Ghost in the Pentagon." *National Interest* 19 (Spring):13–20.

———. 1973. "Can Nuclear Deterrence Last Out the Century?" *Foreign Affairs* 51 (January):267–285.

———. 1971. *Every War Must End.* New York: Columbia University Press.

James, William. 1911. *Memories and Studies.* New York: Longmans, Green.

Jervis, Robert. 1989. *The Meaning of the Nuclear Revolution.* Ithaca, NY: Cornell University Press.

———. 1988. "The Political Effects of Nuclear Weapons." *International Security* 13 (Fall):80–90.

————. 1986. "The Nuclear Revolution and the Common Defense." *Political Science Quarterly* 101, no. 5:689–703.

————. 1985. "Introduction." In Robert Jervis, Richard Ned Lebow, and Janice Gross Stein, eds., *Psychology and Deterrence*, pp. 1–12. Baltimore, MD: Johns Hopkins University Press.

————. 1984. *The Illogic of American Nuclear Strategy*. Ithaca, NY: Cornell University Press.

————. 1982. "Security Regimes." *International Organization* 36 (Spring):357–378.

————. 1979. "Deterrence Theory Revisited." *World Politics* 31 (January):289–324.

————. 1976. *Perception and Misperception in International Relations*. Princeton, NJ: Princeton University Press.

Johansen, Robert C. 1991. "Do Preparations for War Increase or Decrease International Security?" In Charles W. Kegley, Jr., ed., *The Long Postwar Peace*, pp. 224–244. New York: Harper Collins.

————. 1989. "Global Security Without Nuclear Deterrence." In Charles W. Kegley, Jr., and Eugene R. Wittkopf, eds., *The Nuclear Reader*, 2d ed., pp. 72–80. New York: St. Martin's Press.

John Paul II. 1982. "World Day of Peace Message." *Origins* 11:476.

Johnson, James Turner. 1987. *The Quest for Peace: Three Moral Traditions in Western Cultural History*. Princeton, NJ: Princeton University Press.

————. 1984. *Can Modern War Be Just?* New Haven, CT: Yale University Press.

————. 1981. *Just War Tradition and the Restraint of War*. Princeton, NJ: Princeton University Press.

————. 1975. *Ideology, Reason, and the Limitation of War*. Princeton, NJ: Princeton University Press.

Jury, Mark. 1971. *The Vietnam Photo Book*. New York: Grossman.

Kaeuper, Richard W. 1988. *War, Justice, and Public Order: England and France in the Later Middle Ages*. Oxford: Oxford University Press.

Kahn, Herman. 1968. *On Escalation*. Baltimore, MD: Penguin.

————. 1966. *Thinking About the Unthinkable*. New York: Avon.

————. 1960. *On Thermonuclear War*. Princeton, NJ: Princeton University Press.

Kaplan, Fred. 1983. *The Wizards of Armageddon*. New York: Simon and Schuster.

Kattenburg, Paul. 1985. "MAD Is the Moral Position." In Charles W. Kegley, Jr., and Eugene R. Wittkopf, eds., *The Nuclear Reader*, pp. 77–84. New York: St. Martin's Press.

Kavka, Gregory S. 1987. *Moral Paradoxes of Nuclear Deterrence*. New York: Cambridge University Press.

Kaysen, Carl. 1990. "Is War Obsolete?" *International Security* 14 (Spring):42–64.

Keegan, John. 1987. "The Evolution of Battle and the Prospects of Peace." In John R. Challinor and Robert L. Beisner, eds., *Arms at Rest*, pp. 189–201. New York: Greenwood.

Keeny, Spurgeon M., Jr., and Wolfgang K.H. Panofsky. 1981–1982. "MAD Versus NUTS: Can Doctrine or Weaponry Remedy the Mutual Hostage Relationship of the Superpowers?" *Foreign Affairs* 60 (Winter):287–304.

Kegley, Charles W., Jr. 1991. "The New Containment Myth: Realism and the Anomaly of European Integration." *Ethics and International Affairs* 5. Forthcoming.

———. 1989. "The Bush Administration and the Future of American Foreign Policy: Pragmatism or Procrastination?" *Presidential Studies Quarterly* 19 (Fall):717–731.

Kegley, Charles W., Jr., ed. 1991. *The Long Postwar Peace.* New York: Harper Collins.

Kegley, Charles W., Jr., and Gregory A. Raymond. 1991. "Alliances and the Preservation of the Postwar Peace: Weighing the Contribution." In Charles W. Kegley, Jr., ed., *The Long Postwar Peace,* pp. 270–289. New York: Harper Collins.

———. 1990a. "The End of Alliances?" *USA Today* 118 (May):32–34.

———. 1990b. *When Trust Breaks Down: Alliance Norms and World Politics.* Columbia, SC: University of South Carolina Press.

———. 1989. "Going It Alone: The Decay of Alliance Norms." *Harvard International Review* 12 (Fall):39–43.

Kegley, Charles W., Jr., and Eugene R. Wittkopf. 1991. *American Foreign Policy: Pattern and Process,* 4th ed. New York: St. Martin's Press.

———. 1989. *World Politics: Trend and Transformation,* 3d ed. New York: St. Martin's Press.

Kegley, Charles W., Jr., and Eugene R. Wittkopf, eds. 1989. *The Nuclear Reader: Strategy, Weapons, War,* 2d ed. New York: St. Martin's Press.

Kennan, George F. 1983. *The Nuclear Delusion.* New York: Pantheon.

———. ["X"]. 1947. "The Sources of Soviet Conduct." *Foreign Affairs* 25 (July):566–582.

Kennedy, Paul. 1989. "Can the US Remain Number One?" *New York Review of Books* 36 (March 16):36–42.

———. 1988. "Why We Can't Give Up the Bomb." *Atlantic* 262 (August):77–79.

———. 1987. *The Rise and Fall of the Great Powers.* New York: Random House.

Kenny, Anthony. 1985. *The Logic of Deterrence.* Chicago: University of Chicago Press.

Keohane, Robert O. 1989. *International Institutions and State Power: Essays in International Relations Theory.* Boulder, CO: Westview Press.

Keohane, Robert O., and Joseph S. Nye, Jr. 1989. *Power and Interdependence,* 2d ed. Glenview, IL: Scott, Foresman/Little, Brown.

Kershaw, Ian. 1987. *The Hitler Myth: Image and Reality in the Third Reich.* Oxford: Oxford University Press.

Khrushchev, Nikita. 1974. *Khrushchev Remembers.* Edited by Strobe Talbott. Boston: Little, Brown.

Kissinger, Henry. 1961. *The Necessity for Choice.* New York: Harper.

———. 1957. *Nuclear Weapons and Foreign Policy.* New York: Harper.

Knorr, Klaus. 1966. *On the Uses of Military Power in the Nuclear Age.* Princeton, NJ: Princeton University Press.

Knox, MacGregor. 1984. "Conquest, Foreign and Domestic, in Fascist Italy and Nazi Germany." *Journal of Modern History* 56 (March):1–57.

Krauthammer, Charles. 1985. "On Nuclear Morality." In James Sterba, ed., *The Ethics of War and Nuclear Deterrence*, pp. 147–154. Belmont, CA: Wadsworth.

Kristol, Irving. 1990. "The Map of the World Has Changed." *Wall Street Journal* (January 3):A6.

Kruzel, Joseph. 1991. "Arms Control, Disarmament, and the Stability of the Postwar Era." In Charles W. Kegley, Jr., ed., *The Long Postwar Peace*, pp. 247–269. New York: Harper Collins.

Kugler, Jacek. 1984. "Terror Without Deterrence." *Journal of Conflict Resolution* 28 (September):470–506.

Kugler, Jacek, and Frank C. Zagare, eds., 1990. "The Long-Term Stability of Deterrence." *International Interactions* 15, nos. 3–4:255–278.

Kuhn, Thomas S. 1970. *The Structure of Scientific Revolutions*. Chicago: University of Chicago Press.

Kupperman, Robert H., and Debra Van Opstal. 1988. "Yesterday's Arms Control Will Not Prevent Nuclear War." *Annals* 500 (November):59–72.

Lackey, Douglas P. 1989. *The Ethics of War and Peace*. Englewood Cliffs, NJ: Prentice-Hall.

——— . 1984. *Moral Principles and Nuclear Weapons*. Totowa, NJ: Rowman and Allanheld.

Lebow, Richard Ned. 1987a. "Is Crisis Management Always Possible?" *Political Science Quarterly* 102 (Summer):181–192.

——— . 1987b. *Nuclear Crisis Management: A Dangerous Illusion*. Ithaca, NY: Cornell University Press.

——— . 1985. "The Deterrence Deadlock: Is There a Way Out?" In Robert Jervis, Richard Ned Lebow, and Janice Gross Stein, eds., *Psychology and Deterrence*, pp. 180–232. Baltimore, MD: Johns Hopkins University Press.

——— . 1981. *Between Peace and War: The Nature of International Crises*. Baltimore, MD: Johns Hopkins University Press.

Lebow, Richard Ned, and Janice Stein. 1990. "Deterrence: The Elusive Dependent Variable." *World Politics* 42 (April):336–369.

Lefever, Ernest W. 1957. *Ethics and U.S. Foreign Policy*. New York: Meridian Books.

Levy, Jack S. 1991. "Long Cycles, Hegemonic Transitions, and the Long Peace." In Charles W. Kegley, Jr., ed., *The Long Postwar Peace*, pp. 147–176. New York: Harper Collins.

——— . 1983. *War in the Modern Great Power System, 1495–1975*. Lexington, KY: University of Kentucky Press.

Lifton, Robert Jay, and Richard Falk. 1982. *Indefensible Weapons: The Political and Psychological Case Against Nuclearism*. New York: Basic Books.

Linderman, Gerald F. 1987. *Embattled Courage: The Experience of Combat in the Civil War*. New York: Free Press.

Lindsey, Hal. 1977. *The Late Great Planet Earth*. New York: Bantam Books.

Lippmann, Walter. 1947. *The Cold War*. New York: Harper.

Love, Janice. 1986. "When Deterrence Doesn't Deter." *Christianity and Crisis* 46 (November):412–414.

Luard, Evan. 1986. *War in International Society: A Study in International Sociology*. New Haven, CT: Yale University Press.

Lutheran Church in America. 1984. "Peace and Politics." Resolution adopted by the Twelfth Biennial Convention, June 28–July 5.

McGeehan, Robert. 1990. "The United States and NATO After the Cold War." *NATO Review* 35 (February):7–13.

McGwire, Michael. 1987. *Military Objectives in Soviet Foreign Policy.* Washington, DC: Brookings Institution.

——— . 1985. "Deterrence: The Problem, Not the Solution." *SAIS Review* 5 (Summer-Fall):105–124.

Machiavelli, Niccolo. 1950. *The Prince and the Discourses.* New York: Modern Library.

McNamara, Robert S. 1989. "The Military Role of Nuclear Weapons." In Charles W. Kegley, Jr., and Eugene R. Wittkopf, eds., *The Nuclear Reader,* 2d ed., pp. 174–185. New York: St. Martin's Press.

——— . 1987. *Blundering Into Disaster.* New York: Pantheon.

——— . 1962. "The United States and Western Europe: Concrete Problems of Maintaining a Free Community." *Vital Speeches* 28 (August 1):626–629.

McNaugher, Thomas L. 1989. *New Weapons, Old Politics: America's Military Procurement Muddle.* Washington, DC: Brookings Institution.

Mandelbaum, Michael. 1988. *The Fate of Nations: The Search for National Security in the Nineteenth and Twentieth Centuries.* Cambridge: Cambridge University Press.

Mavrodes, George I. 1985. "Conventions and the Morality of War." In James Sterba, ed., *The Ethics of War and Nuclear Deterrence,* pp. 50–60. Belmont, CA: Wadsworth.

Maynes, Charles William. 1990. "America Without the Cold War." *Foreign Policy* 78 (Spring):3–25.

Mead, Walter Russell. 1990. "On the Road to Ruin." *Harper's* 280 (March):59–64.

——— . 1987. *Mortal Splendor: The American Empire in Transition.* Boston, MA: Houghton Mifflin.

Mearsheimer, John. 1983. *Conventional Deterrence.* Ithaca, NY: Cornell University Press.

Midlarsky, Manus I. 1988. *The Onset of World War.* Boston, MA: Unwin Hyman.

Milburn, Thomas W. 1959. "What Constitutes Effective U.S. Deterrence?" *Journal of Conflict Resolution* 3 (June):138–145.

Milhollin, Gary. 1990. "The West Is Making It Easier to Acquire the Bank." *International Herald Tribune* (July 26):8.

Miller, James N., Jr. 1988. "Zero and Minimal Nuclear Weapons." In Joseph S. Nye, Jr., Graham T. Allison, and Albert Carnesale, eds., *Fateful Visions: Avoiding Nuclear Catastrophe,* pp. 11–32. Cambridge, MA: Ballinger.

Moore, Molly. 1990. "Pentagon Said to Imply Need Has Faded for Atom Arms in Europe." *Washington Post* (March 14):A12.

Moravian Church in America, Northern Province, Provincial Synod. 1982. "Nuclear Non-proliferation and World Peace." Resolution adopted in the Tenth Plenary Session.

Moravian Church in America, Southern Province, Provincial Elders' Conference. 1982. "A Covenant for Peacemaking and Nuclear Disarmament." Resolution adopted July 29.

Morgan, Patrick M. 1983. *Deterrence: A Conceptual Analysis.* 2d ed. Beverly Hills, CA: Sage.

———. 1977. *Deterrence: A Conceptual Analysis.* Beverly Hills, CA: Sage.

Morgenthau, Hans J. 1956. "Has Atomic War Really Become Impossible?" *Bulletin of Atomic Scientists* 12 (January):7–9.

Mueller, John. 1991. "Changing Attitudes Toward War: The Impact of World War I." *British Journal of Political Science* (January). Forthcoming.

———. 1989. *Retreat from Doomsday: The Obsolescence of Major War.* New York: Basic Books.

———. 1988. "The Essential Irrelevance of Nuclear Weapons: Stability in the Postwar World." *International Security* 13 (Fall):55–79.

———. 1968. *Deterrence, Numbers, and History.* Los Angeles: University of California, Security Studies Project.

Murnion, Philip, ed. 1983. *Catholics and Nuclear War.* New York: Crossroads Publishing Company.

Murray, John Courtney. 1959. *Morality and Modern War.* New York: Council on Religion and International Affairs.

Naroll, Raoul, Vern L. Bullough, and Frada Naroll, eds. 1974. *Military Deterrence in History.* Albany, NY: State University of New York Press.

Nathan, Otto, and Heinz Norden, eds. 1960. *Einstein on Peace.* New York: Simon and Schuster.

National Conference of Catholic Bishops. 1989. "Nuclear Strategy and the Challenge of Peace: The Moral Evaluation of Deterrence in Light of Policy Developments, 1983–1988." In Charles W. Kegley, Jr., and Eugene R. Wittkopf, eds., *The Nuclear Reader,* 2d ed., pp. 54–71. New York: St. Martin's Press.

———. 1988. *Building Peace: A Pastoral Reflection on the Response to the Challenge of Peace and a Report on the Challenge of Peace and Policy Developments 1983–1988.* Washington, DC: United States Catholic Conference.

———. 1983. *The Challenge of Peace.* Washington, DC: United States Catholic Conference.

National Council of Churches of Christ in the USA. 1983. "Peacemaking and Ecumenism: A Celebration of the Catholic Bishops' Pastoral Letter." Resolution adopted by the Governing Board, May 13.

———. 1977. *To Preserve and Not to Destroy: Statements on Disarmament.* New York: National Council of Churches.

Newhouse, John. 1989. "Nuclear Hair Trigger Persists." *Christian Science Monitor* (February 27):19.

Niebuhr, Reinhold. 1959. *The Structure of Nations and Empires.* New York: Charles Scribner's Sons.

———. 1932. *Moral Man and Immoral Society.* New York: Charles Scribner's Sons.

Nitze, Paul. 1960. *The Recovery of Ethics.* New York: Council on Religion and International Affairs.

Nixon, Richard. 1989. "American Foreign Policy: The Bush Agenda." *Foreign Affairs* 68, no. 1:199–219.

Nogee, Joseph L., and John Spanier. 1988. *Peace Impossible—War Unlikely: The Cold War Between the United States and the Soviet Union.* Glenview, IL: Scott, Foresman/Little, Brown.

Nolan, Janne E. 1989. *Guardians of the Arsenal: The Politics of Nuclear Strategy.* New York: Basic Books.

Novak, Michael. 1983. *Moral Clarity in the Nuclear Age.* Nashville, TN: Thomas Nelson.

Nye, Joseph S., Jr. 1989a. "Deep Cuts and the Risks of Nuclear War." In Charles W. Kegley, Jr., and Eugene R. Wittkopf, eds., *The Nuclear Reader,* 2d ed., pp. 196–198. New York: St. Martin's Press.

———. 1989b. "The Long-Term Future of Deterrence." In Charles W. Kegley, Jr., and Eugene R. Wittkopf, eds., *The Nuclear Reader,* 2d ed., pp. 81–89. New York: St. Martin's Press.

———. 1987. "Nuclear Learning and U.S.-Soviet Security Regimes." *International Organization* 41 (Summer):371–402.

———. 1986. *Nuclear Ethics.* New York: Free Press.

Nye, Joseph S., Jr., Graham T. Allison, and Albert Carnesale, eds. 1988. *Fateful Visions: Avoiding Nuclear Catastrophe.* Cambridge, MA: Ballinger.

O'Brien, William V. 1983. "Just War Doctrine in a Nuclear Context." *Theological Studies* 44 (March):191–220.

———. 1981. *The Conduct of Just and Limited War.* New York: Praeger.

O'Brien, William V., and John Langan, eds. 1986. *The Nuclear Dilemma and the Just War Tradition.* Lexington, MA: Lexington Books.

O'Donovan, Oliver. 1989. *Peace and Certainty.* Grand Rapids, MI: Eerdmans.

Oren, Nissan, ed. 1984. *When Patterns Change: Turning Points in International Politics.* New York: St. Martin's Press.

Osgood, Robert E. 1988. *The Nuclear Dilemma in American Strategic Thought.* Boulder, CO: Westview Press.

Palme Commission on Disarmament and Security Issues. 1989. *A World at Peace: Common Security in the Twenty-first Century.* Stockholm: Commission on Disarmament and Security.

Perry, James M. 1986. "They May Poke Fun at the Swiss Navy but Not at the Army." *Wall Street Journal* (December 8):1.

Peterson, Jeannie, and Don Hinrechson, eds. 1982. *Nuclear War: The Aftermath.* New York: Pergamon.

Philadelphia Yearly Meeting of the Religious Society of Friends. *See* Religious Society of Friends, Philadelphia Yearly Meeting.

Pilat, Joseph F., and Paul C. White. 1990. "Technology and Strategy in a Changing World." *Washington Quarterly* 13 (Spring):79–91.

Pipes, Richard. 1984. *Survival Is Not Enough.* New York: Simon and Schuster.

Powaski, Ronald E. 1989. *March to Armageddon: The United States and the Nuclear Arms Race, 1939 to the Present.* New York: Oxford University Press.

Powell, Robert, ed. 1990. *Nuclear Deterrence Theory: The Search for Credibility.* New York: Cambridge University Press.

Presbyterian Church, U.S.A. 1984. *A Composite Review of General Assembly Statements on Peacemaking and the Arms Race.* New York: Office of the General Assembly.

Quester, George. 1982. *American Foreign Policy: The Lost Consensus.* New York: Praeger.

———. 1977. *Offense and Defense in the International System.* New York: Wiley.

———. 1973. *The Politics of Nuclear Proliferation.* Baltimore, MD: Johns Hopkins University Press.

———. 1970. *Nuclear Diplomacy.* New York: Dunellen.

———. 1966. *Deterrence Before Hiroshima.* New York: Wiley.

Ramsey, Paul. 1988. *Speak Up for Just War or Pacifism.* University Park, PA: Pennsylvania State University Press.

———. 1968. *The Just War: Force and Political Responsibility.* New York: Charles Scribner's Sons.

———. 1961. *War and the Christian Conscience.* Durham, NC: Duke University Press.

Rapoport, Anatol. 1964. *Strategy and Conscience.* New York: Schocken Books.

Raspail, Jean. 1974. *The Camp of the Saints.* New York: Simon and Schuster.

Ravenal, Earl C. 1989. "Disengagement from Europe: The Frame of an Argument." In Ted Galen Carpenter, ed., *NATO at Forty: Confronting a Changing World,* pp. 217–237. Lexington, MA: Lexington Books.

Ray, James Lee. 1989. "The Abolition of Slavery and the End of International War." *International Organization* 43 (Summer):405–439.

Raymond, Gregory A., and Charles W. Kegley, Jr. 1987. "Long Cycles and Internationalized Civil War." *Journal of Politics* 49 (May):481–499.

Reagan, Ronald. 1984. "State of the Union Address" to a Joint Session of Congress. *Weekly Compilation of Presidential Documents* 20, no. 4:87–94.

———. 1983. Speech to the Nation, March 23, 1983. In Arms Control Association, *Arms Control and National Security,* p. 74. Washington, DC: Arms Control Association.

Record, Jeffrey. 1988. "The Nukes as Peacemakers." *Sun* (Baltimore) (October 12):5.

Reformed Church in America. 1985. *The Church's Peace Witness in the U.S. Corporate Economy.* New York: Reformed Church in America.

Religious Society of Friends, Philadelphia Yearly Meeting. 1976. "Minute No. 26 on Outlawing War." Adopted April 3.

Renner, Michael. 1989. "National Security: The Economic and Environmental Dimensions." *Worldwatch Paper 89.* Washington, DC: Worldwatch Institute.

Reston, James, Jr. 1984. *Sherman's March and Vietnam.* New York: Macmillan.

Robock, Alan C. 1990. "Nuclear Winter Confirmed." *National Forum* 70 (Winter):17–19.

Rock, Stephen R. 1989. *Why Peace Breaks Out: Great Power Rapprochement in Historical Perspective.* Chapel Hill, NC: University of North Carolina Press.

Rosecrance, Richard. 1986. *The Rise of the Trading State: Commerce and Conquest in the Modern World.* New York: Basic Books.

———. 1975. *Strategic Defense Reconsidered.* Adelphi Paper no. 116 (Spring). London: International Institute for Strategic Studies.

———— . 1963. *Action and Reaction in World Politics.* Boston, MA: Little, Brown.

Rothschild, Emma. 1983. "The Delusions of Deterrence." *New York Review of Books* 29 (April 14):40–50.

Rummel, Rudolph J. 1986. "War Isn't This Century's Biggest Killer." *Wall Street Journal* (July 7):12.

———— . 1983. "Libertarianism and International Violence." *Journal of Conflict Resolution* 27 (March):27–71.

Russett, Bruce M. 1990a. *Controlling the Sword: The Democratic Governance of National Security.* Cambridge, MA: Harvard University Press.

———— . 1990b. "Politics and Alternative Security: Toward a More Democratic, Therefore More Peaceful, World." In Burns H. Weston, ed., *Alternative Security: Living Without Nuclear Deterrence,* pp. 107–136. Boulder, CO: Westview Press.

———— . 1989. "The Real Decline in Nuclear Hegemony." In Ernst-Otto Czempiel and James Rosenau, eds., *Global Changes and Theoretical Challenges: Approaches to World Politics for the 1990s,* pp. 177–193. Lexington, MA: Lexington Books.

———— . 1988. "Extended Deterrence with Nuclear Weapons: How Necessary, How Acceptable?" *Review of Politics* 50 (Spring):282–302.

———— . 1987. "Sensible Deterrence as Arms Control." In Joseph Richard Goldman, ed., *American Security in a Changing World,* pp. 213–230. Washington, DC: University Press of America.

———— . 1986. "Reply to Winters." *Review of Politics* 48 (Summer):456–459.

———— . 1984. "Ethical Dilemmas of Nuclear Deterrence." *International Security* 8 (Spring):36–54.

———— . 1983. *The Prisoners of Insecurity: Nuclear Deterrence, the Arms Race, and Arms Control.* New York: Freeman.

———— . 1974. *Power and Community in World Politics.* New York: Freeman.

———— . 1967. "Pearl Harbor, Deterrence Theory and Decision Theory." *Journal of Peace Research* 4, no. 2:89–105.

———— . 1963. "The Calculus of Deterrence." *Journal of Conflict Resolution* 7 (June):97–109.

Russett, Bruce, and Donald R. DeLuca. 1983. "Theater Nuclear Forces: Public Opinion in Western Europe." *Political Science Quarterly* 98 (Summer):179–196.

Russett, Bruce, and Harvey Starr. 1981. *World Politics: The Menu for Choice.* San Francisco: Freeman.

Ryder, H.I.D. 1899. "The Ethics of War." *Nineteenth Century* 45 (May):716–728.

Sagan, Carl. 1989. "Nuclear War and Climatic Catastrophe: A Nuclear Winter." In Charles W. Kegley, Jr., and Eugene R. Wittkopf, eds., *The Nuclear Reader,* 2d ed., pp. 320–335. New York: St. Martin's Press.

———— . 1983–1984. "Nuclear War and Climatic Catastrophe: Some Policy Implications." *Foreign Affairs* 62 (Winter):257–292.

Sagan, Scott. 1989. *Moving Targets: Nuclear Strategy and National Security.* Princeton, NJ: Princeton University Press.

———— . 1987. "SIOP-62: The Nuclear War Plan Briefing to President Kennedy." *International Security* 12 (Summer):22–51.

Saint-Exupery, Antoine de. 1942. *Night Flight*. New York: Signet.

Sakharov, Andrei. 1983. "The Danger of Thermonuclear War." *Foreign Affairs* 61 (Summer):1001–1016.

Schall, James V., ed. 1984. *Out of Justice, Peace, and Winning the Peace*. San Francisco: Ignatius Press.

Scheer, Robert. 1988. *Thinking Tuna Fish, Talking Death*. New York: Hill and Wang.

———. 1982. *With Enough Shovels: Reagan, Bush, and Nuclear War*. New York: Random House.

Schell, Jonathan. 1984. *The Abolition*. New York: Knopf.

———. 1982. *The Fate of the Earth*. New York: Avon Books.

Schelling, Thomas C. 1966. *Arms and Influence*. New Haven, CT: Yale University Press.

———. 1960. *The Strategy of Conflict*. Cambridge, MA: Harvard University Press.

Schwartz, William A., and Charles Derber. 1990. *The Nuclear Seduction: Why the Arms Race Doesn't Matter—and What Does*. Berkeley, CA: University of California Press.

Scott, Andrew. 1979. *The Dynamics of Interdependence*. Chapel Hill, NC: University of North Carolina Press.

Sederberg, Peter C. 1986. "Nuclear Winter: Paradoxes and Paradigm Shifts." In Peter C. Sederberg, ed., *Nuclear Winter, Deterrence, and the Prevention of Nuclear War*, pp. 3–14. New York: Praeger.

Seib, Gerald F. 1990. "Prodded by Quayle and Cheney, Bush Becomes Fervent Supporter of Strategic Defense Initiative." *Wall Street Journal* (February 23):A12.

Sharp, Gene. 1973. *The Politics of Nonviolent Action*. Boston: Porter Sargent.

Shepherd, William G. 1986. *The Ultimate Deterrent: Inherent Superpower Security Under Stable Competition*. New York: Praeger.

Shevchenko, Arkady N. 1985. *Breaking with Moscow*. New York: Knopf.

Shue, Henry, ed. 1989. *Nuclear Deterrence and Moral Restraint*. New York: Cambridge University Press.

Shulman, Marshall D. 1988. "The Superpowers: Dance of the Dinosaurs." *Foreign Affairs* 66, no. 3:493–515.

———. 1963. *Stalin's Foreign Policy Reappraised*. New York: Atheneum.

Sibley, Mulford Q. 1970. *Political Ideas and Ideologies*. New York: Harper and Row.

———. 1963. *The Quiet Battle*. Chicago: Quadrangle.

Singer, J. David. 1991. "Peace in the Global System: Displacement, Interregnum, or Transformation?" In Charles W. Kegley, Jr., ed., *The Long Postwar Peace*, pp. 56–84. New York: Harper Collins.

———. 1990. "Nuclear Confrontation: Ambivalence, Rationality, and the Doomsday Machine." University of Michigan, unpublished manuscript.

———. 1962. *Deterrence, Arms Control, and Disarmament*. Columbus, OH: Ohio State University Press.

_____ . 1961. "The Level-of-Analysis Problem in International Relations." In Klaus Knorr and Sidney Verba, eds., *The International System: Theoretical Essays*, pp. 77–92. Princeton, NJ: Princeton University Press.

Singer, J. David, and Melvin Small. 1972. *The Wages of War, 1816–1965: A Statistical Handbook*. New York: John Wiley and Sons.

Sivard, Ruth Leger. 1989. *World Military and Social Expenditures 1989*. Washington, DC: World Priorities.

Small, Melvin. 1980. *Was War Necessary: National Security and U.S. Entry Into War*. Beverly Hills, CA: Sage.

Small, Melvin, and J. David Singer. 1982. *Resort to Arms*. Beverly Hills, CA: Sage.

_____ . 1979. "Conflict in the International System, 1816–1977: Historical Trends and Policy Futures." In Charles W. Kegley, Jr., and Patrick J. McGowan, eds., *Challenges to America*, pp. 89–115. Beverly Hills, CA: Sage.

Smith, Gerald C., and Helena Cobban. 1989. "A Blind Eye to Nuclear Proliferation." *Foreign Affairs* 68 (Summer):53–70.

Smith, Michael J. 1987. "Nuclear Deterrence: Behind the Strategic and Ethical Debate." *Virginia Quarterly Review* 64 (Winter):1–22.

Smith, R. Jeffrey. 1990. "Interview with Admiral William Crowe." *Washington Post* (January 8):A1, A4.

Snyder, Glenn H. 1984. "The Security Dilemma in Alliance Politics." *World Politics* 36 (July):461–495.

_____ . 1961. *Deterrence and Defense*. Princeton, NJ: Princeton University Press.

Southern Baptist Convention. 1983. "Resolution on Peace with Justice." Adopted June 14–15, Pittsburgh.

_____ . 1982. "Resolution on Peace with Justice." Adopted June 15–17, New Orleans.

Stein, Janice Gross. 1985. "Calculation, Miscalculation, and Conventional Deterrence." In Robert Jervis, Richard Ned Lebow, and Janice Gross Stein, eds., *Psychology and Deterrence*, pp. 34–59. Baltimore, MD: Johns Hopkins University Press.

Steinbruner, John. 1981–1982. "Nuclear Decapitation." *Foreign Policy* 45 (Winter):16–28.

Sterba, James, ed. 1985. *The Ethics of War and Nuclear Deterrence*. Belmont, CA: Wadsworth.

Stoll, Richard J. 1990. *U.S. National Security Policy and the Soviet Union*. Columbia, SC: University of South Carolina Press.

Stonier, Thomas. 1964. *Nuclear Disaster*. Cleveland, OH: World Publishing Company.

Streit, Clarence. 1939. *Union Now: A Proposal for a Federal Union of Democracies*. New York: Harper.

Summers, Harry G., Jr. 1989. "A Bankrupt Military Strategy." *Atlantic* 263 (June):34–40.

Talbott, Strobe. 1989. *The Master of the Game: Paul Nitze and the Nuclear Peace*. New York: Knopf.

Tamashiro, Howard, Gregory G. Brunk, and Donald Secrest. 1989. "The Underlying Structure of Ethical Beliefs Toward War." *Journal of Peace Research* 26 (May):139–152.

Taubman, William. 1982. *Stalin's American Policy.* New York: Norton.

Teilhard de Chardin, Pierre. 1969. *The Future of Man.* Translated by Norman Denny. New York: Harper and Row.

Thompson, E. P. 1982. "Deterrence and 'Addiction.'" *Yale Review* 72 (October):1–18.

Thompson, William R. 1988. *On Global War: Historical-Structural Approaches to World Politics.* Columbia, SC: University of South Carolina Press.

Tillema, Herbert K. 1989. "Foreign Overt Military Intervention in the Nuclear Age." *Journal of Peace Research* 26 (May):179–196.

Tolstoy, Leo. 1966. *War and Peace.* New York: Norton.

Toth, Robert C. 1989. "U.S. Shifts Nuclear Response Strategy." *Los Angeles Times* (July 23):A1.

Treitschke, Heinrich von. 1916. *Politics.* 2 vols. New York: Macmillan.

Trofimenko, Henry. 1990. "The End of the Cold War, Not History." *Washington Quarterly* 13 (Spring):21–35.

———. 1989. *Windows of Opportunity: From Cold War to Peaceful Competition in U.S.-Soviet Relations.* Cambridge, MA: Ballinger.

Tucker, Robert. 1985a. "Morality and Deterrence." In Russell Hardin et al., eds., *Nuclear Deterrence: Ethics and Strategy,* pp. 53–70. Chicago: University of Chicago Press.

———. 1985b. *The Nuclear Debate.* New York: Holmes and Meier.

———. 1960. *The Just War.* Baltimore, MD: Johns Hopkins University Press.

Tunander, Ola. 1989. "The Logic of Deterrence." *Journal of Peace Research* 26 (November):353–365.

Turner, Stansfield. 1986. "Reagan Is Right: No ICBMs Means No First Strike." *Washington Post* (October 26):B1, B2.

Union of American Hebrew Congregations. 1989. "Halting the Nuclear Arms Race." Resolution adopted November 2–6, New Orleans.

———. 1983. *Preventing the Nuclear Holocaust: A Jewish Response.* New York: Union of American Hebrew Congregations Commission on Social Action of Reform Judaism.

United Church of Christ General Synod 15. 1985. "Pronouncement Affirming the United Church of Christ as a Just Peace Church." In United Church of Christ, *Social Policy Actions,* pp. 5–9. New York: United Church of Christ Office for Church in Society.

United Methodist Council of Bishops. 1986. *In Defense of Creation: The Nuclear Crisis and a Just Peace.* Nashville, TN: Graded Press.

United Methodist General Conference. 1988. "The United Methodist Church and Peace." In Ronald P. Patterson, ed., *Book of Resolutions,* pp. 548–555. Nashville, TN: United Methodist Publishing House.

U.S. Congress, House. 1990. "Hearing of the Committee on Armed Services," with U.S. House of Representatives, Washington, DC, March 13.

U.S. Office of Technology Assessment. 1989. "U.S. Nuclear Strategy." In Charles W. Kegley, Jr., and Eugene R. Wittkopf, eds., *The Nuclear Reader*, 2d ed., pp. 102–120. New York: St. Martin's Press.

Vale, Michael. 1981. *War and Chivalry*. Athens, GA: University of Georgia Press.

van Creveld, Martin. 1988. *Technology and War*. New York: Free Press.

Vasquez, John. 1991. "The Deterrence Myth: Nuclear Weapons and the Prevention of Nuclear War." In Charles W. Kegley, Jr., ed., *The Long Postwar Peace*, pp. 205–223. New York: Harper Collins.

Vasquez, John A., ed. 1990, second edition. *Classics of International Relations*. Englewood Cliffs, NJ: Prentice-Hall.

Villa-Vicencio, Charles. 1987. "The Ecumenical Debate: Violent Revolution and Military Disarmament." In Charles Villa-Vicencio, ed., *Theology and Violence: The South African Debate*, pp. 233–254. Grand Rapids, MI: Eerdmans.

Voslensky, Michael. 1984. *Nomenklatura: The New Soviet Ruling Class*. Garden City, NY: Doubleday.

Waltz, Kenneth N. 1988. "The Origins of War in Neorealist Theory." *Journal of Interdisciplinary History* 18 (Spring):615–628.

_____ . 1971. "The Stability of the Bipolar World." In William D. Coplin and Charles W. Kegley, Jr., eds., *A Multi-Method Introduction to International Politics*, pp. 333–342. Chicago: Markham.

Warner, Edward L., III, and David A. Ochmanek. 1989. *Next Moves: An Arms Control Agenda for the 1990s*. New York: Council on Foreign Relations.

Weede, Erich. 1984. "Democracy and War Involvement." *Journal of Conflict Resolution* 28 (December):649–664.

_____ . 1983. "Extended Deterrence by Superpower Alliance." *Journal of Conflict Resolution* 27 (June):231–254.

Weigel, George. 1987. *Tranquillitas Ordinis*. Oxford: Oxford University Press.

Weinberger, Caspar W. 1988. "Arms Reduction and Deterrence." *Foreign Affairs* 66 (Spring):700–719.

_____ . 1982. *Annual Report of the Secretary of Defense to the Congress, Fiscal Year 1983*. Washington, DC: Government Printing Office.

Weltman, John J. 1974. "On the Obsolescence of War." *International Studies Quarterly* 18 (December):395–416.

White House. 1989. "Statement by President George Bush" aboard the *Maxim Gorky*, Marsaxlokk Harbor, Malta. *White House Press Office*, December 3.

Wildavsky, Aaron. 1989. "Serious Talk About the Nuclear Era." *Wall Street Journal* (March 16):A16.

Williams, Phil. 1976. *Crisis Management: Confrontation and Diplomacy in the Nuclear Age*. New York: Wiley.

Winters, Francis X. 1986. "Bishops and Scholars: The Peace Pastoral Under Siege." *Review of Politics* 48 (Winter):31–59.

Wittkopf, Eugene R. 1990. *Faces of Internationalism: The Foreign Policy Beliefs and Preferences of the American People*. Durham, NC: Duke University Press.

Wohlstetter, Albert. 1985. "Bishops, Statesmen, and Other Strategists on the Bombing of Innocents." In Charles W. Kegley, Jr., and Eugene R. Wittkopf, eds., *The Nuclear Reader*, pp. 58–76. New York: St. Martin's Press. Also, 1983. *Commentary* 75 (June):15–35.

————. 1959. "The Delicate Balance of Terror." *Foreign Affairs* 27 (January):211–234.

Wyatt, Harold F. 1911. "God's Test By War." *Nineteenth Century* 69 (April):591–606.

Yoder, John Howard. 1984. *When War Is Unjust.* Minneapolis, MN: Augsburg Publishing House.

Zelikow, Philip. 1987. "The United States and the Use of Force: A Historical Summary." In George K. Osborn, Asa A. Clark IV, Daniel J. Kaufman, and Douglas E. Lute, eds., *Democracy, Strategy, and Vietnam,* pp. 31–81. Lexington, MA: Lexington Books.

Zuckerman, Solly. 1989. "Converging on Peace?" *New York Review of Books* 36 (September 28):28–31.

————. 1982. *Nuclear Illusion and Reality.* New York: Vintage.

About the Book

The Berlin Wall is down; the focus of the East-West agenda has shifted away from nuclear one-upmanship. What is the role of deterrence—in theory and practice—in the post–Cold War world? Is it now, and was it ever, a moral strategy for preventing war?

After the Cold War is the most up-to-date text on the traditional questions of nuclear deterrence and the unconventional answers posed by the emerging new world order. These wide-ranging and penetrating essays by leading scholars, policymakers, and moral philosophers give students and citizens the background they need to make the transition to thinking about joint survival rather than mutual destruction.

Each essay offers a distinctive point of view—ranging from "deterrence as usual" to "transitional deterrence"—without reducing the long and complex history of the issues or their contemporary recontextualization to the soundbites of summitry these phrases might recall. Especially provocative are John Mueller's contention that more war has been waged on behalf of moral concern than has been prevented by it, and James Turner Johnson's challenge to end the irony implied in the prospect of fighting just wars with immoral weaponry.

In addition to the rich background and argument developed in this volume, special features add to its lasting utility. The introduction by the editors, Charles Kegley and Kenneth Schwab, puts the essays into context, not only with one another but with current scholarship and emerging policy positions. A concluding essay recounts fascinating dialogues among the contributors, giving voice to speculation beyond their essay positions, and a comprehensive bibliographic review of the voluminous literature on nuclear deterrence gives students and researchers a full picture of the debates that precede those in this book.

About the Contributors

Sir Hugh Beach has served as director of the Council for Arms Control in the United Kingdom and is widely regarded as one of Europe's leading authorities on security affairs and arms control. He served in the British armed forces in World War II and later worked as an officer in the Ministry of Defence. He has written extensively about British and European security issues and has in recent years turned his attention to the social and moral dimensions of military doctrines.

Joseph Cardinal Bernardin serves as the archbishop of Chicago. A native of Columbia, South Carolina, and an alumnus of the University of South Carolina, Cardinal Bernardin pursued his academic training at the Catholic University of America, where he received his M.A. degree in 1952. He was ordained to the priesthood in that year and served in the Diocese of Charleston for fourteen years. In 1968, he was elected general secretary of the National Conference of Catholic Bishops and the United States Catholic Conference. Since his appointment as archbishop in 1982, he has initiated numerous, highly acclaimed studies of the moral aspects of political, military, and social problems.

Kenneth E. Boulding, a native of Liverpool, is Distinguished Professor of Economics, Emeritus, at the University of Colorado and a research associate and project director of that university's Institute of Behavioral Science. He received his B.A. in 1931 from the School of Philosophy, Politics, and Economics at Oxford University before becoming a Commonwealth Fellow in 1932 at the University of Chicago. He emigrated to the United States in 1937. The author of more than thirty books on economics and social science, his most recent work is entitled *Three Faces of Power* (1989).

William A. Clark earned his Ph.D. in political science from the University of South Carolina in 1987 and became an assistant professor at Hillsdale College in Michigan. He is presently associate director of the James F. Byrnes International Center at the University of South Carolina. His research focuses on Soviet domestic politics, cadres policy, and Communist party affairs. A former Smith Richardson Foundation Fellow, Clark is the author of *Soviet Regional Elite Mobility After Khrushchev*

(1989). His next book, *Crime and Punishment in Soviet Officialdom,* is scheduled for publication in 1992.

Jonathan Davidson received his M.A. in history at Cambridge University and served as a career diplomat in the British diplomatic service, holding posts in London, India, Thailand, Senegal, and, between 1975 and 1981, in Washington, D.C., as first secretary in the British Embassy. He is presently the director of the Washington Office of the University of South Carolina, where he also serves as a visiting professor. He is the author of numerous reports in the field of international relations and international education and has prepared reports for the U.S. International Education Advisory Board and the U.S. National Commission for UNESCO.

Steven W. Hook is the 1990-1991 John C. West Fellow at the University of South Carolina where he is pursuing a doctoral degree in international studies. He has served at that university as a research fellow in the James F. Byrnes International Center and as a research assistant at the Institute of International Studies. He received his A.B. degree from the University of Michigan in 1982 and his M.A. degree from the University of South Carolina in 1989.

James Turner Johnson received his Ph.D. in religion from Princeton University in 1968. He is professor of religion and university director of international programs at Rutgers University. His scholarship focuses on the historical interaction between religious and nonreligious factors in the shaping of moral and legal doctrine on war, its justification, and its limitation. A former Guggenheim and Rockefeller Foundation Fellow, his books include *Ideology, Reason, and the Limitation of War* (1975), *Just War Tradition and the Restraint of War* (1981), *Can Modern War Be Just?* (1984), and *The Quest for Peace: Three Moral Traditions in Western Cultural History* (1987). He has published over forty articles in U.S. and European scholarly journals. His current research examines the relation between Western and Islamic religious and cultural traditions related to war, peace, and the conduct of statecraft.

Paul M. Kattenburg earned his Ph.D. in international relations from Yale University in 1949. He is a Distinguished Professor, Emeritus, at the University of South Carolina, where he teaches and writes about U.S. foreign policy and national security issues. He served in the U.S. State Department from 1950 until 1973, focusing on U.S. relations with East Asian states. Widely noted as an early critic of U.S. involvement in the Vietnam War, he is the author of *The Vietnam Trauma in American Foreign Policy 1945–1975* and has published extensively in scholarly journals.

Charles W. Kegley, Jr., earned his Ph.D. in international relations from Syracuse University in 1971. He holds the position of Pearce

Professor of International Relations at the University of South Carolina, where he served as chairman of the Department of Government and International Studies from 1981 to 1985 and as director of the James F. Byrnes International Center from 1985 to 1988. He also has taught at the Georgetown University School of Foreign Service, at the University of Texas, and at Rutgers University as the Moses and Annuta Back Peace Scholar. He has coauthored or coedited (with Eugene R. Wittkopf) *American Foreign Policy: Pattern and Process* (4th ed., 1991); *World Politics: Trend and Transformation* (3rd ed., 1989); *The Nuclear Reader: Strategy, Weapons, War* (2nd ed., 1989); and coauthored (with Gregory A. Raymond) *When Trust Breaks Down: Alliance Norms and World Politics* (1990); also, he has edited *The Long Postwar Peace: Contending Explanations and Projections* (1991). His current writing focuses on international security, trends in world politics, and the comparative study of foreign policy.

Janice Love received her Ph.D. from Ohio State University and holds the position of assistant professor in the Department of Government and International Studies at the University of South Carolina. She is a member of the board of directors of the World Council of Churches, chairing its Programme Unit on Justice and Service. She has written extensively on international economics, Third World development, and social change, and her publications include the book *The Anti-Apartheid Movement in the United States* (1985) and articles on South Africa.

John Mueller is professor of political science and director of the Watson Center for the Study of International Peace and Cooperation at the University of Rochester. He has written extensively on social science methodology, public opinion, international relations, and national security issues. His most recent book is *Retreat From Doomsday: The Obsolescence of Major War* (1989). In a different field, he is the author of the prize-winning *Astaire Dancing: The Musical Films* (1985) and scripts for two musical comedies.

Richard Perle received a B.A. in international relations from the University of Southern California in 1964 and a M.A. in politics at Princeton University in 1967. He also took honors at the London School of Economics in 1962–1963. Currently a resident fellow at the American Enterprise Institute for Public Policy Research in Washington, D.C., he served as an assistant secretary of defense for international security policy during the Reagan administration. In that role, he supervised U.S. nuclear weapons policy, coordinated U.S. strategy in the North Atlantic Treaty Organization, and accompanied President Reagan to the U.S.-Soviet summits in Geneva and Reykjavik. He also currently serves as a consultant to the secretary of defense and several U.S. and multinational corporations. Called upon frequently to testify before Congress on national security issues, his advice and opinions appear regularly on the editorial pages of leading newspapers and policy journals, including the *New York Times, Washington Post, U.S. News and World Report,* and *International Economy.*

Bruce Martin Russett earned his Ph.D. in political science from Yale University in 1961 and currently serves as Dean Acheson Professor of International Relations at Yale. He is the author of nineteen books and 130 articles on military issues and world politics, including *What Price Vigilance? The Burdens of National Defense* (1970); *Power and Community in World Politics* (1974); *The Prisoners of Insecurity: Deterrence, the Arms Race, and Arms Control* (1983); and *Controlling the Sword: The Democratic Governance of National Security* (1990). He edits the *Journal of Conflict Resolution* and has served as president of the International Studies Association.

Kenneth L. Schwab received his doctorate in higher education administration in 1978 at Indiana University and is presently the executive vice-president for administration at the University of South Carolina, where he also serves as an associate professor. His research has focused on international educational issues, particularly their application to world peace and order. He served as a senior administrator for ten years at Guilford College in Greensboro, N.C., and has published a wide variety of articles and has worked extensively with other major U.S. universities on program development and student affairs.

Paul C. Warnke earned a law degree from Columbia University in 1948 and has served as the general counsel of the Department of Defense in 1966 and 1967, as assistant secretary of Defense from 1967 until 1969, and as director of the U.S. Arms Control and Disarmament Agency and as chief U.S. arms negotiator from March 1977 to November 1978. He is a past director of the Council on Foreign Relations and executive committee member of the Trilateral Commission. He is currently a partner in the Washington, D.C., law firm of Clifford & Warnke and is a prolific writer on arms control, national security policy, and weapons systems.

Index